FIFTY-SEVEN SAINTS
For Boys and Girls

FIFTY-SEVEN SAINTS

FOR BOYS AND GIRLS

Written and Illustrated
by the Daughters of St. Paul

ST. PAUL EDITIONS

NIHIL OBSTAT:

Rt. Rev. John G. Hogan

Diocesan Censor

IMPRIMATUR:

✠ Richard Cardinal Cushing

ISBN   0-8198-0044-9 cloth
ISBN   0-8198-0045-7 paper

Library of Congress Catalog Card Number: 63-19996

Printed in the U.S.A. by the Daughters of St. Paul
50 St. Paul's Ave., Boston, MA 02130

The Daughters of St. Paul are an international congregation of religious women serving the Church with the communications media.

Acknowledgment

We are deeply grateful to Rev. John Koenig, of the faculty of Immaculate Conception Seminary, Darlington, New Jersey, and author of the well-known series, "Stories for God's Little Ones," for his careful reading and improvement of *Stories of Saints for Boys and Girls*.

DAUGHTERS OF ST. PAUL

Introduction

This is your book. The Church honors the saints so that they will pray to God for us, but also so that we may learn about them and imitate them. God wants all of us to become saints.

Some of the saints in these stories did great things; others did only ordinary things. Yet they all bear a "family resemblance" as Cardinal Cushing calls it—because the likeness of Christ was produced in each one of them. They all spoke with God often in prayer, tried to keep the Ten Commandments perfectly, and were kind and helpful to their fellow men. Every one of us can imitate them in this.

It is not wise to try to imitate the severe penances of the saints, nor their extraordinary deeds without first asking the advice of the priest to whom we go to confession. Let us first learn to pray much and keep the Ten Commandments well, before we try to do still greater things for God.

Each of the saints is famous for some particular virtue. Yet, since all of the virtues belong together, growing in one—for instance, charity—helps us to grow in humility and obedience, too. That is why we should try to imitate the virtues of all the saints.

It is good to choose some particular saints as our patrons and pray to them often. They are close to God and will pray to God for us. And because God loves them very much, He will answer their prayers. We should never feel alone, when we have such powerful friends in Heaven.

Contents

13

Saint Michael Archangel

Prince of the Heavenly Hosts

Boys named Michael and girls named Michelle are privileged to have an Angel for their patron. Although there are legions of Angels, the Archangel Michael is one of the three whose name we really know. The others are Gabriel and Raphael, both Archangels.

The name Michael means, "Who is like God?" And it refers to a battle between the fallen angels—satan and his followers—and the Angels who were faithful to God.

The name rings like a battle cry against those who tried to defy God.

Several places in Scripture Michael is described as the Prince of the Angels because of his zeal in battle against the devils. He was a special protector of the Hebrew nation before the coming of Our Lord, and now he is a special protector of the Church and of the dying. In the Mass for the dead we pray that St. Michael will lead the faithful departed into Heaven's holy light.

Angels are different from men in many ways. Instead of having to investigate and to reason, they know conclusions and communicate thoughts immediately. They have tremendous energy and never become tired; they can operate in one place after another with a speed faster than that of light. This is because they are pure spirits; that is, they have no bodies. We say that they have a different *nature* from ours. Ours is made up of both spirit and matter.

Although the Angels know more than we and are stronger than we, some of them became so proud as to rebel against God. They were cast into hell by God's power. His agent was St. Michael. They are called devils, now, and roam the world tempting us to sin.

We are weak enough, proud enough, and foolish enough as it is, without having a devil meddling in our affairs, too! To keep him away, we should turn often to our Guardian Angel, asking him to inspire us with good thoughts and to protect us from dangers to our soul and body. We should pray to St. Michael too, for the Captain of the Heavenly Army is never too busy to help another soul in distress!

One of the best ways we can imitate St. Michael is by developing a great horror of sin, so that we will do everything we can to avoid it.

Saint Anne

Mother of Our Lady

The name Anne means "grace" or "gracious" and it was certainly a name which God Himself chose, for He had selected Anne to be the mother of the Virgin "full of grace." God gave Anne a super-abundance of graces because of the important duty which would be hers. From early childhood she had a great love of God; she was prayerful, self-sacrificing, pure and kind.

Anne married Joachim, a shepherd descended from the royal family of King David. The name Joachim means "Preparation of the Lord." Legend tells us that Joachim tended his flocks in the hills of Galilee near Nazareth, and that he also owned a house in Jerusalem, near the Temple of Jerusalem.

In that simple house Anne would have performed the daily tasks of a typical pious Hebrew wife. They were ordinary duties, done with such a great love of God that each of them had great merit in His eyes. She carried jars of water; sewed, washed and mended clothes; cleaned house and cooked meals. While doing these things she would pray and meditate. Often, as all good Hebrews did. she would ask God to send the promised Messias. How close to her was the answer to her prayers!

Since the Hebrews believed that a family without children did not have God's blessing, Joachim and Anne, together with all their relatives and friends, were very much disappointed that the holy couple had no child. Years of earnest prayer passed by but still no child came to brighten their poor little home. According to an ancient story which we are not sure is real history, Joachim went to the Temple one feast day to offer a sacrifice to God. "You may not offer sacrifice," said the high priest, Ruben.

"Married people who do not have children are not worthy to present themselves before the Lord."

Poor Joachim! Humbly and sadly he turned and left the Temple.

He could not bear to go home. A deep longing for solitude took hold of him, and he set out into the rugged hill country where he could pray in silence and beg God's blessing on him and his gentle wife.

Meanwhile, Anne was waiting for Joachim's return from the Temple. Where could he be? she wondered. He had promised to return in a few hours, but the time was dragging on and on. . . .

A well-meaning neighbor dropped in, and told Anne what had happened in the Temple.

Poor Joachim, thought Anne. He must have taken it very hard.

The gentle housewife withdrew into a solitary nook and prayed more fervently than ever before, "O Lord God, we beseech You to lift this reproach from us. Give us a child whom we may consecrate to You—a child to give You honor and glory." She remained rapt in prayer a long time.

Suddenly a being clothed with light appeared before her. "Do not grieve any longer," said a melodious voice. "God has heard your prayers. You shall have a child."

Anne was overjoyed. She thanked God ardently. Then she hurried out of the house to search for Joachim. He, coming back from the hills, met her near the Temple gate.

"Joachim, something wonderful has happened!"

"Anne, Anne, we are to have a child! An Angel came and told me!"

"An Angel? Why, he appeared to me, too! How good God is!"

*   *   *

Joyfully Anne made preparations for the birth of the child. She knew that the little one God was sending her would be someone extraordinary. She recalled that another Anne had prayed many years for a child, and that God had sent her Samuel, who grew up to be a holy ruler of His people. Yet Anne could not know that this child of hers was to be far, far holier than Samuel—that already she was utterly free from original sin!

And so in that little house near the great Temple, a child was born—her soul as fair as a lily, radiant as the morning star, already possessed of the very life of God. Did holy Anne know, as she rocked the infant tenderly, that this moment marked the dawn of a new day for mankind?

"Miriam," Anne whispered. "Star of the Sea . . . Noble Lady . . . Mary!" Miriam, or Mary, would be the baby's name.

The child grew. She slept, she toddled, she began to walk and run and dance about. Anne taught her little prayers and simple household tasks. Instructing and guiding, she was helping God to form the most perfect of His creatures. How quickly Mary learned! Her mother marveled, for never had she seen a small child so intelligent! Right away she understood whatever she was taught. God's grace was working at its fullest in that tiny soul.

Joachim and Anne had agreed to take the child to the Temple to offer her to God. History does not tell us how old Mary was at the time, but one legend says that she was very young. She remained in the Temple with other young virgins, praying, studying the Scriptures, and learning to do beautiful needlework.

How empty and bleak Anne's and Joachim's little house seemed now! It was as if a ray of sunshine had danced about in the dark corners and had suddenly disappeared. "But she is happier in the Temple," the good mother thought to herself. "She will study the Scriptures, meditate and pray. If the Messias is born during her lifetime, she may be able to serve Him in some way!" So Anne resumed her daily tasks, the peace of God in her heart.

How long did Joachim and Anne live after they presented their dearest treasure to God? No one knows for certain. But we do know that the holy couple accomplished the great mission God had given them—that of helping Him prepare a worthy tabernacle for His Divine Son, Jesus.

One of the best ways to imitate St. Anne is to do well every one of our duties, such as school work and chores around the home, and offer them all to God.

Saint Joseph

Patron of the Universal Church

"Do not be afraid, Joseph," said a deep voice. "That which is conceived in Mary is of the Holy Spirit, and she shall bring forth a Son, and thou shalt call His name Jesus, for He shall save His people from their sins."

Joseph awoke with a start, and happiness flooded his soul. Past now were the long hours of bewilderment. Not only did God wish Joseph to marry the Virgin Mary, but He had also chosen him to be a special protector of the promised Redeemer!

* * *

Joseph and his gentle bride Mary eagerly awaited the birth of the Child. They knew He would be born in Bethlehem, for the Prophet Micheas had said so, many years before. But how would this come about? Trusting in God, the holy couple waited patiently.

"Everyone must be enrolled!" the Roman soldiers shouted as they marched through Nazareth one cold winter day. "This census is urgent! Caesar wishes it to be taken at once. Everyone must register in his own family's city!"

In his own city! The city of David, their family, was Bethlehem—eighty-five miles away! The weather was cold and raw, and the Child would be born any day now! Joseph was worried. He did not want Mary to attempt the hard journey—yet the law must be obeyed. "We must trust in God," he decided, and proceeded to make preparations for the journey.

A sturdy little donkey would carry his precious spouse. It would also carry a bundle of food supplies and a packet of swaddling clothes which Mary had made ready for the Child. That was all they needed; Joseph and Mary bundled up as well as they could, and set out for Bethlehem.

The air had an icy nip to it, and the Galilean hills were dry and bleak. Up and down, up and down, Joseph tramped along the dusty roads followed by his docile little donkey and his prayerful spouse. Mary said little, but every now and then she gave her anxious husband a peaceful smile.

The nearer they drew to Bethlehem, the more people they found on the road. "I am afraid the inns will be crowded," Joseph remarked with a furrow between his brows. "I hope some of our cousins will have room to take us in." Mary nodded understandingly, and gazed at the horizon where the town of Bethlehem was growing steadily larger. Micheas' prophecy filled her mind.

Conditions in Bethlehem were worse than Joseph's gravest fears. There was no room anywhere; the relatives had taken in as many kinsfolk as their humble dwellings would hold, and the inns were packed to capacity. From door to door they trekked, and at each they were met with, "No, sorry!" or "You're the fifth one we've turned away today!" or "Listen, you ought to know better than to ask if we've got room! We couldn't fit a midget in here!"

Regret, impatience, sarcasm—Joseph and Mary encountered them all.

Joseph was almost frantic as night began to fall and they approached the last inn. "God will provide," Mary reassured him gently. "Don't worry, Joseph."

And then they found it—that hillside cave which had been turned into a stable. "It's the only shelter I can give you," the innkeeper muttered.

"At least we can keep out some of the cold," replied Joseph gratefully. "Thank you."

A loud noise rent the air. It came from the big ox who lived in the stable. The little donkey snorted in answer, while Joseph helped Mary dismount and led her to a pile of straw nearby. He took off his cloak and spread it on the straw. "Now, just rest," he told her. Mary would have preferred to prepare their meager meal, but she knew that Joseph would feel better if she let him do it, so she smiled and settled down on the straw.

Joseph fussed about, kindling a little fire and getting it to blaze up nicely. Then he took out the evening's ration, warmed it a bit, and gave most of it to Mary. She noticed the gesture, and handed a portion back to him.

Nearby the donkey and ox were munching contentedly. Mary and Joseph talked for a little while, more for the sake of charity than anything else, for neither one of them felt like talking. Then Mary grew quiet, and Joseph knew that she was absorbed in silent prayer. He stole away gently and took up watch near the door to be sure that no wild animals would disturb them. He, too, began to pray. "O Lord God," he prayed, "I wish I could have done better for Mary and the Child. Please forgive me!"

How cold and silent was this night! Stars snapped and sparkled brightly above the stable's wooden beams. The hush was deeper than the deepest, stillest well. "My God," marvelled Joseph, "how wonderful is Your universe. . . ."

What strange joy and peace was flooding his heart?

"Joseph!" Mary was calling him, her voice full of wonder and bliss. Hurrying to her, Joseph sank to his knees to adore the radiant Child Mary held in her arms. God had become Man, and had placed Himself in their care! Mary and Joseph bowed their heads in adoration and gratitude.

Mary wrapped her precious Infant in the bands of cloth called swaddling clothes in which all infants were wrapped in those days. Then she placed Him gently in a manger which Joseph had already filled with hay and straw. Too full of wonder to speak, the couple knelt before the Divine Child.

But what were those hushed, excited voices outside? Scrambling to his feet, Joseph hurried to the door. A band of shepherds from the nearby hills had come to adore the Child. "An Angel spoke to us," they exclaimed. "He told us we would find the Savior here!"

"Yes, come in," Joseph replied in hushed tones, and he led the way to the manger. After the shepherds had knelt for a few moments in silent adoration, with joy and gratitude they returned to their flocks, praising God.

Eight days later, when the Child was circumcised, Joseph gave Him the name Jesus as the Angel had told him to do. What a beautiful name it was, he thought. "Jesus" meant "Savior," and this Child was to be the Savior of the whole world.

Weeks passed, while the Infant Jesus grew under the loving care of Mary and Joseph. The time came for Him to be offered to God in the Temple as the Jewish Law prescribed. There in the Temple, an aged man, holy Simeon, took the Infant into his arms and gave thanks to God, saying, "Now do You dismiss Your servant, O Lord, according to Your word in peace; because my eyes have seen Your salvation!" Joseph listened intently as Simeon turned to Mary and added, "Behold this Child is destined for the fall and rise of many in Israel, and for a sign that shall be contradicted. And your own soul a sword shall pierce. . . ."

Poor Joseph! He could hardly bear the thought of his beloved Mary suffering! And the Child? Joseph recalled the prophecies that the Messias would have to suffer to redeem His people. He cringed at the thought of that Innocent One in pain—yet if that were God's Will, it must be carried out.

Once again in Bethlehem, the Holy Family had three more visitors—three kings from the East who had seen a strange star in the heavens, and mindful of an ancient prophecy: "A star shall rise out of Jacob and a sceptre shall spring up from Israel," they had come to pay homage to the King. Were they surprised to find Him but a Babe? History does not tell us whether they were or not, but it *does* say that the three kings fell down and worshipped Him. How Joseph's heart swelled within him as he watched these three earthly princes paying homage to the Infant in his care! He was always joyous to see others recognize the Treasure in their midst.

However, the Magi had no sooner left their famous gifts and departed, than Joseph's joy was turned to dread. He and Mary had settled them-selves for the night with the Infant Jesus sleeping soundly in His improvised cradle between them. Joseph dozed off. Then the same Angel who had come to him before appeared again. "Arise," he said. "Take the Child and His Mother and fly into Egypt, and stay there until I shall tell you to return. For Herod will seek the Child to destroy Him."

Herod! That cruel king who wanted to hold on to his fame and power forever, and would kill anyone who might endanger him! Now he was even stooping to murdering infants—so much did the throne mean to him!

Joseph scrambled to his feet and wakened Mary with a few hasty words of explanation. While she packed their few belongings and a little food, and bundled the Infant securely against the cold, Joseph doused the smoldering fire and readied their little donkey for his long journey. In a matter of minutes, they were on their way.

Desert nights are cold. The very stars seemed to shiver, as by their uncertain light Joseph led the little donkey over the rough terrain toward the southwest. He dared not seek out the highway, for Herod's soldiers might already be storming their way along it. He kept to the hills and gullies, seeking out the shadows as much as possible and praying fervently under his breath. The meek little donkey was docile to his guiding hand, and surefooted despite the rough going.

Was that the sound of pursuit? Joseph paused, and he and Mary looked back. They could hear cries and agonizing screams. The city was out of sight. "The innocent are being slain tonight," Mary whispered. Joseph tugged at the little donkey's bridle, and the faithful beast moved forward again.

As they made their way through the darkness, Joseph recalled how God had led His chosen people out of Egypt. The Pharoah's army had been in hot pursuit, so God had opened the waters of the Red Sea to let the Israelites pass. Surely, He would deliver them now!

Morning found the travelers far from Bethlehem. They pressed on to the Mediterranean, and struck out into the desert to the southwest. For about nine grim days they trekked, weary and hungry, beneath the searing sun and the icy stars. At last, they came to the Nile—and Egypt.

Egypt had always been a land of idolatry and superstition, but now the Son of God Himself had come to sanctify it with His presence. The Holy Family journeyed around a bit, then found lodgings in Heliopolis, where Joseph went to work at once to earn a little bread for them to eat.

How long did they remain in Egypt? No one is sure, but when King Herod died the Angel appeared once more to Joseph and said, "Arise and take the Child and His Mother, and go into the land of Israel: for they are dead that sought the life of the Child."

As always, Joseph obeyed the Angel at once. He took Mary and Jesus—Who was no longer an Infant—and began the long trek back across the desert. Upon reaching their homeland he learned that Herod's wicked son Archelaus was ruling in Judea, so he prayed earnestly to learn where he should settle his family. Again in a dream the Angel directed him. "Go to Nazareth in Galilee," he said. "There you will be safe."

And so it was that Jesus grew up in a hill village of Galilee.

❊   ❊   ❊

When the Child was twelve, Mary and Joseph took Him to Jerusalem for the Feast of the Passover. They spent a week attending the services, and then at the Feast's conclusion they joined the caravan bound for Galilee. At least, two of them did!

It was the custom of the time for the men to walk together and the women to travel in a separate group, while the children attached themselves to either parent. Hence Joseph traveled with the other men, and assumed that Jesus was with His Mother. At nightfall, however, he was startled when Mary hastened up to him and asked, "Joseph, where is Jesus?"

"Hasn't He been with you? I haven't seen Him since morning!"

"No, I thought He was with you!"

For an agonizing moment they stared at one another. Then Joseph, fighting down the wave of alarm that surged within him, murmured, "Why don't you look among the women, while I search among the men?"

They searched half the night, but in vain. The next day relatives and friends joined them, scattering out into the countryside along the caravan route, looking behind every rock and bush and in every gully, but there was no success. "It's all my fault," Joseph told himself.

On the third day, Mary and Joseph reentered Jerusalem and made their way to the Temple. And there, in the midst of a ring of doctors of the Law, discussing the prophecies with them, was Jesus!

Mary hurried to Him. "Son, why have You done this to us? Your father and I have sought You in sorrow!"

Joseph didn't say a word. He just took the Boy's slim hand in his big, rough one and gave it a squeeze. He didn't mind that Jesus had been about His Father's business—just so long as He was safe!

They went home again to Nazareth, and Jesus was subject to Mary and Joseph. Hours, days, years of hard work passed by, with Joseph and Jesus laboring together diligently in their little shop. What a humble virtuous man was this carpenter whom God had chosen for His foster father! He did few things extraordinary, but what love of God he had!

After Jesus had grown to manhood, Joseph died a peaceful death. It was a great comfort to him to die in the arms of Jesus and Mary. That is one reason why St. Joseph is protector of the dying. He is also the patron of workingmen and of the Universal Church. Just as he protected the Infant Jesus from the cruel Herod, St. Joseph now protects the Mystical Christ, His Holy Church.

St. Joseph was always quiet, but he was a hard worker. He knew that it is more important to really do something good than just to talk about it.

Saint Peter

Prince of the Apostles

He was sturdy and sunbronzed, with a curly auburn beard and a sparkling pair of eyes which took in everything around him. His restless gaze usually fell on the same simple surroundings—a battered boat, a mended net, a serious elder brother, a treacherous lake called Galilee and the red tiled roofs of a city called Capharnaum. Simon was a fisherman, and as far as he knew he would be such until the day he died.

Then came the day that his brother Andrew, usually so quiet, rushed up to Simon and cried, "We have found the Messias!" That day marked a turning point in his life.

The Man Jesus, to whom Andrew brought Simon, gazed long and searchingly upon the sturdy fisherman. "From now on you shall be called Cephas," He said at last. *Cephas* means "rock". Another form of the word is *Peter*.

Simon Peter did not understand why Jesus had given him such a name, nor did he really care. All he knew was that there was something wonderful about this strong, gentle Man, and he wished to stay with Him and learn more about Him.

⁂ ⁂ ⁂

Jesus had other followers, too. They were John, Philip and Nathanael. All together, the little group trudged through the high Galilean hills to the town of Cana, where friends of Jesus' Mother were being married.

It was there—at Cana—that Peter and his friends saw an astounding thing. In answer to a plea from His Mother, Jesus changed many gallons of water into strong, red wine! Peter could hardly believe his eyes. Now he was firmly convinced that Jesus was an extraordinary Man. He must, indeed, be the Messias—the long-awaited King of Israel!

Often, during the next few months, Peter listened to Jesus preach. In fact, one morning He gave a sermon from the big fisherman's boat.

It was a morning when Peter was feeling quite out of sorts. It had been a long night out there on the dark water, and his big net held nothing to show for it all, except a stray crab and a snatch of seaweed. Now the hot sun beat down on him and

Andrew as they bent over their net, scraping away barnacles and muck, making ready for another try. Nearby, John and his brother James, their father Zebedee and their crew were doing the same. They, too, had had a profitless night.

Then a babble of voices came from the hilltop behind them. Looking up, Peter saw an eager mob milling about the tall, straight figure of Jesus! He scrambled to his feet.

It was a large crowd, and growing larger moment by moment. How they swarmed about the Master, almost crushing Him! Peter watched with concern as Jesus drew near. "They'll push Him into the lake any minute now," he muttered. "Why don't the ninnies look where they're going?"

Jesus reached Peter's boat resting there with its prow in the sand, and stepped over the gunwale. He asked Peter to put out a little from the shore. The big fisherman jumped to obey. After poling out a few feet, he dropped anchor and sat there, listening to Jesus speak and watching the faces of the crowd. How intent they were!

When the sermon was ended, Jesus turned to Peter and said, "Put out into the deep, and lower your nets for a catch."

A catch? But night was the time to catch fish, and they had caught no fish from sundown to sunrise! "Master, the whole night we have toiled and have taken nothing; but at Your word I will lower the net!"

What could they possibly catch? But Peter would have done *anything* that Jesus told him to do.

The net was lowered. The net was . . . *filled* in a matter of minutes! Peter could hardly believe his eyes, for as he and Andrew tried to haul it in, the meshes began to break from the weight of all the fish. He waved his arms like a windmill. Zebedee and his crew pushed off from the shore and rushed to help. Fish after fish tumbled into each boat, as the sturdy seamen hauled them in.

"We're likely to sink!" panted Andrew.

But Peter was thinking of other things. Who was he, rude and impatient as he was, to have such a great favor done to him? Such a wonderful thing could have been done only by the power of God. Jesus must be a very holy man—and he, Peter, was not worthy of His company.

Heedless of the flopping fish, he fell to his knees at Jesus' feet. "Depart from me, for I am a sinful man, O Lord!"

Jesus' reply was reassuring: "Do not be afraid. From now on you will catch men."

And when they had returned to the shore, they left everything to Zebedee and his crew and followed Jesus.

* * *

From that time on, Peter was almost always with Jesus, hanging onto the Master's every word, watching with eyes big with wonder His many cures of the sick. How kind He was—and how powerful!

The group of disciples grew and grew. People heard of Jesus' miracles and came from all over to see Him and hear Him speak. One night, when the Master wished to retire into solitude to pray, the disciples and a large crowd followed Him. They camped on a hillside near where He had hidden Himself to pray.

On that hillside the following morning, Jesus chose twelve of the disciples to be His most particular followers. "Peter!" He called. Peter's tanned face broke into a broad grin. He had hoped to be chosen, but had never expected to be called ahead of John and James. "Andrew. James. John. Philip. Bartholomew. Matthew. Thomas. James. Simon. Jude. Judas."

The group of Twelve was complete, and Jesus began to preach to the crowd. He told them, "Blessed are the poor in spirit, for theirs is the kingdom of Heaven. Blessed are the meek, for they shall possess the earth. Blessed are they who mourn, for they shall be comforted. Blessed are they who hunger and thirst for holiness, for they shall be satisfied. Blessed are the merciful, for they shall obtain mercy. Blessed are the pure of heart, for they shall see God. Blessed are the peacemakers, for they shall be called children of God. Blessed are those who suffer persecution for justice's sake, for theirs is the kingdom of Heaven."

Here was the Master, the Messias, the future king of Israel, speaking of docility rather than valor, of kindness rather than fierceness. What a strange sort of king He would be! Peter, now the Master's right-hand man, was worried. "We won't last a week at that rate," he muttered to himself. Kings had to be warriors and they needed fierce fighting men around them.

But Peter's bewilderment was replaced by admiration as the disciples followed Jesus from village to village, watching crowds press about Him, witnessing the many miracles He worked. One day the disciples saw Jesus feed a crowd of over five thousand, just from five loaves of bread and two little fish. But that same evening they were in for an even greater jolt.

They were across the lake from Capharnaum, and as the day began to wane Jesus said, "Take the boat and return to the other shore. I will remain here for a time and will rejoin you later." So Peter and his companions set sail for Capharnaum.

As darkness fell, the breeze freshened, and it became necessary to take to the oars to hold the boat on her course. She tossed and pitched and seemed to make no headway at all. They fought the choppy sea for hours. Then they saw something!

It was a tall, pale form gliding across the water toward them. "A ghost!" someone gulped. Frantically the disciples strained at the oars.

"Take courage!" a gentle voice called. "It is I; do not be afraid."

"It is the Master," cried Peter happily. How glad he was to see Him! "Lord, if it is really You," he called, "tell me to come to You upon the water!"

"Come," Jesus replied.

In a flash, Peter was over the side of the boat, hurrying across the waves toward Jesus. When he had almost reached Him, he reflected on what he was doing. Why, this could not be—one could not walk on the tops of waves—waves were soft and one sank into them. . . . Peter looked down in terror, and—sure enough—he was beginning to sink. The black water was surging up all around him. Another second and he would be under. . . . "Master!" he wailed, "save me!"

And then he felt the grip of Jesus' strong hand, and he was atop the waves again.

"Oh you of little faith," said the Master gently, "why did you doubt?"

And standing beside Jesus on the plunging wavetops, Peter felt very small and very ashamed indeed.

*   *   *

One day Jesus asked His disciples who the people thought He was.

"Some say Elias; and others, Jeremias or another of the prophets."

"And you—" Jesus asked, "who do you say that I am?"

And then Peter knew—knew why Jesus seemed to be more than man. "You are the Christ, the Son of the living God."

"Blessed are you, Simon son of John," the Master replied. "Flesh and blood has not revealed this to you, but My Father in Heaven. And I say to you, you are Peter and upon this rock I will build My Church, and the gates of hell shall not prevail against it. . . .

"But say nothing of this to anyone else."

Soon thereafter as the little band of disciples walked along a dusty road, Jesus told them that He would one day suffer and die, but that He would rise again on the third day. Peter was amazed. Such a thing was not possible! As soon as he had a chance, he stole up alongside the Master and said softly, "Far be it from You, O Lord; this will never happen to You."

Jesus turned and looked him straight in the eyes. "Get behind me, satan. You are a scandal to Me, for you do not mind the affairs of God but those of men."

The other disciples heard the rebuke, too. Seeing their wide eyes and open mouths, Jesus continued, "If anyone wishes to come after Me, let him deny himself, and take up his cross and follow Me."

Peter mulled over the strange words. Satan! His Master said he had taken the part of the devil because he had said He would never suffer and die. And then He had said that one must suffer in order to follow Him! How little I understand the Master and His kingdom, Peter mused. And yet He has chosen me to be one of His closest followers. How much I have to learn!

Six days later Peter was in for another surprise. Jesus took him together with James and John to the top of Mount Tabor, where He became as radiant as the sun. Moses and Elias stood speaking with Him, and then a bright cloud came overhead and a voice from the cloud said, "This is My beloved Son in Whom I am well pleased; hear Him."

It was an experience which would give Peter much courage during the trials which lay ahead of him.

✿   ✿   ✿

On the Feast of the Passover, almost three years after his first meeting with Jesus, Peter witnessed the institution of the Holy Eucharist. The Master had told His disciples before, that those who ate His Flesh and drank His Blood would have life everlasting. Now He took bread and giving thanks, broke it and distributed it among them saying, "This is My Body which is being given for you; do this in remembrance of Me." He also took a cup of wine and passed it among them, saying, "This cup is the new covenant in My Blood, which shall be shed for you."

Which shall be shed. . . . Those mysterious words again. Jesus was sure He was to suffer and die—and indeed danger seemed to be lurking on all sides these days, so openly hostile were the scribes and pharisees.

And now the Master was speaking again, telling His disciples to serve one another, and that the greatest among them should act as the least. Indeed before the supper He had washed their feet as an example of the service they should give one another. He turned to Peter and added, "Simon, Simon, Satan has desired to have you so that he may sift you as wheat. But I have prayed for you that your faith may not fail, and once you have turned again; strengthen your brothers."

Once he had turned again? "Lord," protested the fisherman, "I am ready to go to prison with You and even to death!"

Then Jesus spoke even more plainly, "I tell you, Peter, before a cock crows twice you will deny Me three times."

* * *

Jesus lead His little band—they were eleven now for suddenly Judas was missing—across the valley of Cedron and up a slope to the garden of Gethsemane where the rays of the paschal moon filtered down between the olive trees. The air was very still.

"Come." Jesus motioned Peter, James and John to climb farther up the hillside with Him. Peter noticed the change in his Master's expression. All evening He had seemed sad, but now there was utter dread in His eyes. Seeing Peter's concern, Jesus explained, "My soul is sad, sad even to death. Wait here and pray."

The three watched Him move on among the trees and drop to His knees a few yards away. They, too, knelt. "Father," they heard Jesus say, "all things are possible to You. If it is Your will, remove this cup from Me—but Your will, not Mine, be done."

Peter tried to pray, too. He had never seen his Master so sad. He had never.... His eyes were closing. It had been a long day, with a big meal at the end of it. He forced his eyes open again and looked toward Jesus. He was praying. Peter must try to pray, too. Jesus wanted him to....

"Simon, are you sleeping? Could you not watch for even an hour? Watch and pray that you may not enter into temptation."

Peter stared up at the Master in confusion. He struggled to his knees as Jesus added, "The spirit is willing, but the flesh is weak." He turned and walked away.

Peter listened to Jesus repeat His prayer to the Father: "Not My will but Yours be done, not My will but Yours . . ." And suddenly the Master was bending over him again. "Simon," He reproved. The three disciples looked up at Him tongue-tied. They did not know what to say. Silently He left them and returned to His place of prayer.

This time the Master fell to the ground in agony. It was as if He bore the weight of all the world on His shoulders. Later Peter would understand that it was the weight of all the sins which would ever be committed that bore his Master to the ground. Those sins placed a deep, dark gulf between Jesus and the infinite purity of His Father. And Jesus' face became dark with drops of blood, so violent was the torment in His soul.

Peter did not see the Angel who came to strengthen Jesus, to keep Him from dying of sorrow; Peter's eyelids had closed again.

"Sleep on now," came the weary voice cutting through Peter's dream. "Take your rest." The fisherman opened his eyes as if in a daze.

"The hour has come," Jesus went on. "The Son of Man has been betrayed into the hands of sinners. Rise, let us go. He who will betray Me is at hand."

The disciples staggered to their feet. Strange noises filled the air; strange lights came flickering toward them. A large group of men was coming through the trees, carrying clubs and swords. In their lead loomed a familiar figure—Judas.

"Hail, Rabbi." And Judas kissed Jesus in greeting. Jesus looked into the depths of the betrayer's soul and asked, "Do you betray the Son of Man with a kiss?"

Men rushed forward and grasped Him. He did not resist. "Shall we strike them, Master?" asked one of the disciples. Peter seized one of the two swords they had brought, and looked about fiercely. Then he lunged at one of the high priest's servants and sliced off his ear.

"Put back your sword," Jesus told him. "Those who use the sword will perish by it. Do you not know that My Father would send more than twelve legions of Angels if I asked Him? How else can the Scriptures be fulfilled that this *must* take place?" And reaching out, He healed the man's ear in an instant.

The mob was pressing in about Him. He was speaking to them, asking why they had come at night, with weapons, as if He were a criminal. Peter slipped into the shadows. From his hiding place he watched them lead his Master away. Then he followed.

❊ ❊ ❊

It was to the high priest's palace that they took Jesus first. The place was heavily guarded and Peter hesitated, for he knew that he would not be admitted. John, instead, entered the palace, for he knew the high priest. Soon he approached the maid who watched the gate and asked her to admit Peter. "Are you also one of this Man's disciples?" she asked him.

"I don't know what you are talking about," replied Peter. He pushed his way into the courtyard, where palace guards and other servants were warming themselves around a fire. So as not to attract attention, he joined the group, meanwhile straining his ears for news of what was going on within. Suddenly he heard fierce cries of, "Death! Death!" and a babble of shrieks and curses. He shuddered, and his concern showed in his face.

"This is one of them," the maid exclaimed, pointing toward Peter.

"No," Peter replied. "Not I!"

But a relative of the man whose ear had been cut off was gazing at him intently. "Did I not see you in the garden with Him?"

This time Peter was emphatic. He swore with an oath, "I do not know this Man you are talking about!"

The din inside the house had grown louder, but above it could be heard the shrill crowing of a cock. At the same time, Peter saw men leading Jesus through the courtyard. For an agonizing instant, the Master turned and looked straight upon him. And then Peter knew what he had done!

He turned and fled through the crowd, stumbled out into the blackness, and became lost in the night—lost in his own sea of bitterness.

No one knows where he went or what he did for the next two days. Many think that he stood at the edge of the crowd which gathered before Pilate—that he saw the high priest's agents moving among the people, rousing them to scream out "Crucify Him! Crucify Him!" Probably he followed the painful procession to Calvary and watched from afar the agony of the crucifixion. He dared not approach the cross; he could not bear to face Mary, Jesus' Mother.

The following Sunday morning Peter and John were together when Mary Magdalen came rushing up to tell them that Jesus' Body had vanished from the tomb. The disciples ran to the open sepulchre, and found that it was so. Yet they were not sure what this meant.

Sometime during the day the risen Jesus appeared to Peter alone. No one knows what happened in their meeting. We can imagine how glad Peter was to see his Master, and how grateful he felt when Jesus forgave him his sin of betrayal. However, he would always remember his denial with tears of sorrow.

In Galilee a few weeks later, Peter and some of his companions were fishing on the lake, when Jesus called to them from the beach. As soon as he knew it was Jesus, Peter plunged into the water and swam ashore; he was so eager to see his Master that he couldn't wait for the boat to bring him to land!

After they had eaten together, the Master turned to Peter and asked, "Simon, son of John, do you love Me more than these do?"

"Yes, Lord, You know that I love You!"

"Feed My lambs."

Then Jesus repeated His question, "Simon, son of John, do you love Me?"

"Yes, Lord, You know that I love You!"

"Feed My lambs."

A third time Jesus asked Peter, "Simon, son of John, do you love Me?"

"Lord," the big fisherman replied, "You know all things, You know that I love You!"

"Feed My sheep."

And that was how Peter made a triple declaration of love in reparation for his triple denial. At the same time he received from Jesus the command to take care of the entire Church—the lambs, or faithful, and the sheep, or clergy.

Forty days after His Resurrection, Jesus ascended into Heaven. His Mother, Peter with the other apostles, and several disciples stood on the crest of Mount Olivet watching their Master rise steadily into the sky. Finally a small cloud hid Him from their view. They were alone, but Jesus had said, "I shall not leave you as orphans; I will send you another Advocate." The little band made its way back to Jerusalem to await His coming.

For nine days they prayed together in that large room where they had celebrated the Pasch. At about nine in the morning of the tenth day, they heard a roaring sound as if a mighty wind were blowing. Then they saw parted tongues of flames above one another's head. And all at once, those things which Jesus had said to them which they had found so hard to understand became clear in their minds! They understood His mission—and their own!

Peter and his companions hurried out into the street, where they found a growing crowd of Jewish people who had come from almost every part of the known world to celebrate the harvest feast of Pentecost. The sound of the rushing wind had attracted them. At once Peter and his companions began to tell them of Jesus—how He had fulfilled the prophecies, how He had been crucified, had risen from the dead and ascended into Heaven— how He had been God Himself!

The listeners understood, too, for God's Spirit had poured forth His grace in abundance. "What shall we do, brothers?" came the cry.

"Repent of your sins and be baptized every one of you in the name of Jesus Christ. . . . "

By nightfall three thousand people had been baptized.

* * *

The sacrifice of the cross, renewed as Jesus had taught in the Last Supper, became the center of these men's lives. They found themselves being transformed by the Eucharist and by the Spirit, until they were truly practicing the humility and charity that Jesus had spoken of in His Sermon on the Mount. St. Luke would soon write, "The multitude of believers were of one heart and one soul."

And so the infant Church began to grow. It grew in spite of persecutions from the high priest's followers. It grew to include Gentiles, for Peter learned in a vision that these, too, were to be admitted into its ranks. All men were to be saved, if they but desired it and cooperated with the grace of God.

After a time, Peter went to live in Antioch, a much larger city than Jerusalem, which had become an important center of apostolate. It was there that members of the young Church were first called "Christians." Later, Peter went to Rome, the center of the Empire.

He took up residence in the Jewish section of the city, and began preaching in its fourteen synagogues. Some of the people believed him and were baptized in the Tiber.

After a short journey to Jerusalem, Peter settled in Rome for good.

About that time he wrote two epistles, or letters, to the Christians in Asia Minor who needed a special word of comfort. Many were being persecuted. Suffering—he wrote—is a source of merit for the Christian and must be accepted. He urged them to be humble and kind and to give good example to the pagans around them.

John Mark, nephew of the Apostle Barnabas, was in Rome with Peter, and he wrote down the life of Jesus as he had heard Peter tell it many times. Mark's book became the Second Gospel, and it is especially interesting because of its many details— for Peter remembered those events clearly as if they had happened just a year before, instead of thirty years before.

Suddenly the Emperor Nero's persecution of the Christians broke out. Peter was seized, imprisoned, and sentenced to death, together with Paul, who was also laboring in Rome at that time. They were led out of the prison together, and Paul was taken away to be beheaded, for he was a Roman citizen. Peter, instead, was led to a hill called the Vatican. He recalled something Jesus had once told him. "When you grow old, you will stretch out your hands, and someone will bind you and take you where you do not wish to go." Ahead of him, Peter saw a strong soldier carrying a cross which he himself was too weak to bear.

They reached the hill. Peter recalled another hill—that of Golgotha—and another cross. I am unworthy to die as the Master did, he thought.

"If you don't mind," he requested, "crucify me upside down."

They placed him upside down on the cross, and the agony began—pain seemed to tear at every limb and organ until his blood-filled eyes could see no more and numbness overcame him. And then he saw the gates of Paradise opening wide before him, and he gazed again on the face of that gentle Master whom he loved so well.

One of the most beautiful qualities St. Peter had was his willingness to admit he was wrong and to accept corrections well. If we imitate him in this we will acquire the virtue of humility.

Saint Paul

Apostle of the Gentiles

When Rome ruled all the lands around about the blue Mediterranean Sea, and Jesus Himself walked the dusty roads of Palestine, there was a seaport city in Asia Minor called Tarsus. Many rich Jewish families lived there, and in one of those families was a boy named Saul.

Saul's father was a Pharisee. This meant that he followed many strict religious rules and that Saul would have to live according to all those rules, too. Bright and active, the boy began his schooling at the age of five, with the study of the Bible.

As he grew older, his adventurous spirit often led Saul down to the harbor, where he watched the ships bringing goods in from foreign lands and taking away other goods which had come in from the Orient by camel caravan. Soon he could recognize the different types of ships and where they were from. "This one is Roman," he would say to his comrades. "That one is from Greece; do you hear the sailors' accent? Those merchants over there are from Rome, too; you can tell from the way they speak their Latin. . . ." When Saul wasn't at the waterfront, he was usually watching the games in the stadium. Never a dull moment for him! Life was too interesting, too exciting!

Even wealthy Jewish boys learned to work with their hands in those days. Saul's trade was to be tentmaking, and he began to learn it while still quite small. Little did he realize how useful tent-making would be to him one day.

"Come, O Lord, and don't delay," the boy often prayed, for like all Jewish children he was awaiting the coming of the Messias whom God had promised to His people. No one knew that the Messias was living in a little town called Nazareth, learning the carpenter's trade from his foster father; everyone was waiting for a mighty prince who would come to free Israel from the Roman armies and conquer the whole world. Everyone was in for a big surprise!

While Jesus was still living His quiet, hidden life in Nazareth of Galilee, Saul set out with a camel caravan which was going up to Jerusalem. The boy was now twelve years old, and ready to undertake the studies which would prepare him to become a rabbi, or teacher of the Hebrew Law. What a joy it was to glimpse the Holy City for the first time! The majestic Temple of Jerusalem towered up into the sky, a dazzling tribute to the true God. Here, Saul would learn to know and serve Him in the best way he could. His heart beat expectantly. . . .

School was fascinating. One learned the history of the Jewish people and read the prophecies of the Messias. Then there were all the rules and regulations which the Pharisees had to follow. Saul studied hard and learned quickly. Often he debated with another bright boy who had opinions very different from his own. The years slipped quickly by.

At last, Saul was preparing to return to Tarsus. "Shall we ever meet again, Stephen?" he asked the schoolchum with whom he had debated so much.

"Let us hope so," replied Stephen sincerely, "in that era of love and kindness and peace which is to come." Strange words, those, and a prophecy which Saul did not recognize at the time.

Saul was in Tarsus when Jesus began His public ministry and proclaimed Himself to be the Messias. He was in Tarsus when the angry Pharisees refused to admit that the poor Man Who spoke of a spiritual kingdom was really the leader promised by God to His people. Saul was in Tarsus when word came that the leaders in Jerusalem had killed Jesus in the most horrible and painful and shameful way they could.

* * *

What had come over Stephen? Saul wondered, as he stood talking with his old classmate in the streets of Jerusalem. Something was different about him now; there was a light in his eyes which Saul had never seen before. "Jesus is the Messias, Saul!" Stephen said excitedly. "He has proven what He said with His miracles. All the prophecies are fulfilled in Him! He has risen from the dead!"

As far as Saul was concerned, Jesus had been a heretic who had caused disputes among the people. "Keep still!" he roared at Stephen. "Be still or I'll beat you!"

It wasn't long after that, that the Jews arrested Stephen. He had disturbed them too much with the miracles he was working and with all the conversions he was making to the new religion that followed Jesus.

The stoning of Stephen

"You are fighting against the grace of the Holy Spirit," Stephen told the angry mob which surrounded him.

"Traitor!" they screamed back.

Nobody wanted to listen to Stephen. They had what they called a trial, but the judges had decided he was guilty before the trial even began. "Stone him!" the mob yelled, and they dragged him away through the city streets until they found an open space where they could all stand around and heave heavy rocks at the young man with the gentle expression in his eyes.

"Kill the Nazarene! Kill him!" It was Saul shouting; Saul with his eyes afire with fury, with hatred for the religion he believed was false. He leaped to the top of a pile of stones.

"Hold my cloak, Saul!" shouted one of the mob.

"Mine, too!" screamed another. "I can aim better now!"

Stephen fell beneath a hail of stones. Blood gushed from wound after wound and soaked into the sand as stones continued to rain down about him. Saul could still see the young man's face. Strange, that peaceful expression it bore! He looked almost joyful in the midst of such agony. . . .

"O Lord," the martyr murmured, "do not lay this sin to their charge!" Those were his last words.

*   *   *

Stephen's death did not end the persecution of the new religion. Fiery and bold, Saul began a campaign of tracking down Jesus' followers and seizing them. He stormed through the cities and towns of Palestine; without meaning to, he was actually spreading the new religion, for Jesus' followers fled from city to city before him.

"We must go to Damascus," Saul decided. He knew that this city had become a new center of the "Nazarenes" because of his persecution. With a band of soldiers he set out across the desert in search of the fugitives.

After days of travel, Saul saw the city before him. His hopes soared; everything was carefully planned and he felt that not a soul would escape him. Even the horses quickened their gait expectantly, for they sensed that they were near their destination. What a great thing he was about to do . . . Saul thought. He would . . . What was that strange sound in his ears? Why did his horse stop suddenly and stand still trembling so violently? The very air about him seemed to explode with light, and an unknown power threw him to the ground. Head ringing, gasping for breath, he struggled to open his eyes.

"Saul, Saul, why do you persecute Me?" The Voice was gentle, reproaching.

"Lord," the dazed man said weakly, "Who are You?"

What terror the reply must have struck into his heart, for the Voice answered, "I am Jesus, Whom you persecute."

Jesus!

Jesus was indeed alive. Therefore, He *was* the Messias. Not only that, but He identified Himself

Saul receiving the letters

with those whom Saul had persecuted. Saul felt sick; what a terrible, terrible blunder he had made!

"It is hard for you to kick against the goad," added the Voice kindly. Yes, Saul thought, it was very hard indeed. He could not deny the facts that were facing him, even though he shrank from admitting that he had been wrong all his life.

Swallowing his pride and foresaking his past, he asked, "Lord, what will You have me do?"

And Jesus sent Saul into the city to the house of a man named Jude, who cared for him, because Saul had become blind.

* * *

"Ananias."

"Here I am, Lord."

Ananias, one of the Nazarene leaders, was having a dream. Or was it a dream? At any rate, he heard the Voice of Jesus urging him, "Go to the Street called Straight. Look in the home of Jude for a man from Tarsus named Saul, for he is praying."

Saul? Saul of Tarsus? Praying? That persecutor?

"Lord," protested Ananias. He explained to Jesus about the persecution. Had the Lord forgotten those things?

"Go," was the reply. Then came words which are unforgettable: "This man has been chosen to make Me known throughout the world. I will show him how much he must suffer for My Name."

No longer hesitant, Ananias hurried to the home of Jude and asked to be taken to Saul. He found him, indeed, praying as the Lord had said.

Saul could see again!

He was like a man groping in the blackness for a light. "Saul, my brother," said Ananias, "the Lord Jesus has sent me to you so that you may see and be filled with the Holy Spirit." Suddenly Saul felt peace in his soul, and he found, too, that he could see once more.

Ananias baptized Saul, thus making him a member of that Church which he had hated, a follower of the Christ Whom he had persecuted. Now he must do everything in his power to spread the Faith; how else could he thank Jesus for the great mercy He had shown him?

Saul sat down and ate a hearty meal (his first in three days) and walked out of Jude's house a new man in body and in soul. The grace of God had changed a bold persecutor into an ardent apostle!

The Nazarenes, or Christians as they would soon be called, received Saul kindly. They forgave him all the harm he had done them, for they knew Our Lord wanted it that way. They watched with interest as Saul boldly went among his people to preach Christ to them. They saw how his sincerity and his burning love for Christ brought about many conversions.

The leaders became alarmed. Saul had been a powerful man to have on their side; now, fortified by divine grace, he was much more powerful against them! Something had to be done.

"Let us kill him!"

But the Christians found out about the plot and warned Saul. The new apostle, disguised as an Arab, strode off into the lonely desert wastes.

Alone with God

In the desert, Saul was alone with God. Jesus instructed him with inspirations and revelations. Saul did penance for his sins and prayed fervently. He became as rugged in spirit as the stern countryside around him. It wasn't until three years later that he returned to Damascus.

Saul's enthusiasm led him to preach again to his people. As before, he put himself in danger. "They're after you again, Saul, " came the warning. This time, it took a little more ingenuity to sneak him out of the city. The gates were being watched, so his friends lowered him over the city wall in a large basket, like those used by traders. They watched him merge with the shadows of the night. Saul was now bound for Jerusalem.

The apostles, who led the young Church with St. Peter as their head, had heard of Saul's conversion but had never met him since, nor had they any proof that he was now, truly, one of them. They were cautious and cool when he came to them in Jerusalem. It was not until one of the disciples, Barnabas, believed in Saul's sincerity and spoke to the others, that the new apostle was accepted by the Twelve.

Saul spent fifteen days in Jerusalem. With Peter, he walked the way which Jesus had followed to Calvary, prayed at the tomb, and recalled the anguish he himself had caused Jesus. "I persecuted Him."

"I denied Him," said Peter, and both thanked God from the depths of their hearts for the mercy He had shown them.

The escape

Burning with eagerness to atone for his past, Saul went to Jerusalem to preach that Jesus was the Messias, but he found that their hearts were hardened; they had no wish to believe. Soon they were plotting to kill him.

One day, when Saul was praying in the Temple, Jesus appeared before him and greeted him with these words: "Do not be discouraged, but hurry and leave the city. I shall send you to the peoples of distant nations."

Saul obeyed. He went home to Tarsus, and established a fervent community of Christians there while he awaited further instructions from the Lord.

* * *

A few years had slipped by when Barnabas appeared on the scene. "Come to Antioch, Saul; we need you there!"

Now, Antioch in Syria was the third largest city in the whole Roman Empire, so it was good news indeed that there were already many Christians there. In fact, it was in Antioch that members of the Church were first called by the name, Christian. Saul found that his days in Antioch were full indeed, as he preached, instructed, baptized. . . .

One day there was bad news from Jerusalem: "Famine!" The Christians living there might starve unless Antioch could send help. Quickly the faithful of that great city gathered together a sum of money for their brother Christians. Saul and Barnabas were chosen to deliver it.

How much Jerusalem had changed! The city and its buildings were the same, but its people were

In the Master's footsteps

openly hostile. James, one of the apostles who had been closest to the Lord, had been arrested and his head had been sliced off. Now Peter himself was in prison awaiting trial. It was an anxious band of Christians which gathered in the home of Mary, Mark's mother, to pray.

Peter was to be put to death the next day. What would become of the little flock should it lose its sturdy chief? No one dared to think of it; they literally stormed heaven with their prayers.

What was that rapping at the door at this hour of the night? Perhaps their enemies had come to seize them, too. Peter's followers stared at one another in terror.

At last a serving girl went to investigate. "Peter! It's you!"

"An Angel of the Lord delivered me," said Peter humbly. "Let us all give thanks to God."

* * *

Saul and Barnabas, accompanied by Barnabas' cousin Mark, were setting out on a missionary journey. What a thrill it would be to tell the Gentiles about Christ! Their hearts beat high with excitement as they set sail for the Mediterranean Island of Cyprus.

They had departed in peace, for the persecution was over. The hand of the Lord had smote the evil king, Herod Agrippa. The Church was again free to grow.

"Where is the synagogue?" the missionaries asked as soon as they set foot on Cyprus soil. After all, they found it natural to go first to the Jewish people, for they themselves were Jewish. How would the synagogues of Cyprus receive them?

"Thank God," Saul was able to say a few days later, "we've made a goodly number of conversions. It must be because of that, that the Roman governor has asked to see us."

It was an honor, indeed, to be called to meet the governor, and a splendid opportunity to speak about the Faith. But someone was ready and waiting to cause trouble for the apostles.

In those days there was a great deal of magic, and the governor, Sergius Paulus, had a crafty magician named Elymas living in his household. Elymas urged Paulus not to listen to Saul and Barnabas. "They're prating about a lot of nonsense," he said scornfully.

"Son of the devil!" retorted Saul. He suddenly felt himself full of the power of the Holy Spirit. "Here! As punishment you shall be blind for a time!" And Elymas gave a little cry; he began to grope about; it was plain to all who watched that the magician could no longer see.

Needless to say, the governor was amazed. Truly, he thought, men that possessed such great power must indeed be representatives of the true God. "Saul, will you baptize me into your Faith?" he asked. And so, Sergius Paulus became a fervent Christian.

It was at about this time that Saul changed his name. Perhaps he took the name *Paul* in honor of the governor, Paulus, or perhaps he had always had two names—the Hebrew to be used among his own nation and the Latin among his fellow citizens of Rome, for let us not forget that Paul had been born a Roman citizen. At any rate, from then on (for the rest of his life and all the centuries of history which followed) he has been known as the Apostle Paul.

* * *

There was a misunderstanding between Paul and Mark when the missionaries prepared to leave Cyprus. Mark returned home to Jerusalem alone, while Paul and Barnabas set sail for Asia Minor— there to tramp for miles through wild forests until they reached the city of Pisidian Antioch. There they spoke in the synagogue. Many Jews welcomed the new religon eagerly, and some of the Gentiles did, too, but as everywhere else, the leaders were angered at this. Persecution soon broke out, and Paul and Barnabas moved on to the next town, Iconium.

It was there that Paul converted the noble and virtuous maiden, Thecla, who was to be the first woman martyr of the Church. The Apostles made other conversions, too, but then the usual persecution broke out and they moved on again.

Something very strange happened in the next city, Lystra. A cripple was listening to the apostles' preaching. Paul looked at the poor man, and knew that he had faith. "Arise," said Paul, "and walk." The man arose; he was healed!

"It's Zeus himself," whispered one of the pagan mob to a companion. "It's Zeus, Zeus and Hermes!"

rose the cry. The pagans milled about in confusion. They were suddenly sure that Barnabas and Paul were their pagan gods! "To the temple!" shouted one. "Deck them with flowers; summon the priests!"

For a moment the poor apostles did not realize what all the shouting was about. Then it dawned on them. Paul was greatly angered. What a horrible thing it was to see the power of God Almighty attributed to Barnabas and himself—to see themselves considered Greek gods! Paul's words glowed with fire as he told the excited mob the truth. It was only through the power of the One and Only God Who made Heaven and earth that the crippled man had regained his health. He and Barnabas were only mere men like the pagans themselves.

A murmur passed through the throng. One moment they had been all happy and excited, eager for a festival and merry-making. Now they were silent and uneasy. The next moment they were furious. "It's a trick!" they shouted. "These vagabonds tricked us!" Someone picked up a stone. "That's right; let them have it! Stone them! Stone them! Stone them!"

A bruising hail of stones descended upon the apostles. Blow after blow. . .wound after wound. . . . "We'll have our procession!" And the enraged mob of pagans seized the limp forms of Paul and Barnabas and dragged them through the city streets. Once outside the walls, they left them in a heap on the ground. "They're dead for sure."

A good friend is a treasure, and Paul and Barnabas had made friends wherever they went—friends

Left for dead

for God and for themselves. Now some of them, Paul's most recent converts, approached the still forms. They had hope; perhaps the apostles were yet alive. Eagerly those good friends set to work to revive them.

Paul and Barnabas thus opened their eyes once more in the midst of a circle of anxious and compassionate faces, those of the new Christians who had begun already to practice their great Faith.

Tenderly cared for, the apostles recovered quickly in spite of the harsh treatment the pagans had given them. The next day saw Paul and Barnabas tramping the long road to the next city, aching in every muscle but full of hopes for more conversions. And they received them. After all, wasn't it likely that God would be generous with those who had been generous in doing what He wished?

※　※　※

Four years is a long time, especially if you pack as much as you can into each moment, trying to do everything in the best way possible so that God will give you a beautiful reward. So it was with Paul and Barnabas; they had done so much for the young Church in those few years—more than most men do in a lifetime. Now, Paul's first missionary journey was ending; the apostles returned to Antioch, anxious to tell their old friends of the many conversions they had made in Asia.

Of course, Paul went up to Jerusalem to see his chief, the Prince of the Apostles, to tell him of the new churches he had founded. Peter rejoiced, and had high hopes for Paul as he set out on his second journey, accompanied by a fellow Christian named Silas.

The apostles returned to Asia Minor. En route they passed through many of the cities visited on the last trip. One of them was Lystra, where a young Christian named Timothy asked to join the apostles. Paul welcomed the eager lad, for he read the sincerity in his heart. Timothy was to become a fervent apostle and a great saint.

After many days of walking and preaching, the missionaries reached Troas, a city near the sea. Across the water lay the mountainous lands of Greece and Macedonia.

"Come over to Macedonia and help us!" Paul heard those words distinctly one night as he lay sleeping. In his dream he saw an angel dressed as a Macedonian, begging him to bring those poor pagans the knowledge of Christ which he had taken to so many in Asia. Of course, Paul could not resist such an appeal, for he burned with the desire to bring the whole world to the feet of Jesus.

In Philippi, the first European city that the apostles visited, they gained some very good converts. One of them was a woman named Lydia who will always be remembered for her generosity and kindness. By this time, too, Paul and his companions had been joined by a physician and artist named Luke, that skilled writer who would one day record the Acts of the Apostles.

While they were in Philippi, the missionaries often met a slave girl who told fortunes. She would

Paul and Timothy

be amusing the crowds on a public street (and thus making some money for her masters) when the apostles passed. "These men are servants of the most high God," screamed the slave girl. Of course, what she said was true, but from the strange way she was acting, it seemed that she was possessed by the devil. Paul endured the screams for a few days, then he turned and said to the spirit who possessed the girl, "I command you in the name of Jesus Christ to go out of her!" At once the girl was herself again, and overjoyed to be free of the demon.

But the girl's masters were angry. She could no longer tell fortunes! How could they make money any more? Furious, they called on the city officials and complained that the apostles were preaching a religion that was against the law.

"Arrest them!" was the decision. And Paul and Silas were seized and beaten severely, then thrown into prison. Bruised and bleeding, they huddled in a dismal cell in the dark of night. "How good it is to be worthy to suffer for Christ!" exclaimed Paul. "Let's sing, brother!"

They sang. In spite of their pain, the apostles' voices rang out loud and clear, echoing through the prison and drifting out upon the cool night air. The other prisoners listened to them in wonder.

And suddenly the prison trembled with a violent earthquake; the cells shuddered as if they would be torn apart; their doors burst open.

"Brother," murmured Paul, "the earth has shaken and my bonds are broken."

"So are mine!" exclaimed Silas. "The Angel of the Lord has visited us!"

The jailor had wakened, and was terrified. "If the prisoners have escaped, I'm lost," he thought, knowing the cruelty of the city officials. "There's nothing I can do but kill myself." Following the example of many other Romans, he drew his sword and was prepared to plunge it into his heart.

"Wait!" cried Paul. "Don't hurt yourself; we're all here!"

The jailor was amazed. Fetters burst; doors opened; the Christians could have easily walked out and yet they were standing before him, calm and smiling!

Such character amazed him. Sinking to the floor at the apostles' feet, he asked, "What shall I do to be saved?"

"Believe in the Lord Jesus, and you and your family shall be saved."

While the jailor bathed the cruel sores which Paul and Silas had received from their scourging, the apostles instructed him in the Faith. Before morning, he and his family were baptised Christians!

Meanwhile, the city officials had changed their minds. They sent soldiers to set the apostles free. When he learned this, Paul protested that the officials themselves should come to free the apostles, since he and Silas were Roman citizens and, according to law, should not have been scourged. So, to the great embarrassment of the city leaders, they had to come personally and escort Paul out of prison!

The little band of missionaries pressed on. Only hearts on fire with love for God could have taken upon themselves what they had taken: the spreading of the Gospel to all men, no matter what hardships they should meet. There were times when everything they were trying to build up seemed to crumble—persecutions became more violent, converts fell into sin and error, words fell upon deaf ears. But Paul and his companions, afire with love of God and of souls, still strove to spend every ounce of energy they had—and more!—in the spread of truth, of love, of the way to salvation.

The next important city on their route was Thessalonica, where some Jews and many Gentiles were converted. One group of people, being jealous, stirred up a mob against the Christians. Many were cast into prison and released only after they paid a sum of money. To quiet the people and make life safer for his little flock, Paul left Thessalonica and went on to that famous Greek city, Athens.

Once Athens had been famous for the great and wise philosophers Socrates, Plato and Aristotle. But those men (who would have undertood Paul and Christianity so well) had died hundreds of years before, and since then the people of Athens had become too worldly and fond of comfort to appreciate the sublime spiritual teachings the apostle preached. Their hearts were small and hard; they laughed.

Only Dionysius, a wise judge, and Damaris, a kind woman, were converted and became faithful followers of the apostle.

In the big and bustling city of Corinth, Paul found the people more willing to accept the Faith. He remained there a year and a half, living with a couple named Aquila and Priscilla, and working as a tentmaker side by side with Aquila. The apostle found that the Corinthians were simple people. They received the Faith well. But after Paul left, they began to fall away from some of their Christian practices. When Paul received the word of that, he wrote them a letter which is sometimes read on Sunday during Holy Mass. In that letter is a beautiful passage on love for God and our neighbor. It is one of the many beautiful letters of St. Paul which help us to understand our Faith better.

The apostle did a great deal of penance for the conversion of souls. He spent his nights praying and working; he slept very little. Often he skipped supper. He had only possessions which he absolutely needed—nothing else. Another penance was his patient suffering of malaria fever, which came upon him often in those warm lands.

After Paul returned to Jerusalem to report on his second missionary journey, he revisited Antioch and returned to Asia. He wished to strengthen the faith of the Christians in those churches which he had founded in other years. In the seaport city of Ephesus he spent three years and worked many miracles. Even objects which he had touched gained the power of healing the sick and casting out devils—so great were God's gifts to His faithful servant.

People brought Paul evil books, filled with magic and superstition, so that he could make a great pile of them and burn them in the public square. What a grand blaze they made! To the people of Ephesus, that bright bonfire represented the light of the new Faith which Paul had brought to them.

Soon Paul's restless soul urged him to search for other people to bring to Christ. He boarded a ship for Macedonia and Greece. Then he returned to Asia, to the seaport of Troas. There an exciting thing happened to him.

He was celebrating Holy Mass in an upper room. The room was crowded full of Christians eager to assist at the holy Sacrifice and to hear Paul speak. During the sermon, some of the boys sat on the window sills, and as Paul spoke on and on about the great love of Jesus for every one of us, one of the young fellows became sleepy. His head began to sag. He nodded, caught himself, and sat upright. But in a minute his head was drooping again ... and all of a sudden it was too late ... he felt himself falling, falling!

"Eutychus!" screamed one of his companions. They rushed wildly down the stairs and out into the street. "Paul, Eutychus is dead!"

Paul had rushed down the stairs behind them. He shouldered his way through the crowd and knelt beside that still form. The boy had fallen three stories—onto the hard stones of the street. What could save him?

The power of God could save him! Paul gently took Eutychus into his arms, praying silently. After a moment he said, "It's all right; he's still alive!"

Sure enough! Eutychus was moving. His eyes opened. He blinked, and smiled up at Paul. "Praised be Jesus Christ," murmured one of the onlookers. Exclamations of joy ran through the crowd.

With their hearts full of love and thanks, the Christians returned to their upper room to continue their assistance at Mass.

After his short stay in Troas, Paul pushed on to Ephesus. How dear to his fatherly heart were the Christians who greeted him there! Perhaps he would never see them again, he thought. "Be true to the Faith," he urged them. They cried for sorrow as he prepared to board a ship for Jerusalem, and Paul himself had to wipe tears from his eyes.

The boat docked at a port in Palestine, and Paul set out on the overland journey to Jerusalem. Part way, he met an old prophet named Agabus, who was enlightened by the Holy Spirit. He came up to Paul, took his belt, and tied his own hands and feet together with it. "The man who owns this belt shall be bound just this way in Jerusalem," he said. There could be no doubt that he meant Paul!

"Paul, turn back now," his friends urged him. "You're risking your life! Your enemies must be waiting for you!" Luke was almost at the point of tears.

"What do you mean by weeping and breaking my heart?" Paul retorted. "I'm ready to be chained or even killed in Jerusalem—for the honor and glory of Jesus my Lord!"

Yes, Paul was determined. "God's will be done," said Luke softly.

Jerusalem! Tense and expectant, the little group entered the great city. They sought out the Christian meeting place, and were greeted with joy by James and their other friends. Peter was away on a secret mission, and had left James, the cousin of Jesus, in charge of the flock.

How eagerly the Jerusalem Christians listened to Paul's stories about conversions among the pagan Gentiles! But somehow word got around to the others—those who had never accepted Christianity. They were outraged. This man was telling the pagans about the one God! That was as bad as feeding good food to pigs! It was a sacrilege, according to their way of thinking.

They ganged up on Paul in the streets, suddenly storming down on him from all sides. "Beat him! Kill him!" they shouted. There was *thud* after *thud* as blow after blow fell on the apostle. Paul staggered; he was going to fall. . . .

"Here, now, what's all this?" It was a grim-faced Roman officer, who had come just in time to see Paul's enemies closing in for the kill. "Arrest this man," the officer barked to his soldiers. "Bind him in chains. Take him to the prison." Certainly this man must be a great criminal to have angered such a crowd so greatly.

Paul was chained and led away by the soldiers, while the mob followed, crying, "Kill him! Kill him!"

"Please let me speak to them," Paul urged the officer. Covered with blood and spittle, his clothing torn, the apostle turned toward the angry mob and lifted his chained hands. He began to tell the story of the mission God had given him. The crowd quieted down a little and listened, until Paul reached the point where Jesus had commanded him to preach to the Gentiles. Then savage howls burst forth from the throng. Some scooped up handfuls of dirt and flung it at the apostle.

The Roman officer watched with concern. He did not understand the Aramaic language and so did not know why these people had become so furious. The only thing he could think of was that Paul had committed a very great crime. "Take him and throw him into the prison." he ordered his soldiers.

Meanwhile, a plot was being hatched. Over forty men met together in secret and swore an oath that they would not eat or drink again until they had killed Paul. Their strategy was all mapped out . . . but it was not God's will that His apostle die at that time, for He permitted a young boy, Paul's nephew, to overhear the evil plans. The excited lad hurried to the Romans and told them of the plotted murder. Hastily the officer placed Paul under a heavy guard and sent him out of Jerusalem to the palace of the governor, Felix, where he would be safe until his trial came up.

For two years Paul remained in the dungeon of Felix's palace. It was not until a new governor, Festus, took office that the apostle was brought forward and questioned about his supposed crimes. From that questioning Festus was unable to find any guilt at all in Paul, but he kept him in prison anyway, for he knew how angry his enemies would be if Paul went free.

"I appeal to Caesar," Paul said at last. That was the right of everyone who was a Roman citizen, and Paul had inherited Roman citizenship from his father, who had purchased it at a great price. When a man appealed to Caesar, he had to go to Rome for his trial.

Two devoted friends, Luke and Aristarchus, set out for Rome with Paul. Of course, the apostle was still a prisoner, so a Roman centurion named Julius was sent along as a guard. He proved to be a very kind and considerate man who developed a great respect for Paul during the long and dangerous sea voyage.

When the little sailing vessel ran into a storm, Paul urged its captain to take shelter in a safe harbor. Paul had been shipwrecked in these same waters three times, and he knew the treacherous conditions very well. Unfortunately the captain did not listen, and he held the ship to its original course until violent winds began to buffet it and huge waves towered above her decks on all sides. Now it was too late to seek any port!

The little ship would be submerged unless she unloaded her heavy cargo. The captain gave the order; his crew began to haul the precious goods from the hold and heave them into the sea, while the passengers waited in terror for some great wave to come crashing down upon the ship and smother it completely. Only Paul was not afraid. He knew that he was to preach the Gospel in Rome before he died. Confidently, he begged God to spare all his companions also.

The storm raged for fourteen days and nights. At last, when it seemed that land of some sort was nearby, the sailors decided to abandon the passengers to destruction and escape in the lifeboat. Paul found out. Knowing that the passengers would perish without the sailors, he warned his Roman guards, who cut the lifeboat loose and sent it drifting over the sea.

Soon after this, the ship ran aground on a sandbar within sight of an unfamiliar coast. The crew, soldiers, and prisoners threw themselves into the sea and made for the shore, either swimming or paddling along, clutching pieces of wreckage to keep themselves afloat. No one drowned; everyone reached the beach in safety.

They found themselves on the island of Malta, inhabited by superstitious pagans, some of whom built a fire to warm the shipwrecked travelers, while others scouted about for wood to keep it ablaze. Paul joined them in their search. Suddenly a poisonous snake glided out from a pile of sticks and sank its fangs into the apostle's hand! The natives gasped in horror. "Surely, this man must have done a great evil," they thought. "Even though he escaped death at sea, he has been punished by this deadly snakebite."

They watched, and waited for Paul to become ill, keel over, and die. But nothing happened! Paul continued to look as cheerful as ever. He kept on gathering wood. It was a miracle!

The superstitious natives were filled with awe at this evidence of the power of Almighty God. During the travelers' three-month stay among them, they treated them with great respect, and we can imagine that they were not at all surprised when the apostle healed the Roman governor's father.

Italy at last! As Paul, Luke, Aristarchus and their guards took the overland route to Rome they were greeted by little groups of the faithful, for already Christianity had reached those shores so far from Palestine. Paul spoke often with those Christians in the days which followed. He was once more awaiting trial, but his guards were lenient; they permitted him to live in a regular room, to have visitors, to write letters to his converts in the distant provinces. And Paul took advantage of all these opportunities. He made many converts (even among his guards!) to swell the ranks of the Christians in Rome. When at last his trial came up, he was declared innocent of any major crime and set free.

The apostle sailed westward to Spain, then returned to his beloved churches in Greece and Macedonia for the last time. While in Corinth he met Peter, and together with him returned to Rome to give aid and comfort to their fellow Christians, who were now being persecuted by the cruel Emperor Nero. This emperor was crazy, and had a great fire lit which destroyed a whole section of the city. Then to calm the angry Romans he blamed the fire on the Christians and launched a terrible persecution against them.

Peter and Paul were not long in the city when they, too, were seized and flung into prison. They were sentenced to death.

Paul found time to write a few last letters to his comrades in the Faith. When he wrote to Timothy, he said, "I have fought the good fight; I have finished the course; I have kept the Faith." Now he was looking forward to the Eternal Reward.

That reward was not long in coming. On the same day, June 29, in the year 67, Peter and Paul were led out of the great prison, and parted company with mingled sorrow and joy. In just a short time these two pillars of the Church would be reunited forever.

Peter was not a Roman citizen, so the Romans could kill him as they wished. They chose the worst form of execution—crucifixion—and led Peter out to the spot where the Vatican now stands. Peter saw crucifixion as an honor, since it was the death Our Lord Himself had died, and he humbly asked to be fastened to the cross head downward because he was unworthy to be crucified in the same way as his Master.

Meanwhile, Paul was led outside the city walls and scourged cruelly, then blindfolded. The executioner lifted a sharp sword over his head and brought it down swiftly. The apostle's head fell to the earth and bounced three times. At each spot a fountain of water sprang up. "Jesus!" cried the tongue which had pronounced that Name so often in life, while pure milk gushed from the martyr's veins.

Chained but undefeated

Is it any wonder that Paul's executioner was converted?

We can well believe that the apostle was welcomed into Heaven by St. Stephen, the first martyr, who had prayed for his conversion at the time of his own martyrdom.

From Heaven, St. Peter and St. Paul have watched over the Church down through the centuries. They were the two great instruments which Jesus used in founding and spreading His Church, and so it is fitting that they have been its special protectors ever since the beginning. Their spirit lives on in the beautiful letters which they wrote while they were on earth—letters which explained the Faith and urged the Christians to love God and to lead good lives. The epistle which is read in each Mass is a section of one of these letters.

St. Paul wrote fourteen epistles. In them, he speaks to us, just as kindly and earnestly as he spoke to the people for whom they were first written. Anyone who reads these epistles with faith will be inspired to walk in the steps of the Master with some of the love of the great St. Paul.

Many people are full of energy, but they do not use it to help their neighbor as St. Paul did. If we do good to our neighbor for the love of God, we, too, will earn a beautiful reward.

Saint Thecla

Valiant Virgin

St. Thecla the Virgin was the first martyr among Christian women, as St. Stephen was the first of the men.

She was born in the year 30 A.D. in the city of Iconium, Asia Minor, the daughter of an important citizen, whose house was noted for its wealth and the great number of banquets that were given there. Thecla's family was very much attached to pagan superstition and to the worship of idols.

According to the Greek customs of the time, the girl grew up in much luxury and studied great works of art and literature. But the more learning she gained, especially in philosophy, the more unhappy Thecla felt.

Often, after long hours of study, she would go out on the balcony and gaze at the sunset sky, wondering silently: "If my soul is to die out like that setting sun, why was it created? If it is to go on living after death, what will happen to it? Will some God take it to live with Him? If so, Who will He be?" Her heart would speak to that unknown God, saying, "O mysterious Being Who made me out of nothingness, if You exist, if You love me as I believe, make Yourself known to me!"

Thecla was eighteen when her parents began to think of finding a husband for her. She herself had no interest in marriage, but her father at last chose Tamiridus, a rich and powerful young man, to be her fiance.

Tamiridus was wild with joy, and he had reason to be. Everyone envied him, for Thecla was not only rich, but she also had the most beautiful qualities which can be desired in a young bride. She was lovely, graceful, firm, brilliant, and kept up a lively conversation. Above all, her modesty set off her other gifts like a white background setting off a brilliant bouquet of flowers.

But while her parents and fiance were busily preparing for the wedding, something happened that would change the whole course of Thecla's life. The Apostles Paul and Barnabas came to Iconium.

Coming home one night, Thecla passed close to the temple of Castor and Pollux. She heard the voices of two speakers who had gone down among the people and were teaching them.

"Who are those philosophers?" Thecla asked, ordering her litter bearers to stop.

"Two preachers who come from Antioch," she was told.

"Of what do they speak?"

"Of a God, Creator of Heaven and earth, Who is our Father."

Thecla was excited. Could this be the God Whom she had sought for such a long time? Could it be Him Whom she loved? She continued on her way with a fast-beating heart.

Thecla didn't sleep a wink that night. The unknown men filled her imagination, and she felt sorry that she had not spoken to them.

Thecla's courtyard

At daybreak, she made a sudden resolution, and, attended by a nurse, she hurried to the temple of Castor and Pollux. A man directed her to where Paul and Barnabas knelt in prayer in a dark corner.

"Speak to me," she begged them. "Speak to me about your God. I have need to know Him!"

Paul stood up, thanking God in his heart for the new grace he knew was coming. He greeted the young girl kindly.

How happy Thecla was when she heard the words of the apostle, describing the life of Jesus! And when the great mystery of the Holy Eucharist was revealed to her, Thecla was astonished at God's infinite love! Warm, tender tears wet her cheeks. She desired to receive Baptism immediately, and asked Paul to complete her religious instruction as soon as possible.

Together with her faithful nurse, who had also become a Christian, Thecla assisted often at holy Mass. She wore a white veil and held a lighted candle in her hand; the one was a symbol of her purity; the other, of her love. When she received the Body of Jesus Christ, she was inflamed with a love which made her completely forget the world.

Thecla's family and Tamiridus were terribly angry when she told them that she was a Christian. She also told them that she would not marry Tamiridus because she was now consecrated to God. With kindness and with threats they tried to make her change her mind, but it was no use. Thecla held fast to her Christian Faith.

Finally Thecla was charged with being a Christian and taken before the governor, who tried to make her give up her belief. "For your own good, young lady, leave this new religion to the miserable and to the poor for whom it seems to have been made. Sacrifice to the gods of Greece with me!"

"No, I cannot obey you. . . It is not right to disobey God in order to obey a man."

"Not even your governor?"

"Not even; God is much more."

"Proud and superstitious girl," he retorted, "I'm sure that the devil has taken possession of you so that you can no longer listen to reason. Stubborn girl. . . . Guards, take her to the prison!"

Thecla was put in chains and shut up in a dark, filthy cell, where anyone else would have been overcome by hunger, weakness, loneliness, and the awful smell. Not so Thecla, who placed all her hope in the Lord. Angels came from Heaven to comfort her in the silence of that dark den.

Calm in the face of death

Eight days later, she was taken before the governor in the arena, appearing more beautiful, more joyful, more radiant than ever before. She still refused to give up her Faith, so the governor ordered a tall stake to be placed in a corner of the forum. The trumpets sounded, announcing a death sentence.

The soldiers tied Thecla to the stake, piled the wood around her, and lit a fire. Soon, thick, choking smoke filled the air. The flames sent out long, writhing tongues, which licked about Thecla's delicate body.

A shiver of horror went through the onlookers. Some screamed. Others called for silence. Some hoped that she would change her mind. Others wished that they could save this noble and beautiful girl. But all in vain!

Yet, what was happening? Thecla made the sign of the cross and stood calmly amidst the flames, her face shining with celestial beauty. Her gaze was fixed on the sky, for she was deep in prayer.

A miracle! God had saved His faithful servant. The fire had broken its laws and had shown itself kind toward God's handmaid!

The governor had had enough. He ordered that Thecla be heavily guarded and sent to the city of Antioch. There she was to be taken to the arena and fed to the lions.

A large crowd turned out to see the spectacle of a Christian girl being fed to the lions. They murmured excitedly as her frail form appeared at the edge of the arena; they grew silent as she walked out into the very center, knelt down, and made the sign of the cross. Some of those heartless and cruel people even felt pity for the girl. Mothers embraced their daughters, as they thought with horror of what would soon happen to the poor girl in the arena. Even the governor was touched—and that had never happened to him before! Someone suggested that Thecla be freed, but then superstition won out again, and the crowd began to cry, "The Christian to the lions, the Christian to the lions!"

The attendants opened the cage door. A huge, fiery-eyed lion leaped out. He stretched himself and yawned—showing two rows of fierce teeth and a mouth which made even the governor shiver.

As though to make sure that he was really free, the lion pawed the ground, shook his long mane, and began to run around the arena. Only after running around to his heart's content, did he stop and look at Thecla. He switched his sides with his tail, then let out a great roar and crept toward the girl. The people held their breath.

Only Thecla seemed unworried. Although the lion's breath was now hot on her face, she stood looking up toward the sky and smiling. She seemed like a beautiful marble statue.

The lion lowered his large head and lay down beside her. He began to lick her feet!

Thecla humbly lowered her eyes and thanked God. She gently laid her hand on the lion's head and then sat down on its back!

A murmur of astonishment arose from all sides.

"Another lion!" the governor shouted angrily.

A short-furred lioness leaped out of the cage. She also ran about the arena, roared fiercely and pawed the ground. Then, attracted by the angelic virgin, she joyfully approached, and rubbed up against Thecla's hands and gown as a little kitten would have done!

At this sight, the wonder and anger of the spectators grew. The governor was furious.

The next day, he had her tied to wild bulls, hoping to see her virgin body torn to bits, but the ropes broke, and Thecla was again unharmed.

Next, she was lowered into a pit of poisonous snakes. Now the governor was sure that Thecla would die. But the poison lost its power, and Thecla was found alive and singing, as if she were in a garden of roses and lilies instead of a den of snakes.

The last miracle moved a few important citizens who managed to have Thecla freed. She retired to a little cave in the country, where people from all the cities around came to hear her talk about Jesus and His Redemption of mankind. Many became Christians. Thecla had been generous with Our Lord, so now He was using her as His instrument to lead others to Him.

Thecla died a holy death at the age of ninety. She is called the Church's first woman martyr because she certainly would have been martyred if God had not spared her. She was completely ready to die for Him.

When early Christians wished to praise a woman for her courage, they would say, "She's like another Thecla!"

St. Thecla was brave because she knew that her newly-found Faith was the most precious treasure she could ever find. If we truly appreciate our religion, we will always be proud to be followers of Christ, though we must never look down on anyone who has not received this precious gift. Like Thecla, we should thank God for His goodness.

Saint Cecilia

Martyr with a Singing Heart

In the days of the Roman Empire, there lived a little girl named Cecilia. Her father was a wealthy pagan, but her mother was a Christian, so Cecilia, too, was baptized a Christian when she was very small.

Cecilia was a normal baby who enjoyed playing, sleeping and eating, just as your little brother or sister does. As soon as she could walk, she would run all through the large house in which she lived. Yes, little Cecilia was a happy, active child. Dressed in her tiny tunic and sandals, she would dance about the house, singing, and smiling at everybody. Oh, how lovable she looked as she gaily ran, first to help her mother, and then back to see her father.

Cecilia had a rich, pagan friend, Cornelia, whom she loved very much. Cornelia was the only

A little ray of sunshine

child in her family, so she was spoiled by everyone. She had four slaves of her own, slaves who were very much older than she. But Cornelia was free— she was rich. Although she was very young, she had a quick temper. She would order her slaves around as if they were her age. When they would not do exactly as she commanded them, she would have her father punish them. Poor slaves! She was too cruel to them, but they could not even complain.

Cecilia felt sorry for Cornelia, but even more so for the slaves. She had always been taught by her mother that slaves are just as human as free people are, because slaves have a soul, too.

Often Cecilia's mother would walk with her on the lawn and say: "Pray for our brothers and sisters, the Christians, Cecilia. The cruel rulers of Rome call the Christians foolish, because they worship Jesus of Nazareth. The rulers can't understand. They love the world too much to think about God, the Creator."

Although she was young, Cecilia understood what her mother meant. "Mother, won't they ever stop persecuting the Christians? Each day so many die in the arena, while the people laugh. Oh Mother, I feel so sorry for them."

Cecilia's mother patted her on the head and said: "It is good to feel sorry for them, but we should be happy, too. The martyrs go straight to Heaven. This martyrdom is a great grace."

Cecilia lifted up her head and asked: "Can only the poor people become martyrs?"

"Oh no, Cecilia! We must all be ready to die for the Faith."

With her eyes shining, Cecilia exclaimed. "I want to be a martyr, too!"

Cecilia talked with her mother many times about dying as a martyr. If her mother was busy, Cecilia would talk with one of the slaves, whom she loved and treated as a sister. She loved to think about martyrdom and could not conceal her great desire for it.

Once Cecilia was talking with her slave, Lyda, about how Christians should love one another. Cornelia was walking just outside the door. As Cecilia was saying how sorry she felt for the martyrs, Cornelia laughed and stepped into the room.

She began to tell Cecilia how worthless the Christians were, and how she enjoyed seeing them tortured. With tears in her eyes, Cecilia tried to convince Cornelia how wrong she was, but she saw that it was impossible just then, so she smiled and changed the subject.

Days passed and summer approached. It was Cecilia's birthday. In the large Roman court, many of Cecilia's friends were attending her party. It was time for the party to begin, and Cecilia still was not there. Her mother ran back and forth, looking for her. Finally she saw her in a small room. Cecilia was crying.

"Why are you crying, my little Cecilia? You should be happy. Today you are a young lady! All your friends are waiting downstairs for you."

Smiling through her tears, Cecilia stood up and straightened her dress. How could she resist those tears of joy? Yes, today she was a young lady —a special young lady. So, she answered: "I will go down now, Mother. Thank you for calling me."

Cecilia ran downstairs to where her friends were waiting. For the rest of the afternoon she played with them, and feasted on all the good things that were prepared for her birthday.

Soon it was getting late, and all Cecilia's friends began to leave. Only Cecilia was left in the court.

But soon she was gone, too. Her mother looked all over for her and finally found her. Where was she? She was in the kitchen, washing dishes.

"Cecilia, what are you doing?" Cecilia's mother was shocked to see her own daughter working like a servant. "Why didn't you call that slave girl, Lyda, to do it?"

Cecilia was surprised, but she calmly answered: "I am no better than Lyda is, Mother. I must work, too. Besides, I don't mind washing dishes."

"Never mind, Cecilia. Come here and talk with me. I want to know why you were crying today. Did Cornelia hurt you?"

Cecilia was looking at the floor. In a low voice she answered: "No, Mother."

Once again her mother questioned her. "Then why did you cry? Are you unhappy? Or, do you want something? If you do, just ask; you know you can have anything you desire."

Cecilia tossed her head back and forth. "Oh no, Mother. I am very happy with what I have. I don't want anything else. If I did, I would ask for it and I am certain that I would receive it. Well, I was crying today, because I am so happy to be a Christian. But I want to be more. I want to love and please Jesus Christ by doing something special for Him. For two weeks now I have been thinking of what to do. I have talked to the priest at our church in Rome. I have decided to consecrate myself to God. I want to be a virgin forever."

Cecilia's mother was silent for a few moments. Finally she said: "Cecilia, my daughter, you are much too young to think of such things. Wait a few years, and then think about it. I will not say anything to your father, because he will not like this."

Cecilia's mother began to cry, and ran from the room. She rushed down a long hall and turned a corner. Then she stopped for breath. Suddenly, she saw her husband.

"Why do you cry, my wife?" asked Cecilia's father in a gentle voice.

"Don't mind me, because I am just being silly." She wiped her tears.

But her husband wanted to know why she was crying. He asked again in a stern voice: "Why are you crying?"

Cecilia's mother lowered her head and answered him. "It is Cecilia. She talks of wanting never to marry. She wants to remain a virgin all her life. She is in love with God."

Now her husband was angry. "In love with God? What foolishness! I will teach Cecilia to be wise. Of course she will marry. She will marry the wealthiest Roman senator. I will see to that."

And then he walked quickly down the long hall to Cecilia's room. He stopped outside the door and called: "Cecilia, open the door!" He could hear her jump up and wait for a moment. Then she pushed the curtain aside and unlocked the door.

"Cecilia, my daughter, it isn't true! You don't want to hurt me by remaining a virgin all your life, do you?" Cecilia's father tried to act kindly.

"I don't intend to hurt you, Father. You have always told me that you would let me do what I wanted. This is what I want. Won't you let me do it?"

At once her father grew angry. "Never speak of this again, Cecilia. I will not listen to you now, because you don't know what you are saying. You are tired—go to bed!"

Obediently, Cecilia turned and closed the curtain. In a soft voice she said: "Goodnight, Father."

Poor Cecilia did not sleep all that night. She kept thinking of what her father had said. She prayed that God would protect her. She never spoke of it again, because she knew that her father would be angry. But she worked cheerfully all the time.

Three years passed. In this time that had passed, Cecilia's father had brought a young pagan to meet Cecilia. He wanted to marry her. After her father had heard this, he began to arrange for the marriage. Cecilia had no choice; she would have to marry him.

One day there was great excitement in Cecilia's home. Slaves were decorating a large room. Others were preparing a delicate feast. When it was ten o'clock, Cecilia's mother ran upstairs and called out: "Cecilia, are you ready? Valerian is waiting downstairs. Let me see you, Cecilia, before you go down. This is the day of your wedding, and I am so happy for you."

Cecilia opened the door and stepped back. Her mother smiled and kissed her. "Cecilia, you look lovely! Your hair is so shiny and wavy today, and that white tunic is so beautiful."

Then she reached up and fixed the white roses that crowned Cecilia's head. "Now," she continued, "let's go down to meet your future husband."

Valerian was a handsome young man who had asked Cecilia to marry him. Cecilia's father had not even asked her for her decision. He told her that she must marry Valerian. Cecilia wanted to live as a virgin, but she had to obey her parents. She had not forgotten her vow, but she had to tell Valerian about it. She wondered how she would tell him, and what he would say after she told him.

All through the marriage ceremony, Cecilia thought about these things. During the big feast that followed, Cecilia tried to be gay. She tried to show that she was not worrying. The feast lasted all day, and part of the night. Finally, she took Valerian aside and told him of her vow. She told him that she was the bride of Jesus Christ. Valerian wanted to know more about her "Bridegroom." As she explained, he understood more and more.

After long months of instruction about Jesus Christ and the Church, Valerian was baptized. His brother Tiburtius was also baptized with him, by Pope Urban. Together, all three worked among the poor Christians and buried the martyrs. But one day the emperor found out that Valerian and Tiburtius were Christians. He ordered them to be killed in the arena. They were happy to die for Jesus, because they wanted to go to Heaven. But poor Cecilia! She was left by herself now. Although she was sad, she was happy for her husband and his brother.

After their death, she waited until everyone had left the arena. Then, with the help of friends, she took their bodies and accompanied them to the catacombs.

Each day she prayed that God would grant her the joy of dying a martyr for Him. She did not have to wait long, because one day two Roman soldiers came to take her before the emperor, who condemned her to death. She was to be martyred in a large room which would be heated to an intense degree in order to suffocate her. But Cecilia was happy. She entered the deathroom, knelt down and said:

"Oh Jesus, I thank You for having given me the great grace to die a martyr for the Faith. I believe and hope in You, O Lord. I love You with all my heart! I go now to my death, a day for which I have waited so very long. I die for You, dear Jesus. Take me to Paradise quickly. Have mercy on all those people who don't know You. Bless all the Christians, and protect them, that they may worship You in peace. Amen."

The soldiers turned their backs when they saw her continue to pray silently. They closed and locked the door. For about three hours they left her alone, expecting to finally see her dead. Suddenly they heard music from the room. The soldiers jumped up and rushed into the room. There was Cecilia, standing up with her arms outstretched, singing and praising God.

The captain of the soldiers was startled. After a few moments he ordered a soldier: "Go to tell the emperor of this—oh, poor me! What will he say? Oh, poor, poor me!"

In fifteen minutes the royal carriage stopped in front of Cecilia's house. The emperor, in all his glory and majesty, walked into the house. He had never been seen so angry. "So, she did not die?" he roared. "Then we will kill her in another way! You fools didn't heat the room enough, that's why she didn't die. But now she will suffer more. Take your sword and behead her!"

At once two soldiers went to force Cecilia to place her head over a wooden platform. Before they reached her, she had already parted her hair from her head. She put her head down. The captain of soldiers had his sword raised. He let it fall once swiftly, then again. The head would not separate from the body.

Fearfully, the captain turned to the emperor and said: "The head will not detach itself from the body. What shall I do?"

The cruel emperor smiled. "Let her suffer," he commanded. "Let her die in misery." Then he turned and left the room.

Cecilia's friends gathered around her, crying. Her eyes opened, and she gazed upon them all. She was silently blessing them, and praying for them. Then her eyes closed and remained that way. At the end of the second day, Cecilia again opened her eyes. She looked at her friends, and then toward Heaven. Her friends gathered closer, hoping she would give a sign. But no, she was looking at Someone they could not see. In her heart she was talking with God. The hours passed slowly, while Cecilia remained in the same position. At the beginning of the third day, she moved a little. Her eyes opened once again, and she looked to Heaven. One friend went close to her and watched her for a few moments. Then this friend turned to all the others and whispered: "Jesus Christ came to take Cecilia just now. Let us pray for our beloved sister, who is now a saint in Heaven."

And all her friends knelt down to pray to and for their beloved sister. They prayed, asking her to intercede for all the Christians. They asked her to pray for each of them, too, for they knew that she was now very close to Jesus and Mary.

St. Cecilia loved everyone sincerely whether they were proud nobles or simple slaves, because God made them all. We can imitate her very well in this if we think only kind thoughts about everyone we know.

Saint Tarcisius

First Martyr of the Holy Eucharist

Long ago, in the year 258 A.D., the mighty Roman Empire was ruled by the Emperor Valerian.

For about five years, the Christians had not been persecuted for their Faith. It seemed a time of peace. But the Prefect Macrian was thinking,

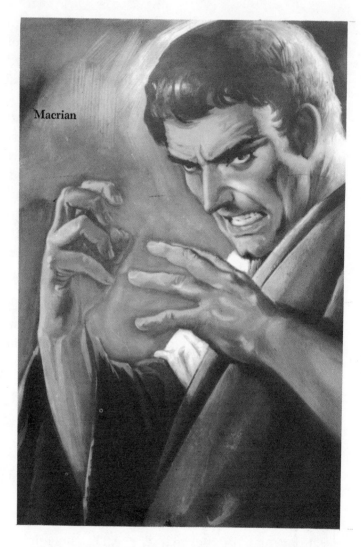

Macrian

"Who cares if the common people follow the teachings of that Hebrew, Jesus Christ! It is a religion for poor people. . . . But when the great noblemen and soldiers join it, that's too much!"

Macrian told the emperor what he had been thinking.

"You are right!" said Valerian. "I must order a persecution of the Christians. It shall begin today! Rome cannot bow to the commandments of the Hebrew Jesus."

And so Valerian ordered that anyone who declared himself a Christian should be punished with death. The only ones who would be set free would be those who denied Christ and honored the gods of Rome.

That very night, the elderly Pope Sixtus II called the Christians together in the catacombs.

"My brothers and sisters and beloved children in our Lord Jesus Christ," he began. "As you already know, the persecution has begun once again! And I want you to know also that some of the faithful have already been taken into the cold, dark prison. Let us pray for them!"

The persecution raged in all its fury. The hunt for the Christians grew more and more cruel with every passing day. Into their homes went the emperor's soldiers and dragged the Christians away. The prisons were packed. And every evening when the sun was setting, the condemned Christians lifted their voices in hymns to God. The beautiful sound of their singing floated up from the damp, dark underground jails.

One evening a young boy was walking up and down near the horrible prisons. His name was Tarcisius and he was the son of the Senator Tarsente.

With his heart full of pity, Tarcisius was listening to the singing of the condemned Christians. Going up closer, he knelt down by the barred windows, and stayed there, listening. How sorry he felt for the poor prisoners!

Sad homecoming

Tarcisius returned home late. His governess was waiting for him in the doorway.

"Why so late, Tarcisius? I was worried about you! Especially since your father is not at home. He had to go into hiding. They are trying to find him to question him."

"He went into hiding?"

"Yes, Tarcisius, for your sake."

"But if they find him, he won't deny Christ—he won't betray Him, will he?" the boy asked.

"Oh, no! Now come inside, supper is ready."

It was a sad supper without his father. Tarcisius ate slowly. Suddenly he asked, "I have heard people say that my mother was martyred. Is that right?"

"Yes," replied his governess, "under the Emperor Decian. Your father was going to tell you some day."

"When?"

"When you would be older."

"But I'm already old!" exclaimed Tarcisius. Then he pleaded, "Please tell me more about my mother."

"Yes, yes, I will, Tarcisius, my boy. Your mother told me that she would be waiting for you in Heaven. She loved you very much."

Tarcisius' eyes glowed at the kind woman's words. "Tell me more," he begged.

"Your mother was young and beautiful, Tarcisius, and although she loved you so much, she was faithful to Christ." The governess went on with her story. Then, later that evening, she and Tarcisius went down into the catacombs.

The Pope was facing them, seated on a stone chair, the chair of Peter. His face was pale and marked with suffering, but his bright eyes shone with piety and tender affection.

"Brothers, many of our number will be judged tomorrow," he said. "Their fate is certain—they'll all be killed!" Sighs and low moans were heard in the crowd. Quadratus, a tall, strong young man, stepped forward. He was a Roman soldier who had become a follower of Christ. He said,

"Holy Father, I have seen them! Today I was on guard at the prison. They made me promise to ask you to send them the Bread of Heaven."

"How can we get the Holy Eucharist to them?" sighed Pope Sixtus. "Who will dare to go into the prison? You?"

"Not I," answered Quadratus. "I cannot. Tomorrow I shall be on guard on the Appian Way."

"Who dares to undertake this dangerous mission?" asked the Pope. "Who will take the risk?"

There was a chorus of "I!" "I!" "No, I!"

Tarcisius made his way forward through the crowd of people until he was standing before Pope Sixtus.

"Holy Father, send me!" he cried.

"You Tarcisius—so young?" said Pope Sixtus in surprise. "Why, you're just a boy!"

"Because I am only a boy, no one will pay any attention to me," answered Tarcisius hopefully.

Pope Sixtus looked at him intently for a long moment. In Tarcisius' eyes he saw a strong, ardent desire to carry Jesus to the prisoners.

Sorrowful news

"All right," he decided. "You shall be the one. I'll entrust the Eucharistic Jesus to you, in this little case."

"I'll carry It on my heart," promised Tarcisius joyfully. "I'll hold It tight like this! I am ready to die to keep from exposing It to the gaze of unbelievers."

The next day, some schoolmates of Tarcisius were sitting on a pile of stones, on the Appian Way. With them was Fabian, the little friend of Tarcisius.

"Fabian, where's Tarcisius?" asked one of the boys. "How come your protector isn't here?"

"Oh, he'll come. He always comes to play."

"Yes, and we'll have some stone-throwing," said another boy named Mark. "I can't wait. Here's a nice pile of stones handy for us, too. Somebody will have a hard job piling them up, afterwards!" He laughed coarsely.

The other pagan boys laughed loudly with him. They were afraid of the bully Mark, and always did what he told them to do.

The minutes slipped by, yet still there was no sign of Tarcisius.

Mark grew impatient. He was anxious to begin the game of throwing stones.

"Tarcisius is taking his time to come," said Fabritius.

"He'll come and he'll win the stone-throwing game, too," stated Fabian. "He's the best player just as he's the best at school."

"He was," said Mark. "Lately, he's always sleepy. His head rolls from one side to the other . . .

like this!" The boys laughed at him.

Fabritius said, "The teacher has begun to notice it, too."

"Maybe Tarcisius doesn't feel well," Fabian defended. "Anyway, he'll beat you just the same— he's a born winner!"

"And what were you born for, to praise him?" retorted Mark.

"I like him a lot," replied Fabian. "He treats me like a brother."

He was interrupted by Fabritius, who had spied Tarcisius. "Here he comes!"

Tarcisius was coming toward them silently and cautiously. His arms were pressed firmly to his chest.

"Come to play!" called Mark. The other boys took up the cry: "Come on!"

But Tarcisius answered, "I can't. I have an errand to do."

"My, how important you think you are!" sneered Mark. "Cut it out! Come on, let's play."

"I can't really," Tarcisius said firmly. "Let me go. We'll play tomorrow."

"No," put in Fabritius, "we'll play today, right now. Choose your stones."

Again, Tarcisius said, "I can't, I tell you! I can't."

"Oh," sighed Mark in disgust, "you're whining like a baby! Come on fellows, form a circle around him. All right now, let's see—why have you got your arms pressed against your chest? What are you hiding?"

"I don't have to tell you," protested Tarcisius. "I can't tell you."

"Smarty!" sneered Fabritius.

Mark kept up his questioning. "Who are you going to tell, Tarcisius? The emperor's eagles, maybe?"

"Maybe."

"Oh, this is too much," snapped Mark. "All right now. . . ."

In his heart, Tarcisius prayed, "Please, Jesus, make my arms as strong as steel! I'll press You close to me, I'll defend You!"

How the poor boy was suffering! His heart was pounding, and his eyes were nearly blinded with tears. His face was eggshell-white. The boys crowded around him. The circle grew smaller.

"We've had enough, Tarcisius," warned Mark. "I'll give you time to tell us. I'll count to three. One. . . ."

Tarcisius prayed silently, "Oh, Lord, Lord, help me!"

"Two!" said Mark.

"Mark, stop it!" cried Tarcisius. "Let me go, Mark. I'll give you my bow and arrows, all of them. I'll give you anything you want, but please let me continue on my errand!"

"It's no use, Tarcisius!" yelled Mark. "You're hiding something and we're going to find out what it is! I'll start counting just once more." Glaring at Tarcisius, he began, "One, two. . . ."

"No!" cried Tarcisius.

"I'll repeat it!" Mark's eyes were flashing angrily. "Two. . . ."

"Just a second, Mark," interrupted Fabritius. "Fellows, listen to me. I just had an idea."

"I get it!" shouted Mark, in wicked glee. "I had the same idea myself. Tarcisius must be a Christian. And maybe he's carrying around his neck the mysteries!" By that word Mark meant the Holy Eucharist. "Yeah, the mysteries! The mysteries!" shouted the other pagan boys.

Mark glanced at Tarcisius and demanded, "Did you make up your mind, Tarcisius? I said two and—and—"

"I said no, and I meant it!" cried Tarcisius.

"Leave him alone!" pleaded Fabian.

"No, no, Mark, go ahead!" yelled Fabritius.

Tarcisius prayed earnestly, "King of Martyrs, I beg You, don't let me be separated from You. I'd rather die!"

"Three!" shouted Mark.

There was a scramble, and several voices shouting, "Let him have it! Hit him! Hit him!"

Tarcisus fell to the ground and like wild beasts, the boys jumped on top of him. Yet his arms remained crossed over the Mysteries like two iron bands.

With a terrific effort, he struggled to his feet and managed to run a few steps.

"Grab some stones!" yelled Fabritius. "Let him have it!"

They did just that. One after another, stones struck him from all sides, until there was not a part of his poor body that was not bleeding.

Yet, somehow or other, he managed to stumble on, until one stone struck his forehead. Then Tarcisius fell.

"Tarcisius! Tarcisius!" sobbed Fabian in terror. "Leave him alone, you bullies!"

But Mark incited them on, "Come on boys, let's get him and see these 'mysteries.'"

"Let him have it!"

Just then Fabritius yelped, "Look out! A soldier's coming!"

"He's coming right this way, too," put in another boy. "Let's beat it!" In an instant, they were gone.

Only Fabian did not run away. He stayed close beside his dear friend, who was suffering terribly.

"Jesus," murmured Tarcisius. "I am dying, but I defended You. Forgive the boys, forgive them!"

Meanwhile, the soldier had drawn near. It was Quadratus, the Christian. As soon as he caught sight of poor Tarcisius lying on the ground, he exclaimed in horrified dismay, "Poor little fellow! What did they do to you?" Then noticing Fabian, he demanded sharply, "What are you doing here?"

"I'm Tarcisius' friend. I love him," wept Fabian. "I didn't throw stones at him. Let me stay here, near him."

"Tarcisius, open your arms," Quadratus urged tenderly, bending over the boy.

"No," whispered Tarcisius. "I won't open my arms. Bring me to Pope Sixtus. I will give my treasure—Jesus—only to him."

"Are you suffering much?" asked Quadratus. gently raising Tarcisius' head.

"Yes, very much," Tarcisius gasped, "but that doesn't matter. Nobody touched Jesus. He is here, right here with me." He was breathing hard, struggling to talk. Suddenly he said, "I already see the Angels. Take me to the Pope!"

"Don't die, Tarcisius! Don't die!" It was Fabian pleading tearfully. "You have been like a brother to me."

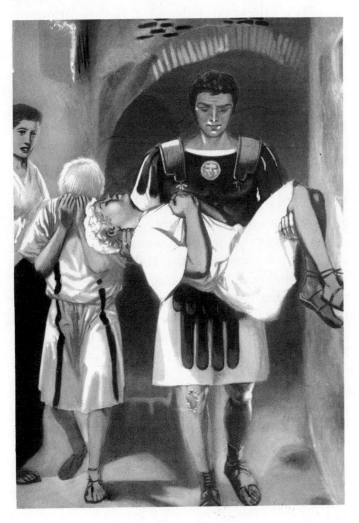

Quadratus carried him gently

"I see the Angels," the little martyr repeated. "My Faith is true. And you,"—he gasped for breath—"you, Fabian, do you believe?"

"Yes," declared Fabian, "I believe, Tarcisius. I want to become a Christian, too. Then we can be together again some day."

Quadratus picked up the dying boy in his arms and carried him to the catacombs.

"Tarcisius," Pope Sixtus whispered gently, when he had gotten over the shock of seeing the boy in such a pitiful condition. "Tarcisius, Jesus is safe because of your loving sacrifice."

Pressing Jesus in the Eucharist close to his heart, Tarcisius died. Then and only then did his arms fall away from his chest.

This was the beautiful way in which St. Tarcisius, the boy martyr of the Holy Eucharist, died—with his beloved Jesus resting on his heart.

A strong, sweet odor of lilies filled the air at that moment. And Tarcisius' soul—joyful and gay—ascended to the throne of God, to the throne of the King Who is waiting for all of us in eternal glory.

Although we may never have the privilege of carrying and protecting the Holy Eucharist, we can show our love for Jesus in the Host by receiving our Communions with love, and by paying little visits to the Blessed Sarcament when we pass a church.

Saint Sebastian

Patron of Soldiers

Sebastian, a young officer in the Roman army, had just found out that two Christians had been put in prison to be killed for their Faith. Sebastian was a Christian himself, although the other soldiers didn't know it. With deep concern he thought of the two brothers—twins, in fact—Mark and Marcellinus, who were not as strong in their faith as they should be. They might abandon it through fear.

"Lord Jesus," prayed Sebastian silently as he hurried toward the prison, "let me die, if need be, but please give the brothers the grace to stand up for the Faith. Don't let them lose Heaven!"

As he burst into the prison, Sebastian found Mark and Marcellinus surrounded by a group of pagan friends. Their own father, also a pagan, was there, too. All of them were urging the twins to give up their Christian Faith and save their lives.

We can imagine how Mark and Marcellinus must have felt! There they were, torn between love for their Heavenly Father and love for their earthly father. Which of them would they choose?

At that point, Sebastian's clear voice rang out, "Christian brothers!" All heads turned in his direction, as he reproached, "You who have always shown yourselves so brave and stout-hearted, will you now turn your backs on the King Who has prepared for you a place of special glory?"

All were silent. Sebastian's face glowed with supernatural light as he continued, "What has this poor world to offer, in the end, but the grave? Will you exchange for a few passing pleasures an eternity of joys?"

The brothers looked at one another silently and bowed their heads. They were won. Even their father and friends had been impressed. They crowded about Sebastian asking questions. And Sebastian, with the fervor of an apostle, spoke on and on.

"I wish to be baptized," said one of the pagans.

"And I!" cried another.

"And I!"

One man only, remained unconvinced. "I need a better proof than your words," he told Sebastian. This man was the Chancellor Nicostratus, and he was known for his hard head. But Sebastian saw Nicostratus' wife beside him, her eyes alight with belief. "You believe, don't you, Zoe?" he asked. "Why don't you speak to your husband? A word from you might show him the light, too."

To Sebastian's surprise, tears began to stream down Zoe's cheeks. What had he said? Why should she start to cry like this?

Nicostratus stepped forward. "Sebastian, don't you know that she is mute?"

Mute! No wonder she had not spoken, Sebastian thought. He knew that God was giving him the chance to save another soul! Lifting his eyes, the young soldier prayed silently for a moment. Then he turned to the woman.

"Zoe, look at me."

She turned her sweet, sad eyes toward him. Sebastian made the sign of the cross on her lips and asked, in a voice that trembled with emotion, "Zoe, do you believe in Our Lord Jesus Christ?"

The woman opened her lips and spoke the first words of her life: "I do believe in Jesus, Our Lord!"

Hardly had she finished speaking when her husband had thrown himself in a heap at Sebastian's feet. He, too, had been won to Christ!

Shortly afterward, the privilege of martyrdom came to Mark and Marcellinus. This time, they did not waver. They suffered bravely for twenty-four hours with their feet nailed to a post. Then they were shot to death with arrows. Surely they received a great reward in Heaven!

Sebastian continued his inspired work of making converts to the Faith and of comforting the Christians who had been captured and sentenced to death. Then, in a vision, he was warned that his own death was near.

✤ ✤ ✤

"That's the man! Seize him!"

The soldiers closed in on Sebastian as their leader had commanded. They bound him fast. How had his Faith been discovered? Sebastian wondered. Then he saw the face of one of his new disciples smirking at him from the shadows. He it was who had betrayed his master!

They led Sebastian before the Emperor Diocletian—the emperor who had prized him above many of his soldiers. Now Diocletian knew the truth about his favorite, and he was very angry. "Death," he snarled. "Death by arrows!"

The tree was sturdy. The ropes were thick. Sebastian was tied securely, and the guards stepped back to let the barbarian archers do their work.

Twang! Twang! Thud! Thud! Bowshot followed bowshot, and the arrows, with a searing pain, buried themselves in Sebastian's flesh. He writhed in pain, but did not cry out. He was willing to suffer this, and even more, for the Lord Jesus. The archers wheeled about and left the field, satisfied that he would die after several hours' torment. They had deliberately avoided shooting him in the heart, for that would have brought death too quickly!

Sebastian's blood bathed the ground around the tree. He could almost *feel* the life leaving his body. Alone, abandoned by men, he prayed to God.

But had he been abandoned? There was a rustle in the bushes, a quick step pattering to his side. Sebastian blinked the blood out of his eyes, and gazed dimly on the face of a pious woman whom he had seen among the Christians in the catacombs!

"I had come to give you a decent burial, my son," she murmured, "but I see there's still hope for you. Let us take you to shelter!"

In the security of the good woman's home, the ex-soldier slowly regained his strength. "Perhaps God has spared me for a reason," he thought. "Perhaps He wills me to try to convert Diocletian from his cruel ways." He pondered and prayed over the question.

How great the pain was!

At last, a little unsteady on his feet, but with the old fire in his eyes, Sebastian came again before the emperor. "The hour of justice has come!" he warned. "Repent. Ask God's pardon for the sins you have committed!"

Diocletian bellowed in rage. "Take that man! Beat him until he is dead!" At once the soldiers fell upon Sebastian. He felt blow after blow, then... nothingness.

And then? Well, they took his *body* and threw it into the sewer, from which the Christians rescued it later and erected a splendid church above it, but Sebastian's *soul* was already happy with God, where it always will be for all eternity.

St. Sebastian always had one thought before him: Heaven. That goal was so precious that he would never do anything that might make him lose it. We all can work for Heaven by avoiding all deliberate sin and by doing what is right.

Saint Lucy

The Shining Light

During the tenth Roman persecution, a sweet and gentle child named Lucy lived on the island of Sicily in the bright Mediterranean Sea. "Lucy" means "Light", and the little girl's sparkling eyes showed that she had been well named.

Lucy's father, a rich pagan, died when she was about six years old. Since she and her mother were both Christians, they went often to meet secretly with others of the Faith in caves beneath the city of Syracuse, assisting there at Mass and receiving Our Lord in Holy Communion. As Lucy grew older her love for Jesus grew stronger. She saw the great difference between the way of life He wishes us to lead and that which many people really *do* lead. Since the world about her was full of sinful pleasures which her religion forbade her to enjoy, she closed her eyes, ears and heart to the temptations surrounding her. For Lucy, God's love was infinitely more precious than anything else in the whole world.

Now in those days every young girl, but especially those from a wealthly family like Lucy's, was supposed to marry and have children. Not to do this was to be a social disgrace. Lucy would have liked a family, too, but after praying over the matter she understood that Jesus was asking her to become His spouse—to be His and only His for all eternity! What an honor!

Of course, Lucy accepted the "proposal". She would remain a virgin forever for Jesus. She didn't mind when a small voice inside her said that this choice would make her suffer. She loved Jesus, and suffering always goes with love.

Happy to know that she belonged to God in a special way, Lucy felt a great contentment for several days. Then her mother broke the news to her. She had arranged for Lucy to be engaged to a pagan youth! How distressed Lucy was, but she didn't say anything to her mother.

Now Lucy's mother had been ill for years, and the girl decided to ask St. Agatha to cure her. So the two set out for the neighboring city of Catania, where they visited the tomb of the virgin martyr, St. Agatha. After assisting at Mass, they remained before the tomb in prayer. Suddenly, in a vision, Lucy saw the saint coming toward her. She was decked in radiant garments and sparkling jewels and was surrounded by Angels.

"Dear sister," said the vision, "why do you ask to obtain your mother's health which your own faith can obtain without my aid? Your mother is well, and all because you have made your body a worthy dwelling place for Our Lord."

The glorious vision continued, "Soon you will become the splendor of Syracuse, just as Jesus has made me the glory of Catania."

The saint disappeared. Lucy rose to her feet and went over to her mother. Indeed, she had been cured!

This seemed to be Lucy's chance to ask her mother two great favors. One was not to go through with the engagement to the pagan; the other was to distribute the family wealth among the poor. Her mother consented to both, but was afraid to tell the pagan suitor!

It must have been quite a shock to the young man when he found out that the poor were swarming to Lucy's home to divide among themselves the wealth that should have been his! At first he couldn't believe his ears, but then he decided to act. At the first flush of dawn, December 11, 304, he arrived on Lucy's doorstep. He was ushered inside, and waited tensely in the entrance hall. As soon as Lucy appeared, he said, "Your mother has promised you to me!"

The dreaded moment had come. Steadily, Lucy replied, "I have already been pledged to Another. Please leave, and permit me to remain true to Him."

Like a flash of light, the suitor saw the truth. Lucy was a Christian! That was the last straw; storming out of the house he rushed toward the palace of the Governor Paschasius.

Very soon, the soldiers were at Lucy's door. Grimly they marched her through the streets, to appear before the governor. She was calm. Paschasius was stern.

"You must sacrifice to the gods of Rome!" he told her.

"I have sacrificed my riches to help the poor, as my Heavenly Bridegroom wished," replied the girl. "The only other possession I have is my body, which I have given to God; I shall sacrifice it for Him, if that is His will.

"Don't tell *me* such things," retorted the governor. "It is my duty to carry out the commands of the Roman emperor."

"Just as you respect the emperors and their laws, so I respect God and His laws," Lucy explained. "In fact, nothing will stop me from obeying His laws."

"Seize her!"

Paschasius stiffened. "You're bold enough, now, but the torturers will change you."

"The words of God are changeless," replied Lucy. "Jesus said that whenever His disciples would be brought before a ruler, the Holy Spirit would speak through us."

"Oh, so you think this Holy Spirit is speaking through you now?"

"He is in everyone who lives in chastity and purity, because such a person is a temple of God."

Fire in his eyes, the governor retorted, "Unless you worship our gods, I'll have you taken to a place where you will lose your purity. Then the Holy Spirit will leave you."

Lucy was fearful, but she hid her feelings and said firmly, "The body does not sin if the will does not consent. Even if you took my hands by force and made me offer incense to pagan idols with them, God would know that I did not want to do so. It would be the same if you stained my body by force; because it would be against my will, I would not lose merit before God."

Nevertheless, Paschasius commanded that Lucy be taken to a place of sin and shame. Four soldiers stepped forward to drag her away, but the calm young woman was praying fervently, and the combined strength of all four could not move her!

Others sprang forward, but their help was of no use. At last Pashasius ordered that she be dragged away by teams of oxen, but those strong animals exhausted their energies without budging the girl.

Nor could pagan magicians move her. "What is the secret of your magic?" the governor asked Lucy in a fury.

"It is not magic," replied the girl. "It is God's goodness towards those who are true to Him."

Curious spectators were thronging in from every side. Paschasius' anger mounted, for he was being made to seem a fool in front of everyone. He shouted for wood, for pitch, for oil! "Light a fire and burn the Christian girl!" he roared.

Materials were brought; the fire was lit. As the flames blazed up, sweeping through the pitch and oil and licking hungrily at the wood, Lucy remained unharmed. She knelt in prayer, now and then speaking to the onlookers. "I have asked God to spare me from the fire," she explained, "so that the faithful may gain new courage from my tortures, and so that unbelievers may cast off their pride and see the beauty and glory of the Christian religion."

But now Lucy's mission had been accomplished. God would delay her flight to Heaven no longer. An executioner was coming forward with a sharp-bladed dagger. Now he plunged the point into Lucy's throat. As blood spurted out and soaked into the ground, the young martyr's soul flew to the waiting arms of Jesus!

St. Lucy had a deep love for God. Such a love comes from prayer—the more we pray and speak to Our Lord, the more we will love Him and want to please Him.

Saint Agnes

Lamb of Jesus

Almost three hundred years after Jesus died for us on the Cross, a family named Clodius lived in the ancient and beautiful city of Rome.

This husband and wife were very noble and rich; they owned a magnificent palace and had many servants.

But although the wealthy couple had much gold and a great number of fine things, the treasure most precious to them was their daughter, Agnes.

The name "Agnes" means "little lamb," and it was just the right name for the golden-haired little girl; she was as sweet and gentle as a lamb.

Agnes was very lovely. Her cheeks were pink, like roses; her eyes, which were a soft blue like the sky, shone with a beautiful light. Often she seemed to be looking far away, toward something unseen but really present—something or someone she loved very much.

She was warm-hearted and kind to everyone, never seeming to think of herself, but always doing good to those around her.

When Agnes had reached the age of thirteen, she seemed to be older, because she was so tall and graceful. Often she wore a snow-white dress with no ornaments or jewels, which made her look very much like a bride—especially since she always looked as happy as a bride, seeming always to be thinking of someone who was very *special* to her.

As she walked to school each morning, returning the same way with her books in the evening, the people whom she passed talked about her gracefulness and charm. She was as pretty as a flower, and so they would call her "a charming blossom" when she passed by, treading lightly upon the close-fitting stones of the old Roman street. Her outward behavior reflected her noble mind, her generous disposition, her tender heart and high moral standards—in short, the whole of her virtuous life.

One day a boy named Procop, who was the son of an important man called the Prefect of Rome, met her and said,

"Stop, Agnes. I want to talk to you."

"What do you wish?" she replied.

"Agnes, I love you because you are beautiful and good. Will you promise me that someday you will marry me?"

"I am already engaged!"

"What?" Procop had heard no news of this.

"Yes, He has pledged me to Him by His betrothal-ring and He has adorned me with immense jewels!"

"To whom are you engaged?" demanded Procop. "Who is richer or more honorable than I? Who has more gold or more servants?"

"He Who has Angels for servants and owns Heaven and earth," Agnes replied. "He Who has put a necklace of precious gems about my neck and has dressed me in white linen woven with pearls. He Who loves the pure and the sweet scent of lilies. . . . He will be my Spouse and He alone!"

Procop went away sad. Because he did not understand what Agnes had said, he thought that she had been teasing him, or else that she was making up daydreams.

Procop

Sorrowful and forlorn, he no longer cared for games. He did not even read or study any more, although he was supposed to be preparing to become the governor.

One night, an old servant of the family said to Procop's father, the prefect, "I know why Agnes refused your son! She must be a Christian. There are many young women who are . . . and many refuse to marry because they say they love someone named Jesus Christ."

The prefect was startled. He himself was a pagan, like most of the Romans, and he hated Christianity because the Christians refused to worship the pagan gods, who were not real but only imaginary.

When the pagans discovered that someone was a Christian, they usually put that person to death in a horrible way. Procop's father decided to make Agnes marry his son by threatening to kill her if she didn't do so.

The prefect went to talk to Agnes' parents.

The warning

"Either Agnes shall promise to marry my son or I will call her to court," he said. "And if she should confess to being a Christian . . . it will be just too bad for her! You know the law of Rome, don't you? It is severe, and it commands enemies of the gods to be wiped out without pity."

Agnes' parents were terrified, for they knew that their daughter was, indeed, a Christian. They themselves were Christians, too—as had been their parents before them.

Many of the noble families of Rome had produced important leaders in the Church. Many of them had become martyrs, too.

Because the pagans hated the Christians so much, the Christians met in secret to assist at Mass, often gathering in tunnels and caves called *catacombs* which were underneath the city; sometimes they even met in the palace of Agnes' family.

Agnes' parents tried to seem calm until the prefect left them. Then they called Agnes and told her what he had threatened.

"Mother! Dad! Have courage," she replied. "I will not betray the Faith you have given me. I will not be a traitor to my Faith even if it means suffering and death! Do not cry for me. Jesus will protect me."

A few days later, the palace of Agnes and her parents was surrounded by armed guards. Agnes was taken to the court where the prefect came forward to accuse her.

"Do you know why you are here?" he asked.

"Don't worry"

"I can guess. It is because I am a Christian."

"Foolish girl! You say something very serious and dangerous and you smile? You should be trembling. Do you know what is going to happen to you?"

"I know," Agnes answered. "But my Spouse said, '*You will be persecuted and tortured because I was. Remember that you were made for My kingdom and not for this world.*' I would give up my life a thousand times rather than give up my Faith."

"Enough! My son is suffering on your account. If you promise to marry him, I shall free you!"

"I am the little spouse of Jesus, and *His* spouse alone. I'm not afraid of you or your soldiers!" she added. "I fear nothing for Jesus' sake. There is an Angel always guarding me and he will not permit Christ's handmaid to suffer any harm!"

"You are so bold!" shouted the prefect. "Guards, take this rebel! Undress her and then make her walk through the streets nude, all the way to the Arena of Alexander. That will humiliate this stubborn girl!"

The guards carried out the shocking command, but—a miracle happened! Agnes' hair began to grow . . . and grow. It grew so long that it covered her from head to foot! Between two astonished guards, she walked down the street.

She walked fearlessly, her head high and her eyes fixed on Heaven.

"O Jesus," she said, "thank You for having saved me from so great a humiliation! O Jesus, You defend those who trust in You! Why don't people want to know and love You? If they would love You, the world would be so much more beautiful."

"If they but knew You, they would all become Christians. Their souls would be washed as clean as the new-fallen snow, and they would become new creatures, reborn through Baptism into a new and immortal life!"

The prefect, his son Procop, the nobles and the ordinary people were waiting at the Arena when Agnes arrived there with the guards. She was led out to the very center of that huge space, but she did not seem disturbed at all. Instead her smile was sweet and cheerful.

Agnes kept very brave, and refused to sacrifice to the pagan idols. She made the Sign of the Cross instead.

Full of anger now, the prefect told Agnes that she would be taken to a horrible place where she would lose her innocence and purity. But she replied, "You may stain your sword with my blood, but you will never be able to profane my body, which is consecrated to Christ."

"My son!"

Right then an Angel came down from Heaven and dressed Agnes in a beautiful long robe. He stayed beside her, holding a flaming sword.

Drawing his own sword, Procop strode out into the Arena and moved toward Agnes. The sword of the Angel flashed like lightning, and Procop crumpled into a heap on the sands of the Arena.

The prefect rushed to the limp form, and found to his horror that Procop was dead. "Son," he cried. "My son!"

He was beside himself with grief. For a moment he had no idea of what to do, then he turned to Agnes.

She was a short distance away, singing hymns of praise to Jesus, Who had protected her.

"Agnes," begged the prefect—seeming to forget all the awful things he had said to her—"if you are innocent, give me back my son!"

"I will pray to Jesus," Agnes replied. "He can do all things."

She sank to her knees and prayed with all the fervor of her young heart.

And it happened—Procop came back to life!

The crowd of onlookers stared at the scene in open-eyed wonder.

On the other hand, the prefect, having his son back again, ordered a man named Aspasian to take his place. He himself took Procop and left the Arena.

Aspasian ordered the soldiers to bring Agnes to the stake to be burned to death.

Without batting an eyelash, the young victim walked up the pile of burning wood. And the flames divided right in half, leaving Agnes untouched at the stake.

There she stood, a little witness to the great King. In a loud voice, she cried,

"O Jesus, thank You for giving me this new proof of Your love. But if You wish, give me martyrdom . . . I want it. I want to come up to You and never leave You."

The sight of her standing there—so sweet and so strong, so calm and so firm—made others want to imitate her, to become as cheerful and generous, as radiant with love for the One Whom she called Jesus. They, too, wanted to embrace her religion.

Aspasian looked around him. The crowds of people who had come to see Agnes die were milling about in fright. Many fell to their knees, shouting, "I want to be a Christian!" "I'm a Christian, too!"

They had never before seen anyone as brave as Agnes, nor anyone who had such a great Faith. They knew that her religion must be truly wonderful.

Aspasian was terribly angry at what was happening. He ordered one of his soldiers to cut off Agnes' head. As Agnes knelt down, a soldier stepped forward with a gleaming blade. Many people began to cry.

Calmly, Agnes pulled back the golden wave of hair from her white neck. She bowed her head, and awaited the death blow with a smile.

As the soldier lifted his blade, the crowd grew still. It was as if everyone was holding his breath.

"Take me, O Lord," Agnes prayed. "Death is really life, the sweet life of eternity. Take me, O Lord."

The executioner was trembling with emotion; for a moment he could not even move. Angrily Aspasian ordered him to discharge his duty. Then the blow fell, and Agnes' head was cut off. Blood spurted forth, dying her dress a deep red and staining the sands of the Arena. Many Christians who had come in secret now sprang forward and began to wipe up the blood with sponges and linen cloths. Savagely the guards turned upon them and many of them, too, were killed or wounded. They gave their lives gladly for their Faith.

The body of Agnes was taken to a spot near the Nomentana Road, not far from Rome. Later on, during the reign of the Emperor Constantine, a church would be built over the place where the little martyr was buried.

On the twenty-eighth of January, Agnes' father and mother were praying at her grave, when Agnes appeared to them! She was in the midst of a group of holy virgins.

Agnes was fair and blonde, and in her arms she held a little white lamb.

"Do not cry for me, my dear ones," she said smilingly, "I am ever so happy . . . with the immaculate spouses of Jesus. And He will have as many spouses as there are stars in the sky—young girls who

The vision

will consecrate themselves to Him in the centuries to come. And I shall be waiting for them near the God of the pure and the strong!"

From then on, on the twenty-eighth of January, after Holy Mass is celebrated in the catacombs of the Via Nomentana in Rome, lambs are blessed and then brought to the Pope. The Holy Father gives them to sisters to raise.

On Wednesday in Holy Week, these lambs are sheared and their wool is used to make the sacred pallia which are sacred vestments for new archbishops and patriarchs.

All this is done in memory of Agnes, to honor this little Lamb of Jesus, who is waiting for us all in the eternal joys of Heaven.

St. Agnes understood well that purity is a virtue very dear to God. One way we can follow her example is always to dress modestly and never listen to impure stories and jokes.

Saint Helen

Seeker of the Cross

Is it ever too late to become a saint? Does one have to be baptized in infancy, or at least converted in youth?

If you think about these questions, you will surely say, No, but perhaps you cannot think of any example of a late conversion. This is the story of such a saint.

Her name was Helen, and details in her early life are so obscure that no one is sure where she came from. Some people say she was born in Britain, the daughter of the Celtic king Coel, and that a Roman officer named Constantius met and married her there. Others say that she was born in the country south of the Black Sea and spent her early years as a waitress in a tavern near one of the great Roman roads up and down which armies marched. They say that Constantius met her in the tavern.

At any rate, Helen married Constantius when she was in her late twenties, and she spent the next fifteen years or so traveling up and down the Empire with him. During this time, Constantine, their son, was born.

Constantius was a brilliant soldier, and won many victories. He rose higher and higher in the army. Finally he became second to the western emperor. That was when the blow fell. The emperor ordered Constantius to *marry* the eastern emperor's daughter—for political reasons!

How could Constantius take another wife when he was already married? Well, we must remember that he and Helen were pagans, so Constantius divorced Helen.

Poor Helen! She really loved her husband, who had many good qualities. It was hard to part from him and from their son, Constantine, who was still only a boy. But she took it as best she could and began to live her lonely life of exile. At that time, she was around forty. The period of exile would last almost twenty years.

Was it during this period that Helen became interested in Christianity and began to learn all she could about it? Again, we are not sure; many things about the life of St. Helen are uncertain. Yet through all this obscurity we catch a glimpse of a remarkable strength of character, which makes us want to know more and more about this good, silent woman.

Constantine became emperor in his father's stead when Helen was about sixty-five. One of the first things that he did was to call his mother from exile, give her the title of empress, and have coins made in her honor. In this latter way we honor kings and presidents even in our day.

At the same time, Helen took instructions in the Faith, and received Baptism. She seemed to be making up for lost time! With Constantine's permission she spent great sums of money to provide food and clothing for the poor and to free many people from prison. She invited consecrated virgins (who lived a life like that of nuns) to dine at the palace, and she herself waited on them, like a serving maid. She had churches built and lavishly decorated. She even went to Jerusalem to oversee the building of a church on Mount Calvary.

Jerusalem had been overrun by the pagans, who had built a temple to Venus, a pagan goddess, on Calvary. This was torn down at Helen's orders, and a basilica was built over the Holy Sepulchre. Helen had another basilica built on the Mount of Olives.

On Calvary, a search was begun for the True Cross, for it had been lost when the pagans had taken over the city. Workmen began to dig, and soon three wooden crosses were discovered! In the earth nearby long, sharp nails were found.

Helen rejoiced—but which cross was the Cross of Christ? She turned for help to the holy Bishop Macarius. "Your Excellency, how are we to distinguish the True Cross?"

"Your Highness," he replied, "let us ask God's help in this matter."

So the bishop and the empress, together with several distinguished people, took the three crosses to the home of a lady who was ill. They said a prayer, and then touched the crosses to the sick woman. At the touch of the True Cross, the lady was miraculously cured!

Helen had a beautiful church built, in which the relic of the True Cross was kept thereafter. News of what she had done spread through the Empire like a fire in a tinsel factory, and men's thoughts came back to the central fact of our Faith— that Christ died on His Cross to redeem us. That was just what Christians needed to think about at that time when the pagan influence was so strong.

Having been God's instrument in reawakening the Christian world, Helen passed peacefully to her reward at the age of eighty. Hers is the story of a remarkable character which patiently rode out the storms of life until at last it saw the beacon, and knew that truly everlasting Haven of Peace.

Sometimes, even when we are young we think it is too late to make a new start in something we feel sorry about. St. Helen's life shows that it is never too late to start over.

Saint Martin of Tours

Soldier of Christ

"Take me with you, Father! I'm not afraid of the long journey." Young Martin's eyes were wide with excitement as he pleaded with his father, a strong Roman officer.

"Yes," agreed Martin's father. "When you come to live in Italy with your mother and me, you will be living in a land very dear to the gods."

"Do you still believe in the gods, Father?" Martin asked. "Don't you realize that there is only one God?"

The father did not reply. He became thoughtful, wondering—as he had wondered before—who could have told his son such strange things?

The truth was that the young Martin, born in the Roman province of Hungary, had learned about the Christian Faith from a woman who had cared for him during his early childhood. She had told him of Jesus and the martyrs who had given their lives for Him.

Now Martin's father was going to take him to Italy. The boy was very excited, for he knew that soon he would see Rome, which was the capital of the entire world.

It was a long journey. Mounted on a single horse, father and son rode through green valleys and up rocky mountain passes. At night they would roll up in their blankets beneath the stars. Some-

Under the stars

Fulfilling his father's dream

times Martin would dream of Jesus. The boy was only about ten, but already he felt a strong desire to become a Christian.

In the family's home in Italy, four or five years slipped by. Then Martin's father told him, "I have always wanted you to become a soldier like me. It is time now for you to begin your training."

Martin felt uneasy. He did not believe he was called to a soldier's life, but to something very different. Yet he did not know what the other life was, so he entered the Roman army as his father wished. Soon he became an officer and was stationed in a Gallic city.

During his off-duty hours, Martin prayed, helped poor and weak people, and told everyone he could about Jesus of Nazareth. He was an unusual soldier indeed! Yet he was not a Christian, although he had begun to take instructions.

One cold night Martin was riding near the city gates when he noticed a ragged, shivering beggar standing beneath a tree. Everyone else was passing right by the poor man without doing a thing to help him.

"Jesus must have intended that *I* should help him," thought Martin. But what could he give? He had no money with him. All that he had was his cloak. . . . Martin drew out his sword, cut the cloak in half, and gave one part to the beggar, while he wrapped the other about himself. Some passers-by laughed, but others felt ashamed because they themselves had not helped the poor beggar.

In the name of Christ . . .

That night Martin had a dream. Jesus appeared to him surrounded by a dazzling light and wearing the half of the cloak he had given to the beggar!

Soon after that, Martin was baptized.

✧ ✧ ✧

One day, the general ordered his army into battle. Martin approached him and said, "Until today I have served you; from now on I wish to serve only the Lord Jesus."

"You're a coward," retorted the general angrily. "You want to run out on us. Till now I thought you were the bravest of my men, but I see that you are really a coward!" And he ordered that Martin be thrown into prison.

Of course, Martin did not change his mind. After a while he was released from prison and discharged from the army. He became a pilgrim, then a hermit. He founded a community of monks. His holiness became well-known. Soon the people of the city of Tours were clamoring to have him for their bishop.

Martin wanted none of it. He felt that honors might keep him from being united with God. But the people tricked him into entering the city, and took him to the church, where he was consecrated bishop.

The honor did not change him at all. He lived just as plainly as before and treated himself just as sternly. He was always very kind to the poor and unfortunate. One day he saw some people mistreating a leper, and thought, "Charity does not only mean giving people food and clothing; it also means giving them a smile and a good word." He went up to the leper and hugged him, saying: "Jesus is suffering in you, my brother."

One day Martin saw a group of men and women, all in chains, in the public square of a village. They were waiting to be beheaded the next day because they could not pay taxes to the powerful Count Avitius. Moved by pity, Martin hurried to the count's palace, but it was night, and every gate was shut. Kneeling before the main entrance, he began to pray: "O Lord, send an Angel to bid him listen to me. O Lord, save those innocent people from such a painful death."

While Count Avitius slumbered in his huge bed and his armed guards slept peacefully nearby, an Angel of the Lord, surrounded by a halo of golden light, appeared to the count in a dream and said, "Arise, Avitius! A servant of Our Lord is waiting for you outside the palace."

Avitius arose and put on his cloak. Trembling, he went out through the main gate. Martin opened his arms and embraced the fiery and powerful warrior, saying, "Come to free the poor people you have sentenced to such a cruel death. Forgive them their trespasses, and God will forgive you yours!"

When near the end of his life, Martin stopped on one of his journeys to see some of the monks who had come to him for guidance. He found them arguing. "If the shepherds are not united," Martin scolded, "what will become of their flock? Be at peace, brothers; be at peace."

Truly sorry, the brothers fell on their knees, and Bishop Martin blessed them. Then he said, "My sons, gladden my last days with your good deeds. I am now over eighty years old, and my ears hear the music of Heaven. Serve God in joy!"

It was the month of November. The leaves were falling from the trees and the sun was hidden by clouds. Martin was dying, and the monks who attended him wept, for they knew how they would miss his encouragement and guidance.

A strange and wonderful thing happened when Martin expired. All the coldness and gloominess of autumn disappeared, and for three days everything was as bright and beautiful as if it had been summer. Of course, no one really needed to see that miracle in order to know that Martin had been a saint; the holiness of his whole life had been proof of that!

When St. Martin was faced with the choice of being called brave and forsaking Christ, or being called a coward and following Christ, he chose the second. It is what we ARE, *which is important, not what people call us.*

Saint Monica

Model of Perseverance

Although St. Monica lived so many years ago, we know much about her life, because of the writings of her great son, St. Augustine. Indeed, St. Monica is noted chiefly for the prayers and mortifications she offered for her son's conversion.

Monica was born in Tagaste, North Africa, in 332. Her parents were fervent Christians, and placed their daughters under the care of an elderly servant who loved the girls very much and corrected them whenever they committed a fault. She taught them to mortify themselves in many ways, one of them being to go thirsty rather than drink between meals.

When Monica was twenty-two, she was given in marriage to a pagan named Patricius, who was much older than she. Her friends were disturbed by the marriage, for Monica was gentle and kind, while Patricius was fiery.

"How do you manage to get along so well with such a sharp tempered husband?" she was asked a few years later. Half-joking, half-serious, Monica replied, "All one has to do is regard the marriage contract as a bond of slavery and not answer back when the master is angry." Of course, she was not serious about the slavery part of it, but she meant what she said about not answering back. She never argued with Patricius, but was always gentle and obedient to him.

She was a great peacemaker, too. She always told people the good things that were said of them, but never the bad. Her patience and meekness also won over her mother-in-law, who had not liked her at first.

Monica went to Mass daily; she gave generously to the poor, in spite of Patricius' criticism. She strove to keep the three children—Augustine, Navigius and Perpetua—unspotted from the world, while she trained them in virtue in preparation for Baptism.

It was the custom of the times for Baptism to be delayed. Monica taught her children to revere the name of Christ, to venerate the martyrs and to desire eternal life. At Augustine's birth she had enrolled him as a catechumen, and when he became very ill, as a child, he begged her to send for a priest to baptise him. But he recovered immediately and, according to custom, his baptism was postponed again.

The boy was highly intelligent, but he did not like to study. Both Patricius and Monica were determined that he should become learned and set him to studying Latin and Greek. In those languages he began to read immoral literature. He began to lie, to steal, to cheat at games.

He was by now attending school in another city, where he came more and more under pagan influence. By the time he was seventeen he had given himself to a life of sinful pleasure.

Meanwhile Monica's twenty years of prayer and good example to Patricius were bearing fruit. He became a catechumen and received Baptism. Reforming his old ways, he passed the next year in peace with God and died a good death. Monica thanked God for having given her such a great grace.

Augustine, now studying in Carthage, came under the influence of a group of heretics called Manichaeans. He joined them. Monica felt as if he had died—and indeed this *was* a spiritual death for her son. For several years, the mother stormed Heaven with her prayers. She made penance; she gave him the good example of her own holy life— all, it seemed, to no avail!

One night God consoled her by means of a dream in which an Angel told her, "Your son is with you."

When she told Augustine about the dream, he said, "Ah, so you are going to join us!"

At once Monica replied, "No; I was not told that I was with you but that you were with me!" In spite of himself Augustine was impressed by his mother's quick retort and recalled it often in the years which followed.

At times, Monica urged bishops and wise priests to speak with her son. Often they told her that he himself with his keen mind would discover that the heresy did not make sense. When she continued to beg one bishop to speak to Augustine, he said, "It is impossible that the child of so many tears should perish."

When Augustine was twenty-nine, he told his mother he was going to Rome to teach. How could she try to help him if he were so far away, Monica thought. She was determined that he should not go—or at least that he should take her with him. At last Augustine said he would wait a few days.

With that trick, he slipped away and boarded a ship for Rome! Sad and silent with grief, Monica stood on the shore and watched the billowing sails grow small in the clear morning light. She had found out—but too late!

Years later, Augustine would recall the pain that he had caused his mother. Later, too, he would recall the deathly sickness which seized him after his arrival in Rome, and how he almost died, without any thought of repenting. Only Monica's prayers, he was sure, saved him.

From Rome Augustine went to Milan where he often listened to St. Ambrose preach—not because of what the bishop was saying, but because he was famous as a speaker. He learned that some teachings of the Church which he had never understood *did* have an explanation, after all. He thought seriously about the Manichaean teachings and decided to abandon the sect.

Meanwhile, his faithful mother made the dangerous trip to Milan to join him. When she learned of St. Ambrose's good influence, Monica was convinced that her son would become a Christian before she died. She redoubled her prayers.

Slowly, slowly, Augustine, aided by St. Ambrose, struggled to understand the Catholic teachings. At last his mind bowed to the truth, but his will still remained in chains, for to be a Christian means to keep the Commandments—to deny oneself. Augustine felt that it was more than he could do.

One summer day, in his garden, he fought it out with himself. He wanted to renounce sin, but he did not completely want to renounce it. Yet he did not want to lose God, Whom he had found after so much searching. Augustine burst into tears of sorrow and begged God not to forsake him. At once it seemed to him that he heard a child's voice saying, "Take up and read."

He had left a book of St. Paul's epistles lying nearby. Hurrying to it, he opened it and read, ". . . and make not provision for the flesh and its concupiscences." And suddenly light and peace flooded his soul. Augustine reentered the house and told his mother that at last he belonged to God.

Augustine was baptized on Easter Sunday, 387, together with some of his friends. Not long afterward the group made its way to the coast in order to set sail for Africa. In the seaport of Ostia, Monica said to her son, "Now I find no delight in anything of this life. What I can still do here and why I am here, I do not know, now that all my hopes in this world have been accomplished."

Hardly five days later she fell sick with a fever. To her sons, Augustine and Navigius, she said, "Here you will bury your mother."

"Not here, Mother," protested Navigius. "Not here in a foreign land!"

Monica stared at him in reproach—she who had often wished to be buried beside Patricius. "Put the body anywhere; don't be disturbed by its care. I ask only this, that wherever you may be, you will remember me at Mass."

Nine days later Monica died.

Augustine did not cry at the funeral, for his mother had died such a holy death. But when he was alone he recalled her loving care for him and her other children, and he broke down and wept for her who had wept for him so often.

"If I am your child, O my God," he wrote, "it is because You gave me such a mother!"

St. Monica shows us that no matter how long we have failed to gain something truly good, we should still keep praying and working for it.

Saint Patrick

Apostle of Ireland

It was the fourth century, about a hundred years after the Roman Emperor Constantine had put an end to the Christian persecution. Though he became a Christian just before he died, Constantine, the son of St. Helen, made a law in 313 called the Edict of Milan which declared that Christianity could be practiced freely throughout the Empire.

Of course, it took a while for the Faith to spread out from the Mediterranean world which St. Paul had converted, to the distant parts of the Empire where pagan tribes hunted and farmed while Roman officials managed their towns and villas.

One of those outlying parts of the Empire was Britain, separated from the heathen Picts by Hadrian's Wall, and from the pagan Irish by a stretch of blue water called the Irish Sea. Britain was a land of forests and farms. Many of its people were Christians who were descended from the Romans.

Patrick belonged to one of these families. He was a sturdy youth in his teens, who loved the fields and forest. He had been baptized a Christian, but had not had very much instruction in the Faith. Nonetheless, he loved God and was determined to become a true soldier of Christ.

One day a fleet of strange warships raided the peaceful British coast. The fierce men who swarmed down on the peaceful villages, burning and killing and carrying off prisoners, were raiders of Niall of the Nine Hostages, the Irish King. How savage they were! They robbed and destroyed, then took away everyone they could capture who was young and strong. Patrick was one of the prisoners.

The hold of the raider ship was dark and crowded. Patrick lay still, cramped, hungry, and aching from his bruises. He listened to the swish and thump of the waves against the ship's hull, and felt the surge and roll of the vessel as she plowed through them. Would he ever see his family again? he wondered. Were his parents alive or dead? Where were these men taking him? Perhaps he was going to Ireland, to be sold into slavery!

"Dear God, be with me, sustain me, protect me," Patrick prayed.

* * *

The slave market was crowded and noisy. The new prisoners stood silently while their captors haggled over prices with the Irish lords and their agents. Their Gaelic phrases grated heavily on Patrick's ears, which were accustomed to the musical flow of Latin. At last a bargain was struck, and Patrick was sold into the service of a lord named Milcho. He set out with the slave buyer toward the northern province which would be his home.

They journeyed through a land of hills and bogs, where wolves howled in the forests by night. This was a wilder land than Patrick's cultivated Britain, but its ruggedness appealed to the boy. He dreamed of escaping and losing himself in those mountain fastnesses, until he could search out a ship that would bear him home.

The estate or dun of Milcho was in the wildest country of all and very well fortified against the wolves and brigands. Patrick, however, was not going to sleep within its walls. His duty would be to tend the sheep in the meadows and the swine in the forest, keeping them safe from wolves and making sure that they did not wander into the cultivated fields to destroy the crops. Trained dogs were given him to help in the task. His home at night was to be a rude hut, with a roaring peat fire blazing at the doorway to drive away the wild beasts. His only comrades would be his dogs.

That was how Patrick passed the next six years. He became toughened to all kinds of weather—bronzed by the sun, hardened against the cold.

Whenever he met one of the Irish, he tried to learn their gutteral Gaelic language. After a time, he knew it well.

Patrick grew to love the people as well. In some ways they were barbaric, but sometimes they were gentler and kinder than any Roman he had known. They worshipped many things in nature, especially the sun. Their priests, called druids, were rather like magicians.

"My Lord Jesus," Patrick would pray, "please give them the grace to see that there are not gods in *things,* but rather that there is One God Who made everything. Give me the chance to study about You so that I can someday explain this great mystery to them. I am too ignorant to do so yet. Please give me a chance to escape!"

Thus Patrick prayed in his solitude on the slopes of Mount Slemish, in the pastures by day, in his hut beneath the stars at night. Before the dawn, he would leave the warmth of his fire and go out to pray in the snow, frost or rain. Looking back on this period of his life a few years later, he would write, "The spirit was fervent within me!"

One night as he slept, he heard the voice of his Guardian Angel say, "Your ship is ready!" Patrick arose and set out at once for the coast.

Indeed, there was a ship, lying at anchor in a sheltered spot. It was preparing to sail. Patrick went up to the captain and asked if he could be taken on as a member of the crew. "Nothing doing!" retorted the captain. Perhaps he could tell that this young man was a runaway slave!

Patrick turned away sad, but began at once to pray. As he walked slowly down the strand, he heard a sudden shout, "Come quickly! The sailors are calling you!"

God had touched their hearts. The captain and crew welcomed Patrick aboard their ship and together they set sail.

After mishaps and hardships, Patrick returned to Britain and rejoined those members of his family who were still living. How glad they were to have him home, after believing him dead! He lingered on with them a few years, until the burning desire to bring Christ to Ireland became too much for him. He resolved to go to France—then called Gaul—to study under his kinsman, St. Martin, Bishop of Tours.

Sadly, Patrick had only spent a few months with his holy relative, when the aged monk passed on to the beautiful reward God had planned for him. Patrick went on to Auxerre, where he became a monk under St. Martin's friend, St. Germanus. In due time he was ordained a priest. He studied more and more diligently, for his Guardian Angel, speaking for the Irish people, had told him in a dream that Ireland was calling him. Indeed, he heard the voices himself: "We beg you, holy youth, return and walk among us!"

God blessed Patrick with an amazingly long life. He was no longer young when the awaited sign from God came to him, but sixty years of preaching lay ahead of him. Most men couldn't have done it, but Patrick still had the fire of his youth, joined to the experience of maturity.

Germanus gave Patrick a blessing, and so also did Pope Celestine. The Pope had already sent a missionary named Palladius to Ireland, but that mission had been unsuccessful. Now Patrick was to take his place. Before he went, he was consecrated first Bishop of Ireland, so that he would have all the authority he needed.

Patrick built the first Christian church in Ireland at a place called Saul—the same spot where he would be buried sixty years later.

He pushed on toward Tara, the palace of the Irish kings. He was in sight of it on Easter Eve, 433, when he and his companions stopped on the hill of Slane to celebrate the Easter vigil. Patrick lit the Paschal fire. It cut the darkness like a knife—the only light that could be seen in that dim, silent world.

Then, from the direction of Tara, cries of rage split the darkness. A few moments, and the galloping of hooves could be heard, and the rumble of chariots. What was happening? Patrick and his comrades turned to face the oncomers.

What had happened was this: Ireland's pagan lords had been celebrating their biggest feast—the Feis of Tara. The druid priests had proclaimed that on that night no fire should be lit in all of Ireland before the fire of Tara. Patrick had disobeyed their law.

And so King Laeghaire and his nobles came thundering up to Patrick. The bishop faced them calmly.

"Who are you?"

"How dare you break the law?"

In a ringing voice Patrick began to explain. He told of his purpose in coming to Ireland. He told the great mysteries of the Christian religion, using the three-leafed shamrock to describe the Holy Trinity.

Naturally the druids challenged Patrick, and a terrible struggle followed between the devilish powers of the druids and the miracles of the Saint. In the end, Patrick won out. Laeghaire was not converted, but he gave the bishop permission to preach in all of Ireland.

There are many inspiring stories told about St. Patrick's journeys through Ireland and the many conversions that he made. Wherever he went, he built chapels and put up crosses as a reminder of Our Lord's Passion. It is said that he remembered the location of every roadside cross and paid a visit to each one whenever he had to pass near it—in order to make an act of love for the Crucified Savior.

One year, at the beginning of Lent, Patrick was travelling along the western coast of Ireland. On inspiration, he climbed the slopes of a rocky crag to fast and pray. For forty days, between the desolate moorland and the wild sea, Patrick battled the devil. Prayer and penance; prayer and penance. He begged God to give the fate of every soul in Ireland, then and for the rest of time, into his own hands. Was it too much to ask for? Perhaps from most men it would have been, but from Patrick, no. He had always had a way of "taking heaven by storm." He prayed with such faith and love that God never refused him—and so it was this time, too. When Patrick came down from his mountain, in the radiance of an Easter morn, he had won, for all of Ireland!

It was after many years of tireless labor for his beloved people, that Patrick passed away, in Saul, on a cold March day in 493. He had converted a nation, and that nation has remained grateful for fifteen hundred years.

The course of history was changed because Patrick wanted to do good to his enemies. Let us, too, see the image of Christ in those who dislike us, and God will bless them, too.

Saint Brigid

Mary of the Gael

Brigid was born during St. Patrick's lifetime— when Ireland was half-pagan and half-Christian. Her father was Duffy, a pagan chieftain, and her mother was Brocessa, a Christian slave. Shortly before Brigid's birth, Duffy sold Brocessa, with the understanding that the child would be returned to him in a few years. Brocessa had the child baptized at the first opportunity and taught her about Jesus and Mary from the beginning.

When Brigid returned to be a slave in her
father's household, she turned out to be different
from ordinary slaves. If a hungry dog came whining
about while she was cooking, he got a piece of meat;
if a begger came by while she was tending the sheep,
she would as likely as not give him one of her woolly
little charges. She seemed to forget that she was
Duffy's slave and to remember only that she was
his daughter.

One day Duffy called her: "Come here with
me in the chariot."

How wonderful! A ride in the chariot! Brigid
scrambled in happily and sat next to her stern-faced
master. A flick of the whip and off they went.

"I'm not doing this to honor you," Duffy said
abruptly.

Brigid gazed up at him wide-eyed.

"I'm going to sell you to the King. You've been
too generous with things that don't belong to you."

Brigid said nothing. How could she explain
that it was impossible to refuse someone who
needed help?

They stopped before a grim fortress. "Wait
here," growled Duffy, and he went in to speak with
the King. Brigid sat quietly in the chariot watching
the horses' tails brushing away the flies, and the
trees and . . . a poor leper trudging down the road.
He came up to the chariot and Brigid looked down
at him, his face all eaten away by the horrible disease and his mournful eyes pleading.

"I have nothing to give him," she thought.

There on the seat beside her was Duffy's sword —a beautiful jeweled sword with a wonderfully keen blade. She took it up and handed it to the beggar. He thanked her and hurried off with the splendid gift.

When Duffy returned to the chariot, he missed the sword at once.

"What have you done with it?" he asked, trying to remain calm.

"A leper came by. . . ."

Duffy let out a roar like an angry bull. "A leper! You gave my jeweled sword to a leper! That sword was worth a fortune!"

"I know," replied Brigid calmly. "That's why I gave it to God."

To God, she said, for all her life Brigid saw God in people who were in need, and that was why she felt she *had* to be generous to everyone.

Duffy pulled Brigid down from the chariot and rushed her into the fortress. "There," he sputtered angrily to the king. "There! She's done it again! She's given my famous jeweled sword to a leper. You see now why I will not keep her!"

The king happened to be a Christian. He looked gravely down at Brigid, who stared back with big, round eyes. Suddenly the king smiled. "She is a Christian," he said, "and a good one. You should be proud of her, Duffy. Take her back home with you, but give her her freedom. After all, she's a chieftain's daughter."

Duffy gulped in dismay. If Brigid were freed, she might give away everything he owned!

But as Duffy was driving home with the quiet little girl beside him, he already had an idea. Yes, he would free Brigid, for she was as fiery and independent as he himself and he *was* proud of her in a way. Hadn't the king himself praised her? Nevertheless, he would marry Brigid off before she could give away half his possessions.

        ❄ ❄ ❄

"Father," said Brigid one day, "I wish to see my mother, Brocessa. May I go to visit her?"

"No," replied Duffy.

But Brigid went anyway, with Duffy-like stubbornness. She went because she was obeying a higher law—that of charity. Her mother, she knew, was feeble and sickly and overworked. Brigid went to take her mother's place grinding corn, churning butter, and tending cows.

Of course, Brigid's generosity went with her. Even though the butter and milk and cream were not hers, she could not help giving them "to God" —to the poor beggars who came daily. And God, Who is the model of all generosity, rewarded her by miraculously keeping the dairy stocked with butter and milk. The master of Brigid's mother was so amazed at this that he looked on Brigid as a saint (although he himself was still a pagan), and he offered to give her the whole dairy and all the cows.

"Rather, give my mother her freedom," begged Brigid—and this the good man did. Later, he became a Christian.

Brigid settled her mother among her own kinsfolk and returned to Duffy. She was now in her late teens—tall and strong with the ruddy cheeks and serene expression that go along with hard work in the pure air. Duffy thought she would make someone a fine wife.

He settled upon a poet, for poets in those days were learned, wealthy and highly respected. Brigid would have a high social position if she married a poet.

Naturally, Brigid had other ideas. As soon as she met the poet of her father's choice, she told him where he could find a wonderful girl who would make him a fine wife. She told him she would pray for that intention. And the poet went on his way.

Duffy was furious, but Brigid was stubborn. "I'm going to be a virgin of Christ," she told him, and what could the irate father do but give in? After all, it was his own hard-headedness she had.

* * *

When Patrick had come to Ireland a few years before, he had begun to found monasteries right away. But he had founded no convents. Many young girls whom he converted longed to consecrate their virginity to Christ, and did so, yet they had to continue living with their parents and brothers and sisters. They prayed, helped the poor, and did needlework for the new churches Patrick had built. But their own families did not understand them. Patrick once wrote, "They do this without their fathers' consent, and suffer persecution and lying reproaches from their kinsfolk."

Brigid had seven good friends, girls about her own age who wanted to belong entirely to God.

"Let us live together in community as the monks do," she proposed to them. "Let us go to Bishop Mel. He will receive our vows in Christ's name." And so the bishop did, and gladly.

By this time, the fiery Duffy had come around almost completely. He gave Brigid the financial support and political backing she needed to begin her foundations. Whether or not he himself became a Christian, we do not know, but in view of all the other triumphs in Brigid's life, we can assume that he did.

Brigid seemed to acquire the friendship and backing of the Irish bishops almost at once. Patrick had died but a few years before; they saw in her much of his spirit and encouraged her missionary labors. Through them Brigid learned how Patrick had thought and felt about various problems and though not repressing her own genius, she strove to imitate him.

We are not sure which convent was Brigid's first, for she founded many in a short space of time. Those early convents were little groups of huts, made of clay and wattles, which the young nuns built themselves. Around the group of huts went a large stone or earthen wall. As soon as Brigid had one community set up, she would leave a capable sister in charge and, taking one or two others with her, she would continue to a new spot, recruit vocations, and build another convent. Like Patrick before her, she traveled the length and breadth of Ireland.

Brigid traveled in a little chariot, drawn by two swift horses. It was a dangerous way to travel on such bumpy roads, and at least twice she was thrown out of the chariot. Once the horses ran away, and came to a halt at the very edge of a cliff!

Courage was one of Brigid's chief qualities, but she was best known for her cheerful generosity. Now that she was a nun and had to look after a whole community, she gave even more generously to the poor than she had as a child. On one occasion the sisters were expecting a visit from some important churchmen. They carefully put aside milk and butter, bread and meat in order to provide a feast worthy of the occasion. But who should appear at the convent gates but a host of beggars! Brigid could not resist and gave them all the food she had prepared.

Another time, she loaned her chariot to a poor family who were carrying all there belongings on their backs.

Once a noble lady brought Brigid a basket of apples. Brigid was delighted. She took all the apples and distributed them to a band of lepers who were standing hopefully near the convent gate.

"I brought them for you, not for those lepers!" the lady exclaimed.

"What is mine is theirs," said Brigid calmly.

Everyone got a royal welcome in Brigid's convents. Bishops, monks, young girls from the neighboring farms, all were feasted on whatever provisions the sisters had on hand. And somehow the food never quite gave out, even if the cows had to be milked an extra time or two! Brigid was always giving "to God" and God would not be outdone.

We often hear people mention Martha and Mary—Martha who was so practical and hardworking, Mary who was always absorbed in God. Brigid had the qualities of both. She loved to pray and to meditate on the lives of Jesus and Mary. Indeed she loved Our Lady so much and imitated her so well that she came to be called, "the Mary of the Gael." But when did Brigid pray and meditate? While milking the convent's cows, churning the butter, baking the bread, reaping the grain, brewing the ale, tending the sheep. One of the most famous lives that has been written about her refers to an unexpected visit from St. Brendan the Voyager: "Brigid came from her sheep to welcome Brendan."

Yet Brigid loved and encouraged studies. In Kildare, the most famous of the convents she founded, scholars poured over manuscripts. The famous age of Saints and Scholars began in the convents and monasteries in Ireland during her lifetime.

Kildare was also known for the beautiful workmanship of its decorated manuscripts, bells and chalices, which went to churches all over Ireland.

Brigid shines down through history as a saint of joy. She liked to play jokes; she enjoyed listening to music; she loved to see people having an innocent good time. She was fond of animals, like other Irish saints, for instance Kieran and Kevin and Columncille. She saw God in everything around her and was forever thanking Him. Yet in spite of all this, Brigid practiced many mortifications. It is very true that mortification and joy go together happily.

When Brigid was born, Ireland was half-pagan and half Christian. At the time of her death—thanks to her labors and those of St. Patrick's other disciples—the Emerald Isle was completely Christian and had begun to send out missionaries to other lands. They went forth with the spirit of Brigid—with fire and courage and a love that embraced the world.

Someone once said that a sad saint is no saint at all. Like St. Brigid, let us see God's beauty in everything around us and thank Him joyfully, always.

Saint Benedict

Patriarch of Western Monks

At the age of fourteen, the young Roman noble Benedict had already sickened of the vanity and corruption of Rome. Thus the youth obtained his parent's permission to retire to the solitude of a of a country villa, where he could pray and study in peace. It was a welcome change from the corrupt life in Rome; yet something else still seemed to call him.

A life of prayer, mortification and penance far from all traces of civilization: such, Benedict felt, was God's will for him. The aged governess who lived with him would take it hard, he knew, but the impulse was so strong that one night the boy left a note and softly slipped away from the villa, bound for the wild, rugged countryside.

He walked on and on. As day broke the going became rougher and rougher—a rocky, steep-sloped terrain—just the sort of country he was looking for! Benedict's smile broadened as he trudged up into the mountains.

Suddenly a deep, silent valley opened before him. There would be no people here; no one would want to live in such desolation except someone like Benedict, who sought only God and wished to avoid all else.

Ah! That cave among the rocks looked perfect; could it be that God was guiding his steps in that direction? He approached the cavern with singing heart. "May You be praised, my Lord!" he exclaimed.

"Now and forever!" a voice replied.

Benedict was startled. He gazed about wildly. He had thought that he was alone, far from any other human creature. Yet a few feet away from him stood an old man, a hermit with a very kind face!

"I wished to live in solitude," Benedict murmured.

"You will easily be able to do that," replied the hermit. "But tell me, who are you?"

In a few words the boy told the story of his life and the great desire God had given him to leave the world and draw close to Him. The holy hermit understood this very well, for God had inspired him, too, in much the same way. He knew that the boy needed to withdraw from the world and concentrate on his own sanctification. Yet, thought the hermit, Benedict was still very young. . . .

"Listen," he said. "I'll leave a bell nearby with a cord attached to it. From time to time I'll come by with a little food, so when the bell rings you will know that there is something to eat waiting for you outside. That way you will not have to see anyone or be disturbed by anything."

Benedict was very grateful; no other arrangement could have pleased him more. Happily he stood at the cave's mouth and watched his new friend stride away along the rocky slope. The hermit turned once to raise his hand in farewell, then he was gone.

Poverty and privation, cold and discomfort, darkness and dampness, these were to be Benedict's life. But he scarcely noticed them, so absorbed was he in prayer and in penances. The length of the days, the passage of the seasons, these were nothing to him.

✻ ✻ ✻

Benedict was a saint, and saints are often attacked by the devil, who envies them for their virtue. One day, Satan snapped the bell cord. Time passed, and the lad grew hungrier and hungrier. He was slowly starving to death, but no welcome jingle sounded from the bell. The holy hermit must have forgotten him, Benedict thought. . . .

But on Easter Sunday a marvelous event occurred a few miles away from Benedict's cave. A good priest was preparing his holiday dinner when he heard a voice say, "While you are eating, My servant Benedict is almost dying of starvation in the cave of Subiaco!"

The good priest did not hesitate. He put all his food into a sack, slung the sack over his shoulder, and set out for the cave of Subiaco! "Good health to you, brother!" he greeted Benedict. "I come in behalf of the Lord!"

What a joyous Easter feast the two men of God had, and what gratitude filled the young hermit's heart for God's goodness to him!

The priest returned to his parish, but Benedict was not left alone for long; although solitude is blessed, sanctity is like a magnet. Others who were also weary of the world and its delusions came to the young hermit and asked him to tell them his rule of life so that they could follow it, too. Benedict accepted them as brothers and formed them into communities of monks. By the year 520, twelve monasteries dotted the rugged countryside.

*　*　*

Like every other great man, Benedict had enemies. Once a man sent him a poisoned loaf of bread. It was set before him at mealtime.

Did Benedict eat it?

No.

Each day at mealtime a crow used to fly down and join the brothers at their meal. Benedict loved animals and was very kind to the crow, which ate right from his hand. This day he gave the crow the poisoned loaf of bread, but he said to it, "Take this bread and carry it far away. Drop it where it will not harm anyone."

The crow obliged by seizing the bread in its beak and winging off into the wide, blue sky. Soon he was gone from sight.

Hours passed by. Had the crow become too greedy and disobeyed Benedict? Had he eaten the poisoned bread? Ah, no! A small black speck appeared in the sky and grew steadily larger; Mr. Crow had returned!

He lit next to Benedict, and we know that if he could have talked he would have said, "Your order was carried out just as you wished. Now I hope you won't refuse me some little crumb!"

And if we know Benedict, of course he did not.

* * *

When Benedict's religious order had built quite a few monasteries he set out to build the greatest of them: Montecassino. The spot chosen was a mountain where a pagan temple stood. "We must conquer this mountain!" the saint told his monks. Singing and praying, they began to climb it. In holy joy, they encircled the temple and demolished it. Then they began prayerfully to build the great church and monastery.

"Pray and work," Benedict always said.

Pray and work. It would become the very *motto* of the Benedictines. A wise and complete plan of life was contained in those three words.

The monks also set to work diligently to cultivate the fields about their new home. Hard work with the plow, shovel, pick and hoe transformed the rough countryside into beautiful fields laced by long silver ribbons of irrigation ditches. Soon, in the Dark Ages, Benedictine monasteries would be little shelters of peace and happiness amid the miseries of the outside world.

Within the monasteries the monks worked in their little rooms copying down the great writings of the Greeks and Romans: works of thought, of poetry.... These were writings that influence our own lives today, and they would not have been preserved through the Dark Ages if it had not been for Benedict and his monks who knew their value and treasured them because of it.

Montecassino! Benedict had lit a bright light which would never be put out, because it was a light of the spirit.

Early in the year 543, the saint told his monks, "Brothers, God is calling me!" The time had come, he knew, for him to join his twin sister, St. Scholastica, who had died a short while before. A high fever seized him. With great fervor he received Holy Communion, and calmly he passed away. But although St. Benedict has been dead for centuries, the world has not forgotten the great debt which it owes to him.

"Pray and work" is the secret of success. If we want to do well in something, we must work hard at it, but we must also pray for God's help.

Saint Kevin

Kevin of the Angels

St. Kevin lived about a hundred years after the great saints, Patrick and Brigid, at a time when Ireland was called a land of saints and scholars. He was baptized by St. Cronan, and a legend says that Angels became visible around the font during the ceremony. Because of this, he is often called Kevin of the Angels.

Kevin's parents were nobles, who could easily have hired tutors for the boy, so that he could grow up among the comforts of home and become a warrior and chieftain. But Kevin's parents were wise. They knew that a good education is better than comfort, and learning to serve God well is the best kind of wealth.

So they sent Kevin away to study under a wise old monk named Petroc. The boy was seven when he started school, and nineteen when he finished. By that time he was certain about what he wished to do with his life—he would become a priest.

That meant more study, but to Kevin it was worth it. He continued to pour over his books under the stern guidance of his uncle Eugene, a serious hard-working priest who expected students to measure up to his standards. Kevin found it hard at times, but he kept plugging, and at last the great day arrived—ordination!

Now that he was a priest Kevin felt a great need to go apart for a while to be alone with God, praying and meditating upon the truths he had learned during his long years of study, making penance and asking for the light to understand and accomplish what God wished of him.

Into the hills of Wicklow he trudged until he reached a wild spot where two lonely lakes mirrored the sky. On one side rose a rocky crag; on the other, a green mountain. The place was called Glendalough, which means the valley of the two lakes.

For seven years Kevin lived in that wild valley, eating berries and nuts and wild plants, meditating and praying. He had a great love for animals, because God made them, and those timid creatures could sense it; they came to him fearlessly and shared his rude hut and glowing fire.

One day a farmer named Dima came walking through the glen. He was a pagan farmer, but he had heard that a holy hermit lived at Glendalough and he was curious. He asked Kevin to tell him about God. Of course, Kevin was eager to do so. Simply and clearly, he told Dima about the beautiful mysteries of the Faith—one God Who made everything from nothing and keeps us in existence; man's sin of pride and disobedience; the Son of God taking man's nature and suffering and dying to make reparation for sin; the supernatural life of grace and the promise of life after death with God for all eternity.

Dima listened spellbound. At last he said, "Will you come down to my farm and teach my children what you have told me?"

Kevin hesitated. "I will pray about it," he said. But almost at once he heard the answer in his heart. *This* was what God wanted him to do with his life. The next day he went down to the farm with Dima and his children.

Soon Kevin was teaching not just one family, but dozens of men and boys from the nearby villages and farms.

"We must build a school," he decided.

Rocks were plentiful. The farmers pitched in and built Kevin a monastery in the solitude of Glendalough. Other monks came to help teach the children of the farmers—and the children of kings and chieftains who heard of the learning and holiness of Kevin of Glendalough. The rich and the poor lived and worked and studied together, and were treated all alike.

More buildings were added to the little settlement including a sturdy stone tower with a cone-shaped top. It became a famous landmark. People came from all over Ireland to tell Kevin their problems and ask his help in solving them.

In order to help others, one must have the help of God, so every Lent, Kevin withdrew up the mountain to live alone in a cave and examine his conscience, do penance, make strong resolutions for the future, and pray for the strength to grow in virtue and the light to help others.

The years slipped by. Kevin's hair and beard grew white, but his eyes still sparkled, and his step was as quick and firm as ever. He longed to go on a missionary journey, as many of his grown-up pupils had done.

"What do you think of the idea?" he asked his friend Kieran, Bishop of Clonmacnoise.

Kieran understood Kevin's longing but he knew that it is better for one missionary to train many others than to leave the others half-trained and go to the missions himself.

"Birds do not hatch their eggs while they are flying," he said.

Kevin saw the point. Not to go was a sacrifice, but he knew now where God's will lay.

So Kevin continued to teach and advise everyone who came to him until the peaceful June night in 618 when his soul sped heavenward to join the Angels and saints around God's throne. From Heaven he prays for missionaries wherever they may be.

St. Kevin knew the importance of sharing what he knew with others. If someone asks us a question about the truths of our faith, we should try to give them a clear and correct answer.

Saint Columban

Missionary Monk

He stood at a gaping cave mouth, a cliff overhanging him—the lean old monk whose face bore lines of suffering and fatigue. His restless, glowing eyes searched the vineyards and olive groves clinging to the slopes below, flicked over a mill grinding grain against the winter, lingered upon a timbered church and a small ring of huts, swept upward to the surging crests of the Apennines. Beloved was this land of Italy, which gave warmth to one's old age!

Autumn was well along; the old monk could feel its twinge in his bones. The foliage was still too dense for him to see what was going on in the valley, but he knew that his monks were down there, toiling in the vineyards and olive groves, gathering the figs and the almonds, making ready for the days of icy blasts and swirling snows. There would be no abundance of food that winter, but the monks would fast so rigidly that their supplies would see them through.

How were his other monasteries faring? the old man wondered. Hundreds of miles to the northwest, beyond the massive Alps thrusting themselves skyward–they nestled among the forested mountains of Eastern Gaul. There, were his monks still leading that life of perfect charity and self-denial which had been their ideal? Did they yet practice those rigid fasts and penances he had taught them? Had outsiders again tried to interfere in their life of labor and solitude, as they had when they had driven the abbot himself into exile?

The old monk pondered in silence, and at length turned back into his cave. During the last two years he had spent many hours at prayer in this retreat. Now he felt he would soon leave the cave for good. . . .

It had been a long life, and an active one. The old monk thought back over the years to that painful day in distant Ireland when he as a youth had made a hard decision and had held to it. . . .

It was right after a severe temptation against purity. Knowing his weakness, he went hurrying off to speak to a friend, a holy hermit woman whose advice he respected. He laid the problem before her.

"What shall I do?"

The pious woman did not waste words: "Do you recall how Eve coaxed and Adam gave in? How the strong Samson was made weak by Dalila? How holy David fell from grace because of Bathsheba, and wise Solomon embraced folly for the love of women? Go, flee from that river in which so many have drowned!"

The boy reflected on this advice and saw how right it was. He was highborn and handsome; wily eyes were already upon him, and he would be given no peace as long as he remained at home. Since he wished to avoid sin at any cost, he must flee.

❊ ❊ ❊

His mother was heartbroken. "I cannot let you go!" she protested, standing firmly in the doorway to block his passage.

"And yet, Mother, I must go," replied the son, as he strove to hide his own inner torment. He reflected that to keep God's laws one must be willing to give up anything.

The weeping mother threw herself on the floor before the open doorway. Taking a firm grip on his emotions, the youth stepped over the prostrate form and set off at a fast pace toward the north, and sanctuary.

* * *

On the island of Cluain in the Lake of Erne, in a monastery under the direction of Abbot Sinell, the youth continued his studies of Latin and of Scripture. After deciding that he wished to become a monk he went on to the monastery of Bangor. There he was ordained.

Long, quiet years followed—years of stern self-discipline which led to a deep union with God. Irish monks fasted severely, studied earnestly, punished themselves harshly, and worked energetically—and he, Father Columban, strove to sacrifice himself completely by those means. We must die to ourselves, he reflected, that we may live to Christ. We cannot live to Him unless we die to our own wills. We must be Christ's, not our own. . . .

And so, over a space of almost thirty years, Columban strove to detach himself from his own tastes and interests so that Christ would be the one love in his heart. One detachment only remained to be made—detachment from the monastery of Bangor itself—and this he finally requested.

"I would rather you remained here," Abbot Comghall replied sadly. "Nevertheless, I shall pray about it, and I will let you know God's will."

And God inspired Comghall not only to grant Columban's desire but also to provide him with twelve companions!

* * *

The little band of monks packed a few possessions—mostly books and sacred vessels—and set sail for the European continent. From Brittany, where they gained more followers, they set out for Eastern Gaul, tramping along crumbling Roman roads which were almost strangled by the dense forests.

Those forests were dangerous for many reasons. In them lurked fugitive soldiers, runaway slaves, robbers and cutthroats, not to mention wild beasts. Sometimes Frankish nobles would come thundering down the old roads on fiery horses—off to some wild battle. The Roman Empire had all but died, and Gaul lay divided among three Frankish kings, Christian in name but pagan in their horrid vices. It was a land that cried for the breath of holiness.

* * *

Columban and his companions were welcomed into Burgundy, the territory of King Gunthram, and there in a wild, desolate region of the Vosges mountains, they came across a ruined Roman fort and a moldering temple to the pagan goddess Diana. Setting to work with a will, they converted the fort into the monastery of Annegray; and the temple into St. Martin's Chapel.

It was wonderful to see how the monks worked together! They obeyed as if they had only one will. They looked after one another as if they had but one soul. They were all patience, humility, gentleness. These things Columban—and Comghall before him—had insisted upon, and many of the graces bestowed by God upon the monks may have been merited by Columban's own inner struggles, for he himself was a person of violent emotions—strong loves and hates which he was forever conquering and reconquering for the love of Christ.

At once these foreign monks won the hearts of the common people, simple folk descended from generations of Christians. These peasants were more virtuous than the nobles. Upon hearing rumors of the monks' holiness, they came flocking to Annegray to ask for prayers for themselves and their sick ones at home. Many young men asked admission to the monastery in order to study and become monks.

* * *

The monks lived chiefly on wild plants, roots, and bark—not an easy diet for such hard workers!—with an occasional fish. The nearby river was a good place for fish, and Gall, one of the priests who had come from Ireland with Columban, was an excellent fisherman—quick, dexterous and patient. However he was not always obedient.

One morning, Gall set out to fish, not in the spot Columban had chosen for him but in another which he thought would be better. His heart leaped when he reached the riverbank, for sure enough there was a school of fish just waiting for him! Skillfully Gall cast his net. But what happened? At once the fish reversed direction and swam away. Patient as always, Gall made another attempt. . . .

And another....

All day long he fished, and returned to the monastery with nothing to show for all his labors.

"Father, I am sorry I have wasted the day like this," he moaned.

"But why did you not obey, and fish where you were told?" Columban replied. "Go back at once to the place I spoke about."

Shamefaced, Gall went down to the right spot and cast his net. At once so many fish swam into it that it took all the monk's strength to pull it to the shore.

* * *

In those mountain fastnesses, where bears roamed and wolves skulked, Father Columban found a cave, its entrance overgrown with brambles. It overlooked the river. There he could retire to pray undisturbed; that solitude and the few greens and berries which he ate increased his union with God as nothing else could have done. Silence and mortification, these are essential for sainthood.

Some of the other monks felt the same need. From time to time they, too, were permitted to go off into the forests and spend a few days in prayer and fasting and bodily penance. Often they would pray for hours with arms extended in the form of a cross. This was no practice for weaklings, and Columban kept an anxious eye on the health of his men.

* * *

The number of monks was increasing. It was time to found another monastery. Father Columban followed the river downstream about eight miles until he came upon the ruins of a Roman town which had been sacked by the Huns. This he chose for the site of his second monastery, Luxeuil.

With joy, the monks set to work–hacking away underbrush, felling trees, hauling stones. They restored the town walls and within them built a church, a school, and a number of little cells. Not long afterward they set about draining the swampland three miles to the south, planting grain to sustain the growing community. There they built another small monastery, Fontaines. Soon the three communities housed sixty monks and over two hundred disciples, mostly noblemen's sons, who would return into the world after finishing their studies, schooled also in self-discipline, in honesty and in kindness. Penitents also flocked to spend a few weeks' time with the monks, for they were treated kindly by them and received from them corrective penances which would help them not to sin again.

          ✻ ✻ ✻

Father Columban believed in utter obedience. One day he entered a room full of sick monks. "Get up," he ordered. "Go help your brothers thresh the harvest!"

Several of the monks sprang at once to their feet and hurried to the threshing floor. They picked up flails and began to pound the wheat. Gladdened at the sight of such faith, the abbot called, "Stop! You must rest after so much sickness and work!"

When the men paused, they discovered that they were completely well, whereas their brothers

in bed were still sick! "And those men will remain
ill for a while yet," Columban remarked dryly.

❊ ❊ ❊

About sixty years before, St. Benedict had
drawn up his famous rule for monastic life. Now
Columban drew up a rule of his own based on the
need for greater penances and stricter discipline
which the Irish monks and their disciples always
felt. The thirst for sacrifice must not be denied, for
that was what bound them together so strongly.
Thus it was that Columban's rule stressed priva-
tions and penalties. But the prime purpose of monastic life, he wrote, was to learn to love God with
all one's mind, heart, and strength and to love one's
neighbor as oneself for love of God.

One must keep one's mind on God and Heav-
en, Columban taught, by seeing all things only as
symbols of eternity or as means to reach that goal.
Nothing should be loved for itself, nor should any
quality be developed so much as to destroy others,
for such a quality would then no longer be virtue.
Virtue is temperate.

Well did Columban understand the truth of
his words, for his whole life had been and would
be a struggle to keep himself on an even keel—to
subject his volcanic emotions to a sober intellect
and an iron will.

❊ ❊ ❊

As abbot, Columban was the spiritual father of
all his monks. He punished them as a good father
would do; he watched over their spiritual life and

health. Above all, he tried never to become attached to them, for one must love one's brother solely for the love of Christ. Yet human nature sometimes plays tricks–and one day Father Columban knelt in the church at Luxeuil praying and weeping because one of his monks was dying.

The younger monk's name was also Columban, and he was one of the twelve who had come from Ireland with the abbot. Now he was at the point of death from a fever, and the elder Columban could not bear to see him go.

As he prayed and wept, he heard a monk come up behind him.

"Father Abbot," came the whisper, "Columban is calling for you!"

Hastily the abbot genuflected and left the church. He rushed to the dying man's bedside.

"Father," pleaded the younger Columban, "why are you keeping me in this burdensome life with your prayers? They are standing by to lead me away"–he glanced about as if he saw Angels surrounding him–"but they are prevented by your prayers and tears. Loose these bonds so that the heavenly kingdom may receive me."

Now Father Columban saw how selfish he had been. At once he had the Last Sacraments administered to the dying man, and the younger Columban's soul sped away in peace. It was the moment young Columban had lived for. Sixteen more times, Father Columban would witness the death of one of his spiritual sons.

❊ ❊ ❊

About twenty years after Father Columban's arrival in Gaul, he stirred up a political hornet's nest. Until that time he had been friendly with the kings of Burgundy, even those who led scandalous lives. Often he had urged the young King Theodoric to change his ways, and that young man had listened respectfully but had gone on doing as he pleased. Then came the day that the abbot paid a visit to Queen Brunhilda, Theodoric's grandmother, with whom he had always been on good terms. He said something in his usual frank way which offended Brunhilda deeply. After the abbot departed, the queen began to urge King Theodoric and the bishops to drive the monks out of Gaul!

One day the young king rode up to Columban's monastery with a band of soldiers. He had often come to Luxeuil as a guest, but today he came as a monarch. He demanded to examine every inch of the monastery. Of course Father Columban replied that certain parts of the monastery were closed to lay people. This was the excuse the king had been waiting for.

"If he will not obey me," he roared to his men, "take him away!" And he had the abbot seized and taken off to Besançon, a city forty miles to the south. Only one of the monks was permitted to go with him.

❊ ❊ ❊

The road back to Luxeuil was under guard, but Columban and his monk were allowed to wander about the city freely. Thinking as always of their fellow men, they went to visit the prison, filled with condemned criminals.

"If you were set free," the abbot asked, "would you lead good lives and do penance for your sins?"

"Yes, yes!" the prisoners clamored.

"Take hold of that iron and pull it," Columban ordered his monk. As the monk obeyed, the iron shattered. In a twinkling all the fetters were off— and Columban was washing the prisoners' feet, as Christ had washed the feet of His Apostles.

"Now go to the church," Columban directed. "Wash away your guilt with tears of repentance."

The prisoners rushed toward the church, for they did not want to be seen in the streets. Columban followed with his companion. All at once shouts filled the air behind them; there was the sound of running feet; a band of soldiers came charging down the street waving swords and spears.

"Save us, Father!" the prisoners shouted. "We cannot open the doors of the church!"

Columban raised his eyes in prayer, and the big doors swung open. As soon as the prisoners had rushed inside, the doors swung shut again. Not even the sexton, with his enormous bunch of keys, could make them open.

"We'd best leave them free!" declared the captain of the soldiers. He wanted no more brushes with the miraculous!

Father Columban was permitted to wander freely about the city, but the bridge and road leading to Luxeuil were guarded. People were kind to him, for after the opening and closing of the great church doors, they knew that he was truly a man of God. He roamed about, biding his time until one Sunday morning when he looked out over the river and saw no guards on the bridge. Then he and his companion set out for home.

* * *

Hardly had Father Columban returned to Luxeuil when a band of horsemen thundered up to the monastery gates. They had orders to search the the place, they said.

The soldiers searched, but all the monks looked alike to them. The captain alone recognized Columban, seated in the entryway of the church reading a book as if nothing at all were happening. The captain pretended he didn't see Columban. "Let us go," he told his men. "This man is hidden by divine power."

The soldiers remounted their horses and rode off.

A few days later, while they were singing the psalms of the Divine Office, Columban and his monks again heard the rumble of horses' hooves, the tramp of feet, the clash of weapons. "Man of God," called a voice, "we beg you to obey the king's commands and ours, to leave this place and return whence you have come." Soldiers poured into the church.

Columban replied slowly, "I do not think it would please the Creator if a man were to walk again that native land he had left for the love of Christ."

The soldiers understood. But they knew that Theodoric could have them killed if they did not obey their orders. "Father, take pity on us," they begged. "We do not want to take you away by force, but if you do not leave Luxeuil, we shall die!"

"And yet," said Columban gently, "Many times I have said that I shall never leave Luxeuil—unless taken away by violence."

"Father, we do not wish to commit such a crime. These are not our wishes but the king's commands."

Columban was moved with compassion. Turning to his monks, he said, "I shall go with them." He began to walk out of the church, the soldiers pressing around him and the monks trailing behind.

Suddenly he stopped and prayed, "O Eternal Creator, prepare a place where we, Your people, may serve You forever." The monks gathered about him. "Do not lose hope," Columban told them gently. "Continue to sing the praises of Almighty God. This sacrifice we are making will be rewarded with many vocations." He paused. These men were like sons to him—how could he leave them?

"If any of you wish to come with me, you may."

A clamor arose. All of them would come, for no one wished to be separated from the abbot.

"No," replied the soldiers. "The king has ordered that only the monks from Ireland and Brittany shall accompany your abbot."

And so Columban left his beloved Luxeuil, accompanied only by a handful of monks, Gall among them. The soldiers went with them all the way, down valley after valley to the River Loire where they all boarded a small boat bound toward the sea. It was, in all, a journey of some six hundred miles. In the cities where they stopped over, many people came out to greet the monks, having heard of their great holiness. Finally the little band reached Nantes, a port from which they were to sail for Ireland.

Columban sat down and wrote a long, anxious letter to his community at Luxeuil and their new abbot, a Burgundian monk named Attala. More than anything else, he feared that disagreements would arise among the monks, and he urged Attala to take all necessary steps to preserve the spirit of union and charity he had insisted upon. He could hardly keep back the tears as he wrote. He reminded the monks that their own sufferings were a share in the Passion of Christ. Then he bade them farewell and posted the letter.

Confident that they had accomplished their mission, Columban's guards had left him. They were not present to witness the fierce storm which blew up, caught the little ship just before it reached the sea, and drove it high and dry onto the shore. They did not know that the same strong wind kept the ship aground for the next three days. They were not present to see the superstitious ship captain unloading the monks and their few belongings— whereupon the wind died down, and the little ship floated off with the tide!

To Columban this was a sign that God did not want him to go to Ireland. Almost at once he and his monks were on the road, trekking north-eastward toward the safety of the kingdom of Theodoric's brother–and enemy–Theodebert. They moved in haste and secrecy. It was a tiring march of several hundred miles, over rough roads.

East of Paris and near to their goal, they stopped at the home of a nobleman named Chagneric, the father of one of Columban's monks at Luxeuil.

"Stay with us a few days," Chagneric urged. "Then we shall send someone with you to guide you on your journey." The nobleman was pleased to have such a distinguished guest as Columban. The monks agreed to stay.

The youngest of the children in that house, a girl of seven, showed a deep affection for the aging abbot. He spoke to her of many things which she was too young to understand, but which she would think about over and over again.

One day he found the little one playing with a head of wheat.

"You have chosen great happiness," he said. "Wheat shall be your portion in life."

The child looked puzzled, and the old monk explained that Christ in His Passion had been beaten like threshed wheat, dying in order that men might be nourished and live eternally.

Indeed that child *would* choose Christ when she grew up. She would found a community of nuns to teach school to noblemen's daughters. The community would follow the rule St. Columban had written for his monks.

Two sons in the same family were to become bishops.

When he had journeyed a bit farther, Columban was approached by a pious couple and their three little boys. He blessed them and continued on his journey. Did he know that all three boys would someday found monasteries?

In Metz, King Theodebert welcomed Columban kindly, for he was only too happy to help the monks whom his brother had exiled. He offered them land on which to build a monastery.

"Since I have decided to journey to Italy, Your Majesty," replied the abbot, "I shall look for a suitable place along the route, and build there."

In a boat loaned by the king, he set off up the Rhine with his Irish and Breton companions, and several monks from Luxeuil, including Attala, who had come to Metz to rejoin him.

They toiled up the Rhine and its tributaries to Lake Zurich in what is present-day Switzerland. It was a land unmatched for beauty. Lakes as smooth as glass reflected the luminous sky; orchards and cornfields on the lower slopes gave way to forested hilltops. Far to the south gleamed snowy alpine summits.

The people were Alemanians, a Germanic tribe. Unlike their cousins the Franks, they had never become Christians. They worshipped gods of earth and sky, of trees, mountains and rivers, and sacrificed to idols.

The missionaries built huts on the lakeshore, and began to preach among the pagans–with little apparent success. These Alemanians had clung to their woodland deities for centuries; they were not about to renounce them now. At last, Gall, with more zeal than prudence, set fire to the little pagan temples and threw the offerings into the lake. A slow wave of hostility surged through the people. Soon Columban was told of a plot to kill Gall.

"We must move on," the abbot told his men. "These people will no longer listen to us, but in the country around Lake Constance we may have more success."

They struck out northeastward, and traveled swiftly and secretly past one Roman ruin after another to the shores of Lake Constance. It was a broad, pale green lake set in the midst of wooded hills. A small Christian community dwelt on its southern shore. The pastor welcomed them eagerly and helped them search for a site for a monastery.

They rowed down the lake about fifteen miles to the ruins of a Roman town, Bregenz. It was a good location. The soil was rich; the view inspiring. With axes and spades, the monks began to clear and cultivate the land. Having built cells for themselves, they removed some bronze idols from St. Aurelia's Chapel which stood nearby, rededicating the church and consecrating its altar.

Gall, spokesman for the group because of his skill with languages, attempted to teach a curious crowd of pagans the truth of Christianity and the falsity of idol worship. At the end of his sermon, he took three idols, broke them and cast them into the lake. Some of the pagans went away in a rage, but a few asked for instruction.

Happy to be settling down at last, the monks built a monastery and planted an orchard. Gall wove nets and set about providing fish for the community. He also acted as interpreter for Columban as he tramped through the forests seeking out the pagans and preaching to them.

One night when Gall was alone on the lake, fishing, he heard a wail from one of the mountain-tops. An answer howled back from the lake. The voices cried back and forth to one another, complaining about the strangers who had come to take the people away from their old gods. Gall made the sign of the cross in the air on each side of him and cried out, "In the name of Our Lord Jesus Christ, I command you to depart from this place and not dare to harm anyone here!"

Later that same night, after the monks had chanted the Office, they heard the voices again, passing from mountain to mountain, until they grew faint in the distance and disappeared altogether. Never again were they heard.

Two years passed quickly; then some of the more obstinate pagans began to stir up trouble. They went to the local duke and told him a lie about the monks driving away the game. The duke flew into a rage, for he enjoyed hunting. At once he ordered the foreigners to leave the region–but before the monks had even begun to pack, two of them were ambushed and murdered by the pagans. Sorrowfully their brothers buried them and prepared to flee.

Some of them would return to Gaul, others would found new monasteries here and there in the wilderness, still others–Gall among them–were to go on to Italy with Columban.

Each assignment was an order.

But Gall was ill with a fever. "Father, I cannot make the journey!" he exclaimed, throwing himself at his abbot's feet.

"Brother," replied Columban, "I know that now it seems a heavy burden to suffer hardship and weariness for my sake. Stay, then, but I command you not to celebrate Mass again as long as I am alive."

It was a stern command, especially when given to one who was closer than a brother, but Columban seldom let his heart get out of hand. He had always taught that a man should obey until death, and Gall had been unwilling to do so. Perhaps the abbot had thought back to his sick men at Luxeuil who had obeyed instantly when told to thresh the grain. One wonders who suffered more when the abbot ordered Gall not to celebrate Mass–Gall himself, or Columban.

And so Gall remained in the wilderness, where he set about building a great monastery and becoming a great saint. When offered silver vessels for the monastery altar, he would refuse them and say, "My blessed teacher, Columban, offers the sacrifice of the Mass in iron vessels because our Savior was fastened to the cross with iron nails."

* * *

The old man in the mountainside cave roused himself from his reverie. He must return to the valley, to the thriving monastery of Bobbio which he and his monks had built on the land given them by the Lombard king of northern Italy. He knew that his death was near.

I shall tell my men, he thought as he took one last glance around the cave, that as soon as I pass out of this life, they must send my walking staff to Gall as a token of absolution.

And, leaning on his staff, the old man made his way down the mountainside. He did not know that his newest monastery, Bobbio, would become one of the greatest cultural centers of Europe, preserving for future generations the treasures of the Italian and Irish civilizations. He did not know that within fifty years his five monasteries would have multiplied into almost a hundred, and that tens of bishops would receive their early training within those walls.

He did not know, either, that one chill November dawn, Gall, in his monastery hundreds of miles away, would tell his deacon, "Prepare the vessels and vestments. I have learned in a vision that my master and father Columban has passed from the miseries of this life into Paradise. Therefore I must offer Mass for the repose of his soul."

Sometimes we are faced with a choice between something we know we ought to do and something we would enjoy doing. When that happens, let us think of the stern self-discipline of St. Columban and his monks, and stick to duty.

Saint Dymphna

Patron of the Emotionally Disturbed

"Where have you been, child?" the little man asked worriedly. "It's not right for you to be out by yourself with night coming on."

Fourteen-year-old Dymphna smiled reassuringly. "Now don't you worry. My Angel was with me every step of the way. When you frown like that, you don't seem at all like the jolly court jester that used to make my good mother laugh so."

The little jester smiled then, and said, "Well, let's go in to eat. The wife has something extra special for us tonight."

Dymphna and the jester entered a small thatched hut. Beside the fire a woman was busily carving thick slices of meat from a roasted goose. She turned and greeted the girl warmly. "At last you're home, Dymphna. You shouldn't stay out so late on your visits to the sick and the poor."

"Yes, 'Auntie', you're right, I know, but didn't our dear Lord Himself stay among the poor until sunset, healing them and giving them encouragement? And besides those good townsfolk have been so kind to us ever since we came upon this little town of Gheel in our flight from Antwerp. . . .

"Where is Father Gerebran?" Dymphna asked in the same breath. Meanwhile she had begun to prepare the table.

"The good Father's been out on errands of mercy like yourself, I expect," the jester growled. "I never saw the like of either of you—so tender-hearted and all that."

Dymphna refused to be fooled. "We're no more tender-hearted than yourself, 'Uncle'," she retorted. "What other than Christ's own compassion prompted you to leave a cozy position in the court of a king to flee into the wilderness with a poor old priest and the king's young daughter?"

"With a holy priest of God and with the saintliest princess I ever knew," replied the woman gently. "There! The goose is ready now. All we're lacking is the good Father to eat it."

"Where did you find the goose, Auntie? It's the first meat we've had these three months. Not that I've minded living on greens," Dymphna added hastily. "It has been a good mortification."

"Yes, but a growing girl needs her strength. I bought it at the market today with some of the coins we carried with us from Ireland. We still have a few left. Oh, Father, here you are!"

Stooped and angular against the rosy sunset, an aged priest made his way into the hut. His eyes were glowing with a beautiful light. "How good God has been to give us the sick and the poor to comfort," he murmured softly. "I feel so much closer to Him now than I did at your father's court, Dymphna."

Dymphna had run for a stool. "Sit down, Father Gerebran, and rest yourself. Tell us about your day."

They were an unusual group, these four—an old priest, a jester and his wife, a young girl. No family ties bound them together, but a far firmer bond—love of God and hatred of sin. This was why they had become exiles in a strange land.

As they ate companionably beside the crackling fire, Dymphna's thoughts drifted back to that murky night when the four of them had huddled together in a frail little boat, watching the powerful forms of oarsmen move back and forth against the mist, listening to the soft swish-thud of the oars. How good those men were to us, to bring us all the way across the sea, Dymphna thought. They were my father's slaves, but they helped us escape his wrath. May God reward them for it.

"Father Gerebran—tomorrow could you offer your Mass for those good slaves who helped us escape? And for the old lady by St. Martin's Chapel whom I visited today?"

"I will put the intentions, my child, and as always I shall offer the Mass for the king, your father, that he may recover his sanity."

"Oh yes. We must *never* stop praying for that. How horrible is his sickness!"

The group fell silent, watching the flickering flames. "You deserve a better life than this, Dymphna," the woman said at last. "It's a pity that you who have grown up in a king's court must now live in a hovel like this."

"Don't be silly!" Dymphna laughed. "Why this is better than a palace and I have Father Gerebran for my director and you for my "family" and Jesus Himself for my only Spouse. What more could any girl want?"

A few days later Dymphna went to the market on an errand for a crippled old man who lived nearby. While she was buying him a large round cheese, she heard a voice say, "Young lady—pardon me."

A tall young farmer stood beside her, twisting his cap awkwardly in his big, red hands.

"Are you the young lady who came here with the good priest Father Gerebran a few months ago?"

"Yes," Dymphna replied.

"Well," gulped the farmer, "I feel I must tell you. Last market day I sold a goose to the woman who lives with you, and yesterday a stranger from Antwerp offered me a sum of money if I could tell him about any Irish fugitives living in the area. The coins which he offered me were just like the ones the woman gave me—so I told him about the four of you. My conscience has bothered me ever since."

Dymphna felt chills run up and down her spine, but she managed a weak smile and said, "Now don't you worry yourself about it. Sure you meant no harm. God will take care of us all."

But as soon as the sad, young farmer had said goodbye, Dymphna snatched up her cheese and hurried into the forest. I must tell Father Gerebran at once, she was thinking. We must flee farther into the countryside. It was not enough for us to come just these few miles inland from Antwerp. Only one person could have sent that spy—my cruel, insane father!

Down the forest path Dymphna ran toward the Chapel of St. Martin. As she had hoped, she found Father Gerebran walking up and down in its shadow reading his breviary. Hastily she poured out the news.

"Let us tell the others at once, my child," he said. "We must be far away before sundown."

But it was already too late. Striding down the path from their little hut came Damon the pagan chieftain, Dymphna's cruel father! Around him milled a mob of savage warriors. It was useless to run.

Damon stopped, motioned his warriors to stand still, and approached Dymphna slowly. "Dymphna, come home with me to Ireland," he said gently, almost purring, like a cat. "You will be very happy there." A strange, wild flicker was in his eyes.

"We know your plans for Dymphna are evil," retorted old Father Gerebran. He drew his bent body erect and faced the pagan squarely. "You have driven yourself insane and have become a tool of the devil. She *shall not* return with you!"

Savage fury twisted the king's features into a terrible mask. "Kill him!" he roared, and the swordsmen leaped forward to seize the priest. A sword flashed—and Father Gerebran's head was severed from his body. The bent, black form crumpled into the dust.

Again Damon's voice became smooth and gentle. "Come home with me, Dymphna. I need you. You won't be sorry."

"Never!" Dymphna's eyes blazed fire. "You are my father but you think as a devil. I know you want me to lead a life of sin. I will not. I will never offend God!"

Now Damon was beside himself with rage. "Seize her!" he bellowed, but this time the warriors did not budge. Princess Dymphna faced them tall and straight, like a little queen. They knew she was good and holy. They could not bear to kill her.

Damon himself fumbled for his dagger, grasped its hilt, wrenched it from its sheath. "Then die!" He lunged at the girl. Dymphna raised her eyes to Heaven and gave her soul to God as her head was severed from her body.

❖   ❖   ❖

Dymphna's true mission of charity began with death. She who had ardently wished for her father's cure, now begged God to cure all the insane, nervous, and emotionally disturbed people who came to pray near her grave. A shrine and later a church were built over her remains and those of St. Gerebran. And to this day, the mentally disturbed come flocking to the town of Gheel in Belgium where the good townspeople take care of them and St. Dymphna intercedes to make them well.

There is a very wise saying which goes, "Hate the sin, but love the sinner." We can imitate Saint Dymphna well by praying for all sinners.

Saint Margaret of Scotland

Patroness of Learning

"Good-bye, England," sighed Princess Margaret, as she watched the rugged coastline disappear beyond the restless gray waves. "Perhaps I shall never see you again; farewell!"

Margaret, a pretty girl of twenty, had grown to love England deeply during the ten years she had lived there. Her grandfather, Edmund, had been king of the rugged little island, but Danish invaders had prevented Margaret's own father from ever wearing the crown. Nor would Edgar, the girl's young brother, ever rule England, for Norman conquerors had seized the throne. Margaret was bound for Hungary with her mother, sister and brother.

The king of Hungary was a relative of theirs and would take them in.'

"Margaret, please come inside the cabin!" her mother called anxiously. "A storm is coming!"

"Yes, Mother," Margaret replied, and stooped to enter the stuffy little cabin. She could hear the oarsmen shouting excitedly to one another. Their little ship was pitching and tossing more and more by the moment, so Margaret wedged herself into a corner and held on, smiling at her young brother, who responded with a broad grin. Edgar had never been on shipboard before, and thought it quite an adventure.

For many hours, the little vessel rode before the furious gale, and when the storm finally abated, the travelers had lost their course completely. The land finally sighted to the northwest was a far wilder, more mountainous countryside than that of England. "It's the Scottish coast, for sure," explained the captain.

"King Malcolm's country," Margaret murmured to her mother. "He was exiled in England for a time before he reconquered the land and regained his father's throne."

"In that case," replied her mother wisely, "prepare yourself to meet some wild and warlike people. Don't expect the Scots to be as civilized and polished as the nobility you have known until now."

However, young King Malcolm's friendly reception surprised both Margaret and her Mother. He was most courteous to them, and invited them to stay for a few months in his big, draughty castle.

"My queen has died, God rest her soul," King Malcolm explained. "This castle is very gloomy when there are no charming ladies to brighten it up. I would be grateful to you if you would stay."

Margaret certainly did brighten up the castle. King Malcolm was much impressed by her beauty and gaiety, but even more so by her kindness to her family, to the courtiers, to the servants, and to himself. He admired her spirit of piety and recollection. It was obvious that Margaret sincerely tried to please God in all things.

One day King Malcolm said to Margaret's mother, "Lady Agatha, your daughter Margaret is both beautiful and good. May I have your permission to court the princess?"

Margaret's mother hesitated a moment. "I am happy that the princess has found favor with Your Majesty. However, Margaret has always intended to become a nun. I believe I must speak to her first."

Margaret was a little upset. She liked King Malcolm, and court life was familiar and pleasing to her. But she loved God, and had always wanted to serve Him in the best way possible. To solve the problem, she turned to prayer.

One morning after receiving Holy Communion and talking heart to heart with Our Lord, Margaret knew what she must do. It was as if He Himself had spoken to her, saying, "This is your place. Here it is that I wish you to serve Me and sanctify yourself. You have a great opportunity for good in this kingdom."

Margaret's doubts were gone, and King Malcolm was overjoyed when she accepted his proposal! The wedding ceremony was solemn and joyous.

Yes, there was a great opportunity to do good in Scotland. The people were poor and spent much of their time raiding the English. Queen Margaret found a solution to the poverty and the raiding, both. She asked King Malcolm to invite some Benedictine monks from England and the Continent to settle in Scotland. These monks began to teach the Scots how to raise good crops in their poor, rocky soil. They also built churches and monasteries–aided by the warriors who had formerly raided English settlements. Children living near the monasteries began to go to school there, receiving an education which their parents never could have had. Many of these children later became priests. Missionaries went out from Scotland to convert the neighboring islands–the Shetlands, the Hebrides, and the Orkneys.

Since the Scottish bishops had been out of contact with the Church of Rome for years, Queen Margaret invited representatives of the Archbishop of Canterbury to meet with the bishops and point out any instances in which they needed to change their customs. This meeting was very successful. At its close, the Church in Scotland was once again observing all the practices of the Universal Church.

Queen Margaret's life was full of activity. Mass, prayer, alms to the poor, visits to the prisons. . . But the energetic queen was never too busy to devote time and attention to her family. She was a loving and attentive wife to Malcolm, for whose salvation she prayed continually. She was a firm but understanding mother to their eight lively children; the Princes Edward, Ethelred, Edmund, Edgar, Alexander and David; and the Princesses Matilda and Mary. "I would rather that each of you died a thousand times than commit one mortal sin," she would tell them. "Pray to the Blessed Virgin; be kind to the poor; avoid all sins of impurity. Lead holy lives, and spread the Catholic Faith."

Edmund was destined to become a monk, while Edgar, Alexander and David would one day be good kings of Scotland. Matilda was to be Queen of England.

Then Queen Margaret became seriously ill. She felt her strength failing day by day. "It is my last illness," she told her chaplain.

At the same time, the English attacked a Scottish castle. King Malcolm said a hasty good-bye to Margaret, gathered his army, and rode off to do battle. Edward and Edgar went with him.

On her deathbed, Margaret prayed anxiously for her husband and sons. She offered her sufferings for their safe return, but more especially for their spiritual well-being.

One day a bruised and battered figure appeared in the doorway of the queen's room. It was her son Edgar. He was covered with caked blood, and dusty from hard riding. Weakly, with sorrow in his face, he crossed the room and knelt at his mother's bedside.

"Your father?" Margaret asked thinly, already sensing the truth.

"Father and Edward have both been killed, Mother," gulped the boy, and he buried his face in his hands.

"Few sorrows could have been greater than this," murmured the queen. "May this suffering cleanse me of some of my sins."

After consoling Edgar and calling a servant to treat his wounds, Margaret sent for her chaplain. "Two things I ask of you," she said. "As long as you live, please remember my husband's soul and my own poor soul in your Masses and prayers–and watch over my children, teaching them to love God and do His will." The chaplain promised, and Margaret, that faithful wife and mother, was at peace. She made her confession, received the Last Sacraments, and left her tiny, war-torn kingdom for the Kingdom of Eternal Peace.

St. Margaret knew that the people we should spend the most time with and do the most for, are our own families. Let us be kind to everyone, but especially to our parents, brothers and sisters.

Saint Francis of Assisi

Herald of the Great King

In the city of Assisi in northern Italy, about seven hundred years ago, as the wife of the rich merchant Peter Bernardone was about to give birth to a baby, a stranger came to her door and said to a servant, "If you wish everything to go all right, tell Peter's wife to go to the stable at once."

A strange command—but it was carried out. And that's how it happened that Francis was born in a stable, as Jesus was!

On that very day, another stranger ran through the streets of Assisi crying, "Peace and happiness!" to the astonishment of everyone.

The baby was named John, but when his father Peter returned from a trip to France, he changed his son's name to Francis, because be liked France so much.

A smart and lively little boy, Francis was his parents' delight. When he began going to school, he did very well in his lessons. He was a good playmate, too—always full of ideas.

Peter Bernardone had great dreams for his son Francis, dreams of great wealth as a merchant. He started to train the boy in business while he was still young, even though this meant taking him out of school.

In a short while, Francis became such a good businessman that Peter's customers were very enthusiastic about him. He was friendly, courteous, and easy to get along with. He won over even those who had not planned to buy anything! Business kept getting better and better.

Francis was not satisfied just with *making* money; he wanted to *spend* a lot, too! He dressed like a royal prince. But his father didn't mind that. He was so happy with the way his business was going.

Singing, dancing, hunting trips, parties—Francis never missed a thing! He was always there—the life of the party! He was so popular that he was proclaimed, "King of the Festivals"!

Peter the merchant, who had become wealthy by working and was not noble by birth, nearly burst with pride when he saw how much the great nobles liked his son! He began to build dream castles in the air every time he thought of Francis. "Perhaps some day he will even have a coat of arms for himself, such as the nobles have," he would say. At such talk, Peter's wife would only sigh and pray for her son.

Francis loved a good time, but he was also a very generous youth. He liked to see everyone happy, and the friends who received rich gifts from him—gifts perfectly suited to each one's taste—were well aware of his generosity. One day, while he was handing out gifts right and left, a poor beggar came up. "In the name of God," said the beggar, "give me an alms!" Francis pretended that he didn't hear the man, but then as he saw him walk away sadly, the youth felt so sorry that he ran after the beggar and gave him a purse full of coins to make up for his unkindness!

When Francis was about seventeen, a war broke out. A thick, solid wall had to be built around Assisi to defend it. It had to have towers and bulwarks for defense. Every man in the city set to work on it, and among them, of course, was Francis, who enthusiastically abandoned his father's store to take part in the work. He learned how to mix mortar and lay stones in place, and he worked so hard and so joyfully that he gave courage to the others and made everything seem easier.

But in spite of its sturdy wall, Assisi was conquered by the attacking force, and many of the defenders were taken prisoner. Among them was Francis. He looked like a nobleman, so he was thrown into a special prison reserved for nobles.

Poor Francis who had been used to complete freedom, to good times and the satisfaction of his every wish, found prison life horrible. But his joyful spirit still ruled him. While the nobles moaned among themselves, Francis went about singing! "How can you sing in prison?" he was asked.

"Why this is nothing," the youth replied. "I shall be venerated throughout the world!" Francis was joking—as usual—but this time he had spoken the truth without knowing it.

After a year in prison, Francis was released. But it was not the same youth who returned to his family. His ambitions were different now. He had decided to become a great soldier.

Right at that time, men were arming for battle. Francis went out and bought the best armor and weapons he could find. His father smiled. If the boy wanted to win fame on the battlefield, that was fine with him!

The night before the soldiers were to leave for the fight, Francis found out that one of the noblemen had no money to buy weapons, and would not be able to go to the battle. Generously, Francis gave him his own best set of weapons and kept only the second set for himself.

That gallant act led to a strange dream. Francis saw a golden palace, and inside it hung weapons of pure gold marked with a cross. "Whose arms are these?" he heard his own voice asking.

A mysterious voice replied, "They belong to you and to your soldiers!"

What a dream! When Francis set out with the other soldiers, he felt as if he were riding on air! What a magnificent leader I will become! he thought.

Yet, while they were on the road, Francis was stricken by a sudden illness. He was forced to stop, while the other soldiers went ahead. "I'll catch up later," he thought.

That night, as he was dozing off, he heard a voice ask, "Francis, is it better to serve the master or the servant?"

"The master."

"Then why are you leaving the master for the servant?"

Deeply troubled, Francis replied, "What shall I do?"

"Return to Assisi, and you will find out," was the answer.

So, as soon as dawn came, Francis mounted his horse with downcast heart and slowly rode back to Assisi. How the people laughed when they saw him return—he who had gone off so dashingly only the day before. "Another one of his stunts," they said. "What will this younger generation do next?"

Francis swung back into his old habits of going out with his friends, singing loudly and gaily, and riding off on hunting parties. He seemed to be the same as ever, but—oh—what bewilderment in his heart!

Then, as he was returning from a party one night, Francis stayed behind his companions. He stood still and gazed up at the beautiful stars in the velvety sky. Suddenly, light seemed to flood his soul! "My God and my All!" he exclaimed over and over.

When his friends came back to look for him, they found him staring off into space. "Dreaming Francis?" they teased. "Thinking of a girl?"

"Of a great Lady," replied Francis slowly. But he didn't tell them who she was. Like every medieval knight, he would have his Lady, but she was not a creature. Poverty—holy poverty—would be his lady. Poverty, because Jesus Christ had loved it so much and had chosen it for Himself.

How was Francis to serve Lady Poverty? He was not sure yet himself. But an inspiration came to him to make a pilgrimage to Rome, and with some money which his mother gladly gave him, he set out for the Holy City.

In Rome, Francis went to St. Peter's Basilica to fill his soul with spiritual joys. Looking around, he saw that the pilgrims were giving small offerings, and with a rush of generosity he offered all the money he had in homage to St. Peter. His great act of charity completely amazed the other pilgrims.

A bit embarrassed, the youth went out. He saw the poor, gathered together at the church entrance, waiting for alms, and he thought that he would never really be able to understand them unless he himself were dressed in a poor man's rags.

What did he do then? He walked up to the most ragged fellow of the whole crowd and asked him to exchange clothes with him—fine, elegant garments for a pitiful, disgusting cloak! The bargain was accepted. Francis shuddered when he felt that greasy, dirty rag on his skin, but the victory he had won over himself filled him with joy.

He went still further. He, who was accustomed to handing out generously, now stretched out his own hand to passersby, for the love of Jesus Christ, Who became poor for our sakes. Francis had given away every cent he had; now to keep from starving, he had to depend on the charity of his neighbor.

✧   ✧   ✧

He returned from Rome completely taken up with this new idea, which was becoming clearer to him all the time. It was not enough to give *money*— he would have to give *himself*.

Gold for the service of God

He was no longer the same. No one at home could understand him. He often went riding in the quiet of the country to think. . . .

One day he saw a leper, and turned away in instinctive horror until an interior voice stopped him: "How can you be a Knight of Christ if you are afraid?"

Francis remembered the words of Jesus: "Amen, I say to you, as long as you did it for one of these, the least of My brothers, you did it for Me." Who could be poorer than that leper, abandoned by everyone? Would Francis run away from Jesus? Never! Back he went at once.

With supernatural heroism, he dismounted from his horse, bent over the sickening sores of the leper, and kissed them. Then he gave the man a generous offering. But his greatest gift was his enchanting smile and tender kiss. That poor wreck of humanity stared at him dumbfounded; he felt so comforted and happy!

Yet Francis was even happier! That victory over his natural inclinations had made him taste heavenly joys. From that time on, he became the comforting angel of all poor lepers, caring for their sores, cheering them up, and talking to them of God!

"I must begin to live a life like that of Jesus," Francis thought. He went into a little country church, dedicated to St. Damian, to pray. There, he heard these words from the crucifix: "Go, and repair My house, which is falling in ruins."

"Yes! I shall do it!" Francis replied at once. He looked about him. The little abandoned church was

It took

all Francis' courage . . .

so shabby; it really would take a lot of work to fix it up. The first step would be to find the priest in charge. Francis hurried off to look for him.

Francis gave the priest what money he had with him and asked him to use it to keep a lamp always burning in front of the crucifix. The priest was surprised, for, of course, he had no idea how dear to Francis that crucifix was!

When the youth reached home, his father looked at him gloomily. He was annoyed because Francis spent so little time in the shop and the business was suffering. But Peter Bernardone's face brightened when he saw Francis take many yards of fine cloth, load them upon his horse, and leave. "At last the boy's getting his sense back," thought Peter. "He's off to make a fine sale!"

But what did Francis do? He sold the cloth, all right, and the horse as well! But the money went— not to Peter Bernardone, but to the priest at St. Damian's.

At least that was what Francis intended! But the priest regretfully said, "I cannot accept money to rebuild the church." Francis threw the money down and went into the church to pray.

Soon the priest learned that Francis' angry father was coming in search of him. He hurried to the praying youth and said, "Come with me! I'll hide you until your father has gone!"

After all, the priest thought, he's a sincere young man—and Peter Bernardone can get awfully angry sometimes!

Francis escaped his father's wrath that time, but not so later on, when Peter Bernardone became so angry that he complained to the city officials about his son. Francis retorted that he was consecrated to God and would be judged only by the bishop. And so it was that he and his father appeared before the bishop's tribunal.

The father was angry and excited; the son, calm and composed. Gently the bishop told Francis, "Return to your father what belongs to him. God would not want for His church money gotten in such a way."

"Your Excellency," replied Francis, "I'll return not only his money, but even his clothes." So saying, he took off all his fine clothes except an undergarment, and added, "I no longer call Peter Bernardone my father; I give everything back to him, and from now on I shall say to God, *Our Father, Who Art in Heaven!*"

The bishop was deeply moved. He put his arms around Francis and covered him with his own robe.

Peter Bernardone was confused and disturbed. He could tell that the people favored Francis more than himself. This was not the outcome he had expected at all. He took up his money—and the clothes—and left!

The bishop's gardener had an old tunic which he gave to Francis to wear. Joyfully, the youth accepted it; he made a large sign of the cross over it to symbolize his consecration to God, and happily left to follow his bright ideal.

Winter's solitude was calling him. Singing hymns of praise to God, Francis began to climb the slope of a mountain. Truly he had reason to sing! He felt that now he was completely "of God."

The singing reached the keen ears of a robber leader and his band who were lurking in the brush. They stole up behind Francis. "Who are you?" their chief demanded.

"I am the herald of the Great King!" replied Francis gaily. Imagine how astonished the robbers were when they found themselves facing a man as poor as they were! Mocking, they fell upon him and began to beat him and roll him in a ditch full of snow. Francis didn't fight back; in fact, he *relished* the blows and insults for the love of Jesus Crucified. When the robbers had gone, he picked himself up out of the snow and continued on his way, still singing!

He felt hunger gnawing inside him. It had been quite a while since he'd had enough to eat, and now there was nothing green to be seen in the chill winter landscape. Coming upon a monastery, he offered himself as a chore boy—he who had once been "the King of the Festivals!"

❖   ❖   ❖

"Repair My house!" Those words still echoed in Francis' ears. But now he had no money. How could he repair the ruined church? Soon an idea clicked in his mind. He could *sing* for money, just as the wandering minstrels did—only instead of singing ballads about love or war, he would sing about God! So Francis began to go through the countryside, singing such hymns of praise to God that people crowded about him to listen. They were deeply moved and willingly gave donations when Francis asked them to help him rebuild the little church.

Soon he had enough material to begin the project. He had learned how to build walls during the time of the war; now he put that talent to good use and developed it more. The good priest watched him with kindly interest, and tried to help him in every way he could. Every night he would prepare supper for Francis, but the youth would never eat it; he preferred to go begging from door to door with a bowl. That was more in keeping with his vow of poverty.

One family would give him a spoonful of soup; another, a bit of salad, another a crust of bread. . . . It all went into the bowl to form an unappetizing mass, but Francis would eat it calmly, with his eyes lifted toward heaven.

There was a certain young nobleman, named Bernard Quintavalle, who was very much impressed by Francis, and wished to know him better. One day he invited him to his home and managed to persuade him to spend the night. They slept in the same room, so Bernard was able to see that as soon as everything was still Francis slipped out of bed and knelt on the floor. He spent the night in prayer, murmuring over and over, "My God and my All," while Bernard breathed deeply in order to pretend that he was sleeping. Bernard watched his holy guest closely. When morning came, he told Francis that he had decided to follow him.

Francis urged him to think it over carefully. Poverty is no easy life for those who have grown up in rich surroundings. This was something that they should pray over.

After assisting at Mass in a nearby church, Francis and Bernard asked the Priest, Peter Cattani, to open the altar missal three times in the name of Jesus. Each time their eyes fell upon passages of the Gospel which spoke of the excellence of holy poverty.

That was enough for Bernard—and for Father Peter, too—for he too had admired Francis for a long time and wished to imitate him. Now Francis knew that God was inspiring him to found a new religious order and that these men were to be its first members. "Brothers, poverty is our way and rule of life. Go and preach."

Soon other men joined the group of "Little Brothers". To all of them Francis said, "God has called us not only for our own sakes, but to save our neighbor, too. We must go out into the world and bring men to do penance and to obey the commandments." Their lives were to be beacon lights to all mankind.

While on one of his journeys, Francis met a young soldier riding down the road. On a sudden inspiration from God, he cried out, "Angelo Tancredi, it is time for you to change the baldric for the cord of penance, the broadsword for the

"Angelo Tancredi . . .!"

cross of Christ. . . . Follow me, and I shall make you a soldier of Jesus Christ!"

The young man knew that only God could have inspired those words that struck him so forcefully. At once he dismounted from his horse and stood before Francis. "I'm ready!" he said.

Another member of Francis' growing spiritual family was Brother Juniper. He was known for his simplicity. One day he was told to prepare the soup for all the brothers for the next meal. The brother in charge gave him some money to go to the market and buy all the food that was needed.

Now, Brother Juniper was a little upset because some of the other brothers spent too much time in preparing the meals. He knew that they were not living in accord with the spirit of St. Francis. So he decided to show them a better way to prepare the meals. In the market, he bought a great quantity of vegetables, many eggs and some chickens. When he had brought them home, he lit a huge fire, filled a great pot with water, and dumped everything into it—eggs with the shells on, vegetables with the stalks and roots, chickens with the feathers and feet—everything!

Tired and hungry, the brothers returned home. Brother Juniper greeted them with a broad smile. "Eat up! Eat up!" he urged them. "I've made enough soup for the next fifteen days. Now we won't need to spend our time in cooking. We can use it completely for the service of God!"

There was a shout of protest! No one could bear to eat that detestable soup. Yet there was noth-

Everything into the pot!

thing else to eat in the little hut. When he understood his mistake, Brother Juniper knelt and begged the pardon of God and of his brothers. But although he had made a mistake, it was due to his great concern for the welfare of souls!

One very cold night, Francis was returning home with Brother Leo. He began to speak about "perfect joy" and what makes it. It could not come from created things or from fame or honors, he said, nor even from prophecies and miracles. It could only come from self-denial and humiliations suffered in imitation of Jesus Who suffered so much for everyone. Brother Leo listened carefully, for Francis was saying something that was very hard to understand. Francis continued, "We cannot glory in any of the gifts God has given us because they are not ours, but we *can* glory in sufferings, because they *are* ours." Brother Leo understood then, and he was so deeply moved that he no longer felt the cold!

Often, the brothers took care of lepers, showing the poor diseased creatures such kindness that they became very grateful to God. If they had been bad before, they began to lead good lives.

But one leper would only curse and blaspheme. He had no use for God, he said. How the brothers' hearts ached when they heard him talking that way! They wanted to abandon him for saying such terrible things, but before taking such an important step, they asked Francis.

"Let me see him," said Francis. He went into the hut where the leper was staying, and offered to serve him in any way he could. Rudely the leper

Off came the loathsome sores

accepted the offer. The first thing he told Francis to do was to give him a bath—because he couldn't stand the horrible smell that came from his sores.

Francis heated water and added some sweet smelling herbs to it; then he bathed the leper very gently. A miracle! Little by little, the sores were disappearing—and not only the body but also the *soul* of the poor man was being cleansed, for he suddenly became humble and repentent! As soon as he could, the man dedicated himself to God in a life of severe penance.

Years later, a beautiful soul from Heaven appeared to Francis. "Do you recognize me?"

"Who are you?"

"I am that leper whom Jesus restored through your merits. May God bless you!"

* * *

One day Francis came upon a grove of trees which was completely filled with chattering birds, while others were flying about in flocks overhead. "Praise the Lord, brother birds," he said. The birds flew up into the air and formed a great cross in the sky. Francis raised his hand in blessing. Then the birds began to sing, and still singing they flew off in every direction—"to preach the Gospel all over the world!"

Francis loved animals. One time there was a huge wolf prowling about devouring cattle and even people. No one dared to go outside without a weapon, and the women and children of the region stayed inside the houses, full of fear.

In pity for those people, Francis begged God to free them from the terror. At the same time, he warned the people that they had a greater need to fear sin than to fear an old wolf. Then, with no weapon at all, he went into the forest to meet the beast. He was followed—at a great distance—by the bravest citizens of the village.

When the fierce wolf saw Francis, he came toward him snarling, his fangs bare. But the saint calmly made the sign of the cross and said, "I command you in the name of God, not to hurt me or anyone else." The wolf stopped and cocked his head to one side. He seemed to listen. . . .

"Brother wolf," continued Francis, "you have done much harm, not only to animals but also to men—who are made in the image of God. Rightfully we are enemies. But now, do not kill anyone again, and I will make peace between you and them in the name of God." The wolf looked penitent!

"Now in a little while your appetite will be satisfied," Francis continued, "because the townspeople will provide for your meals. Promise not to harm any more people or animals?" With a nod of his head and a wag of his tail, the wolf promised; not only that, he put his paw in the saint's hand as a greater proof of his sincerity!

The wolf followed Francis into the town, where a great crowd had gathered in the public square. Francis made the people repeat the promise to the wolf that he would not be harmed, and the wolf again put his paw in the saint's hand. Then Francis

Brother Wolf

spoke to the townspeople about how much more terrible the torments of hell are than the jaws of any wolf! The citizens learned the lesson. Many changed their way of living.

From then on, the wolf went from house to house each day, like a beggar asking alms. Everyone gave to him generously.

Two years later, "brother wolf" died of old age. The people were actually sorry to see him go, for his presence had kept reminding them of what Francis had told them. So that they would never forget, they built a little, wooden tomb over "brother wolf's" remains.

* * *

Because Francis was so good and tried to serve God well in everything, the devil tried especially hard to make him sin.

Once such terrible thoughts came into his mind that he sprang up, rushed out into the snow, and threw himself into a thorny patch of briers. The sharp spines dug into his flesh all over, and drove away the violent temptation. As a sign of how pleased God was, the thorny bushes began to bloom with big, beautiful roses—in the middle of January.

Francis never spared himself in the hard but joyous life to which God had called him. After many years those who knew him best could see that his health was almost gone and that he would soon die.

Francis knew it, too. He asked to be taken to the church of St. Mary of the Angels. On the way, he told his brothers to place him down on the ground,

Defeat for the devil

facing toward Assisi. Slowly he raised his hand and blessed the city. "May you be blessed by God, holy city, because many souls will be saved through you and many of God's servants will live in you. They will be among the elect in the kingdom of eternal life!

Francis blessed all his spiritual children, and as he did so, he saw in his mind's eye all the good they would do in the world in the centuries to come, giving glory to God. He begged them to sing for him the "Sun Song", a beautiful hymn of praise which he had written in thanksgiving to God. He even raised his weak voice and sang with them.

Death came toward evening on October 4, 1226, and Francis' soul went soaring home to Paradise to take its place among the choirs of Angels!

Poverty was Francis' guiding star. Everyone can have the spirit of poverty. Taking good care of clothes, playthings and furniture and cleaning our plates are all according to St. Francis' spirit.

Saint Clare

Patroness of Television

Seven hundred years ago, in the city of Assisi, lived a beautiful and generous girl named Clare. Her father was a rich count, and he planned that she should marry a wealthy nobleman when she grew up. But Clare's mother had other ideas. She often told her five little daughters that money and all the fine things it buys can keep people from thinking about God and how to love Him and serve Him better.

Clare and her little sisters were impressed very much by what their mother told them. They tried never to forget God in all the good times they had together, and they always made sure that the fun they had was "clean fun."

As Clare grew older, she had a desire to do something very special for Our Lord. She did not know what it should be, but she began to understand a little better when she went to hear Francis Bernardone preach.

Francis was the son of a wealthy cloth merchant. Once he had been a very popular young man in the society of the town, but then he had given up his family, friends and good times to be poor like Our Lord. Indeed there wasn't anyone who imitated the poverty of Jesus better than Francis did. The Religious Orders were poor, but not so poor as he. His poverty was like that of the Gospel.

After Clare heard Francis preach, she decided that she should speak to him. With one of her relatives, she went to the little church of St. Mary of the Angels, where Francis and his brothers stayed. The holy young man was not a bit surprised to see the wealthy count's daughter and to learn that she felt God was calling her. He already knew about

Clare
consulted
Francis

Clare, for everyone in Assisi knew how good she was and spoke of her often.

Francis listened to Clare kindly. Then he advised her to think for a while about the seriousness of what she wished to do. It would take a great deal of strength to put her desire into practice and to persevere in it.

Time passed. Clare thought and prayed about the matter, and the desire grew stronger and stronger in her heart. She wanted to become poor and dedicate her whole life to Jesus. At last she begged Francis to consecrate her to God, and Francis said he would.

In Clare's whole big house, only she and her mother knew what was going to happen. The mother was very happy for her daughter, because she knew that she could become very holy in the life she had chosen. She helped Clare prepare for the great event.

One peaceful Palm Sunday Night, Clare dressed up in the most beautiful clothes and jewelry she had. "After all," she thought, "I should look like a bride, for I am going to become a bride of Jesus Christ Himself!" She said goodbye to her dear mother and slipped out an unused door into the cool spring night. A girl friend was waiting in the shadows to go to the church with her.

It was a little church, outside the town, where nobody would go at that time of night except Francis and his brothers. In fact, they were there waiting, each holding a lighted candle. As Clare walked down the aisle, they sang a psalm.

The girl recollected herself in prayer before the altar, which was ablaze with light and adorned with flowers. Then she put aside her jewelry. A rough, grey robe was slipped on, in place of the rich mantle she had worn. A knotted cord went about her waist; wooden sandals went on her feet. Francis sheared off the gleaming, golden curls. A black veil was placed on her head.

And there she was—a bride of Christ, radiant with supernatural joy as she pronounced the vows of obedience, chastity and poverty which would bind her to Him forever! Clare was no longer a rich young lady but a humble sister with her heart set on the infinite treasures of Heaven.

Right away after she made her vows, the brothers took Clare to a nearby Benedictine convent where she would live with the sisters and learn all about cloistered life before starting her own convent.

How surprised and angry Clare's father and uncle were when they found out what she had done! In an armed band, all of Clare's male relatives stormed down upon the Benedictine convent. The young sister saw them coming, and ran into the church, thinking that there she would be safe. She went right up to the altar and held on to it. As her relatives crowded around her angrily, she calmly showed them her shaved head. "From now on, I belong to God alone!" she said. Defeated by her firmness—and by the grace of God—the relatives retreated and left her in peace.

❊   ❊   ❊

Clare's father was afraid that he might lose Agnes, his second daughter, in the same way he had lost Clare. Hurriedly he selected a suitable young man for Agnes to marry, and with the youth's father made arrangements for the engagement. Then he heaved a sigh of relief. Now he would not lose his good, prayerful, sweet Agnes.

At least that's what he thought. Before he knew it, Agnes was missing! She had gone to join Clare! Furious, the father rushed to his brother, Monaldo, who had a band of tough fighting-men. "Bring me back my daughter!" he urged.

The fierce Monaldo needed no coaxing. He rounded up his cutthroats, and off they thundered to the peaceful convent. Pulling up sharply in the open courtyard, the men swung off their horses and rushed into the sacred cloister of the sisters, searching for Agnes' cell. "Here she is!" came the cry. In an instant they had surrounded the girl. Monaldo seized her by the hair, and started to drag her away, blaspheming and cursing all the while.

"Clare! Help me!" cried out Agnes.

Clare heard her, but she did not come out into the open. Instead, she sank to her knees and prayed. God would be their strength. As she prayed the attackers felt themselves growing weaker and weaker, or rather they felt Agnes growing heavier and heavier. She was worse than a millstone! And it wasn't due to any resistance on her part, for the girl had already fainted! The men trembled in fear.

Monaldo seized Agnes

Furious, Monaldo drew out his sword and raised it violently with blasphemy on his lips. If they could not move the girl, at least he could kill her!

But lo! What power stayed his arm from bringing the sword down on Agnes' neck? Monaldo stood frozen, as if he were paralyzed.

Clare arose from her prayer and appeared on the scene. She turned such fiery words and glances on the evil men that they turned around like whipped dogs and walked away.

How was Agnes? Very happy, as soon as she recovered consciousness and learned that Monaldo and his band had gone. How she thanked God! What did it matter that her hair had been practically pulled out by the roots, or that she was covered with bruises? She would soon belong completely to Jesus!

Word of what happened reached Francis, who came hurrying to the convent. He spoke words which only a saint could have said, words which inflamed the hearts of Clare and her sister. Then he said, "This was your 'novitiate', Agnes! We'll consecrate you to God right now!" Need we describe Agnes' bliss?

As time passed, the anger of Clare's relatives cooled. Other wealthy young girls and pious women came to form the first convent of Franciscan Sisters, or Poor Clares, as they are called today. This first house was at the church of St. Damian, which Francis had restored. Clare became the first superior, and she was a model of every perfection and virtue.

The Sisters were always busy. They grew their own food; they sewed, embroidered altar linens, and kept their house spotlessly clean. They did everything for the love of God, and that was what made their poverty joyful. They wore no shoes; they fasted much, and slept on beds made of boards. Nothing was too much for them.

Clare would spend many hours each night in prayer before Jesus in the tabernacle. Yet she was always the first one up in the morning, first to call her companions, first to light the lamps and prepare everything for Mass, first to think of little things to help her sisters spiritually and materially.

Once when Clare was very ill, a horde of Mohammedans who had invaded Italy passed near Assisi. Seeing the convent, they came to attack it. Their horrid shrieks and blasphemies terrified the sisters, who came running frantically to Clare's bedside. Clare stood up. She went to the chapel and took from it the monstrance holding a consecrated Host, praying all the while with ardent faith, "Lord do not abandon the handmaids consecrated to Your love into the hands of these beasts!"

A voice replied, "I shall always be your salvation."

Clare prayed for Assisi, too: "My God, I beg You also to favor my country, so that no danger may overtake it. Help it, through Your love!" Then Clare opened the gate and stood before the infidels, holding the monstrance high in the air.

The Mohammedans stopped stock still. Then, gripped by a mysterious terror, they wheeled and fled—and did no more damage in the whole district! What had they seen so terrible in that gentle woman whose only weapons were the Host and a vivid faith? Only God knows the answer.

Now the danger had passed. The sisters, hearts swelling with gratitude for God's intervention, joined their saintly superior in singing a hymn of gratitude and love to God.

❊   ❊   ❊

It probably surprises us that St. Clare, who lived so long ago, is called the Patroness of Television! How did this come about?

Well, once when Clare was very ill, she was lying in bed on Christmas Eve while all the other sisters went off to assist at Mass. Naturally she felt sad that she could not be with them to sing to the Infant Jesus. But what was that melody? It sounded for all the world like the voices of St. Francis' brothers lifted in a hymn of joy and praise. And then, before her very eyes, Clare saw the beautiful Christmas crib in the church some distance away. She was able to see and hear the entire service perfectly! Because of this vision, St. Clare was recently chosen to be the Patron of Television.

After Clare had spent many years serving God, she knew that she would soon die. She was eager for death because she longed to go to Heaven. After her sisters read the Passion to her, she passed away quietly. One of the sisters saw the Blessed Mother herself come down and take St. Clare away to Heaven.

One of the most beautiful virtues St. Clare pos-sessed was a great trust in God. When everything seems to be going wrong in our lives, we would be wise to remember that everything that happens is permitted by Our Lord for our own good.

Saint Anthony

Wonder Worker of Padua

"Ferdinand, I baptize you in the name of the Father and of the Son and of the Holy Spirit," rang the voice of the priest as he poured the water of Baptism. The church was in Lisbon, Portugal. The infant at the font would one day be known and honored around the world as St. Anthony of Padua.

The boy's childhood was serene and uneventful. With his two brothers and two sisters, Ferdinand grew up in a happy and holy family. When about ten, he became an altar boy.

Severe temptations against purity afflicted Ferdinand during his teens, but he drove them all away and turned to prayer with more fervor than ever before. He felt sure that God was calling him to flee from the world and seek a life of peace with Him, so at fifteen he entered the Order of the Augustinians.

Prayer and study, study and prayer—these became Ferdinand's life. He worked and prayed to become more humble, more meek, more obedient, and more charitable. The only thing that bothered him was the distraction of seeing his relatives and friends so often. They took his thoughts away from God! Thus, after two years, he asked to be transferred to the monastery in distant Coimbra, where his friends and relatives would not disturb his peace!

At Coimbra Ferdinand delved deeply into Sacred Scripture, making every study a prayer, as the great St. Augustine had done before him. He mortified himself often, and practiced great love of God and neighbor. When at last the day of his ordination to the priesthood arrived, he was more nearly worthy of the honor than most men have ever been.

That same year—1219—five missionaries from the new Franciscan Order stopped at the Coimbra monastery. They were going to Morocco where they wished to be martyred for preaching the Faith to the Moslems. Such a noble ideal fired Ferdinand with enthusiasm. As the Franciscans journeyed toward Morocco, he accompanied them with his prayers.

A few months later, those same five Franciscans were slain by the Moors. Their relics were carried back to Coimbra and placed in one of the large churches where the faithful could venerate them. Oh, how Ferdinand was inflamed with zeal to imitate their holy example!

One morning, while celebrating Holy Mass, Ferdinand had a vision, in which he saw a Franciscan hermit's soul going straight to Heaven—without passing through purgatory. "Surely," thought the young priest, "these men lead just the life of perfection I desire." Could not he, too, join this new missionary order and give his life for Christ? "I will take their habit," he resolved. "Like them, I shall throw myself into the battle."

Not long after that, Ferdinand removed the white robe of an Augustinian and put on the rough brown habit of a Franciscan. "Go," said one of the Augustinians kindly. "You will become a great saint!"

How different was the hard simple life of a Franciscan hermitage from the studious routine Ferdinand had followed in the great monastery! This was real poverty—real mortification—and Ferdinand took to it as an eagle takes to the sky. To avoid being tracked down by well-meaning friends, he took a new name, Anthony, the name of an early monk who had lived in the Egyptian desert.

Anthony spent only a few months in that peaceful hermitage. Then he asked his superiors to send him to Morocco so that he could give his life for Christ. In December, 1220, he and a companion landed on African soil. How eager they were to work and suffer to bring the poor Moslems to God's grace and truth!

But sometimes God asks us to sacrifice our dearest dreams, and now He asked Anthony to do just that. A raging fever seized the young priest shortly after he had landed in Africa, and it dragged on for days, weeks and months, weakening him until all knew it was useless for him to remain there. To regain his health, he was ordered to board a ship returning to Portugal. Again God's Providence changed the young priest's plans. As the little ship headed for the Portuguese coast, a great storm arose, tossing the fragile vessel and knocking her about for several days, until she was driven ashore on the Sicilian coast, far from her destination. Anthony found a small Franciscan monastery, and learned from the monks that a general chapter of his Order would soon be held at Assisi. All the monks could attend, and this would be the perfect chance to see St. Francis in person! With a song in his heart, and renewed vigor due to the change of climate, Anthony set out on foot for the cradle of his Order.

What a thrill it was to see over three thousand brown-robed priests and brothers from all over Europe congregating around the little church of St. Mary of the Angels, sleeping by night in little straw huts among the trees! In their midst was St. Francis, guiding his missionary followers and giving them their assignments for the months ahead.

Anthony did not meet St. Francis in person, but another superior assigned the young monk to a small monastery in the Tuscan hills. There he spent long hours in prayer and penance—fasting and scourging himself. Sometimes terrible temptations came, but Anthony, with God's all-powerful grace, always won the battle.

None of the Franciscans knew how holy Anthony was or how much he had studied. He always took over the most unimportant or uninteresting jobs—like scrubbing pots and pans. But one day, at a meeting of priests, he was commanded to give a little sermon, since no other priest was prepared to do so. Anthony began to speak slowly, but soon the words were just pouring out of him—all those beautiful truths which he had read in Scripture and prayed over and meditated in his heart. The Holy Spirit was inspiring him, and everyone who listened was inflamed with love of God.

After that sermon Anthony's days of solitude were over. Someone hastened to tell Francis about this marvelous new preacher, and naturally the holy founder was overjoyed, for he saw that God's grace, working through Anthony, would convert many, many souls. Thus he sent his young spiritual son from city to city, teaching theology to the monks, basic truths of faith to the people, and sound doctrine to the heretics.

Fascinating indeed are the tales of Anthony's conquests of heretics! One legend says that after he had preached for several days to a great crowd of heretics, only to be answered with mockery and scorn, the saint said, "Since you show yourselves unworthy of God's word, I will turn to the fish to show you the foolishness of your unbelief!"

And Anthony went down to the riverbank and said, "Fish of the sea and river, listen to the word of God, because these people are sickened by it." At once a great crowd of fish—of all sizes and kinds—

rose to the surface of the water and remained motionless, while Anthony told them of God's goodness, how He had given them pure water, freedom, and many good things to eat. The fish bowed their heads all together. "God be praised," cried Anthony, "for the fish of the water honor Him more than the heretics!" At the sight of such a miracle, all present knelt and were converted.

Another legend tells us that several heretics invited Anthony to a banquet with the intention of poisoning him. Anthony accepted, but when he was seated in their midst, he said, "God has revealed to me that you intend evil. Brothers do not charge your conscience with this sin. Repent, and do no wrong."

"Why are you so anxious?" replied one of the hosts. "The Gospel says that no food will harm the Minister of Jesus Christ. Let us see if the Gospel speaks the truth."

"If you eat and remain unharmed," chimed in another, "we will submit to your Faith; if not, we shall conclude that the Gospel is false."

"I will do what you wish." replied Anthony calmly, "not to tempt God, but to give you proof of the courageous zeal which I have for your salvation." He made the sign of the cross over the poisoned food and began to eat. At the end of the meal, he was as lively and vigorous as ever. The heretics, red with shame, were converted.

In one of the cities where Anthony spent some time, lived an evil official, who insulted the holy monk frequently. Anthony, on the other hand, treated this man with great courtesy, greeting him always with a respectful bow. This happened many times, until the official's scanty patience was completely worn out and he growled, "Why do you make a fool of me like this? If I didn't fear God's wrath, I would run my sword through you here and now!"

"I venerate a martyr of Jesus Christ," Anthony replied. "I, too, have offered myself for martyrdom, but God did not grant me this grace; you, however, will have it. In that happy moment, please, remember me."

The official laughed harshly, and went his way. However, many years later, he was converted, and joined a Crusade to the Holy Land. There he began to preach to the Moslems, who seized him, tortured him for three days, and put him to death. Before he died, the martyr recalled Anthony's prediction and said it aloud.

These legends of miracles have sprung up about St. Anthony because of his wonderful speaking ability and deep love of God. We know for certain that God used these qualities as His instruments in making thousands of conversions. On the other hand, we are not sure that actual miracles took place during Anthony's lifetime. He is called the Wonder-Worker because of the miracles wrought after his death.

Why is Anthony pictured holding the Infant Jesus? We do not know for certain. However some people tell this story to explain the familiar picture:

One night, Anthony visited a friend and was asked to stay over. At a late hour the host saw a light glimmering in the saint's room, so he crept outside and went up to the window to watch Anthony praying. He saw the Infant Jesus Himself in the kneeling saint's arms! The Holy Child was smiling tenderly. The host watched reverently until the Divine Infant disappeared.

* * *

Of all the cities Anthony visited in his travels, Padua was his favorite because of the lively faith its people had. It was in Padua that Anthony chose to stay whenever he could. It was to Padua that thousands flocked to listen to him. It is Padua today that reveres him as its own.

St. Anthony's final illness came upon him suddenly. He made his last confession, received Holy Viaticum, and then sang his favorite hymn to Mary. Tears began to fill his eyes, and he murmured, "I see my Lord!" Calmly he received the last anointing and passed into the next life, no trace of struggle on his face, as if he had fallen into a deep sleep. He was only thirty-six years old!

Why was Anthony able to accomplish so much? Because he prayed often and well, and because he lovingly meditated the truths of our Faith.

Saint Elizabeth of Hungary

Queen Who Sped to Heaven

This is a story of a brave soul whom nothing could conquer, for she relied in everything on God. It is the story of a young wife and mother who was born a princess and died a saint.

In the land of Hungary, in the year 1207, a baby girl was born to King Andrew and Queen Gertrude. The child was named Elizabeth, which means, "Consecrated to God."

The very first things Elizabeth learned were her prayers. By the time she was three, she was walking around the palace saying, "Jesus and Mary, make me a good girl. Make me a saint!" Her mother was giving her a wonderful training.

In those days, marriages of princes and princesses were planned by their parents, often years before the actual wedding. The little princess would go to live with the prince's family until the two were old enough to marry. That was what happened to Elizabeth. When she was four, she went to live with the Duke of Thuringia, so that she could marry the duke's son Herman when she grew up.

The little girl was cheerful and easy-going, and the duke grew fond of her. But not so the duchess and the other noble people of the court. "She's too holy," they sniffed. "She doesn't fit in with us!"

Poor Elizabeth! Two unexpected sorrows came into her life. The first was the news that her mother, Queen Gertrude, had died. Then, not long after that,

Herman, the boy she was supposed to marry, died also.

"What shall we do with Elizabeth?" pondered the duke. Should they send her home to King Andrew? Should they place her in a convent? He hesitated. He didn't really want to see her go. She was like a little ray of sunshine in his cold, formal palace! "She shall marry the second son, Louis!" decided the duke. So Elizabeth stayed on.

There were many poor people in those days, and they used to gather by the hundreds outside the palace gates to beg food. Whenever she could, Elizabeth went out to them and gave them all the food she could. This annoyed the duchess and the other members of the family and household. "Who does she think she is?" they sneered. They took to scolding the little princess and making fun of her. Because the little girl was sensitive, this bothered her very much, but she tried not to show it. "Dear God, this is the way to show You I love You," she would say softly, just to Him. Two people only, were fond of her—the duke and young Louis.

Then another sorrow entered her life. The beloved duke died. Louis, as soon as he became old enough, was made the new Duke of Thuringia. It was shortly after that, that he and Elizabeth were married. He was twenty-one; she, fourteen.

Young! you say. Yes, but it was the custom in those days. Not only that, they both loved God very much and knew that marriage brings many duties because it is a very holy thing. They were willing and generous, intent on becoming good Christian parents and wise and able rulers of their land.

When Elizabeth was sixteen, their first child, a little boy named Herman, was born. In the years which followed, three little girls blessed the noble family. Each of the children was consecrated to God while still an infant, Elizabeth made sure of that!

She still fed the ragged beggars at the palace gates. Not only that, she would go out to visit the poor families in their little huts, carrying with her baskets of food and clothing. She started an orphanage and a hospital. Sometimes she would go to take care of the sick herself. She would even take care of the wounds of lepers.

One day, in fact, she brought a leper home to the palace, and, after bandaging his ugly sores, she made him lie down on the royal couch to rest. But wouldn't you know it? The old duchess, Louis' mother, found out! She was *shocked!* She rushed to Louis and told him the dreadful news.

Even gentle Louis felt that this was *too much!* Elizabeth was running the risk of them and their children contracting the dread disease. He hurried toward the royal apartment, all ready to give his young wife a good scolding. "Elizabeth!" he stormed as he burst into the room.

Then Louis stopped short. Whatever he had intended to say froze in his throat. There, on his very own couch, lay—not a hideous leper, but Christ Crucified! Awed, astounded, Louis sank to his knees and begged God to forgive him his hot head. "Guests like This One are welcome," he told Elizabeth.

Then there was the time when Louis saw Elizabeth hurrying away from the palace on a cold, snowy day with her apron bulging. "What are you carrying?" he called out as he hurried to catch up with her. He was thinking, "It must be food for the poor, and she's going to catch her death of cold running around with it in weather like this. I'm going to send her right back to the palace!"

Elizabeth smiled and opened her apron. Bread? No! Roses–great, fragrant red and white roses in the dead of winter! "Well," thought Louis to himself, "if God is so pleased with her errands of mercy that He changes bread to roses, who am I to stand in the way?"

Was there ever a couple more devoted to one another? Each thought only of the good of the other and of the children. Louis worried about Elizabeth's health and comfort–especially since she did not seem concerned about either! Elizabeth tried to keep Louis calm and happy in the midst of all his responsibilities as ruler of Thuringia. She was sad whenever he had to go on a journey, and perked up only when he came home again. Then she was radiant with smiles and wore her best dresses. In every way she could think of, she tried to be a help and comfort to him.

"How holy she is," Louis would marvel whenever he awoke at midnight to see her kneeling at the bedside, deep in prayer. He had the same thought as he watched her assist devoutly at Holy Mass or return from a visit to the sick or croon a lullaby to one of their little ones. "Never change," he would tell her, "unless you become even more perfect." And to encourage his young wife in her quest for perfection, Louis wrote to the Pope himself, and asked him to send a very wise priest to be Elizabeth's confessor.

The Holy Father sent a monk named Conrad, who was very strict. Father Conrad asked Elizabeth to take a vow of obedience to him, and then he told her to do a great many things that were unpleasant for her to do, so that she would become completely detached from doing what she wished. He knew that she would become holier that way.

Meanwhile, important events were taking place. Many noble knights of Europe were preparing for a Crusade—a Holy War—to recover Palestine from the Mohammedans so that Christian pilgrims could visit the holy places where Jesus had lived and walked. Often the knights who fought in the Crusades were killed in battle. Often, too, they contracted deadly diseases. No loyal wife rejoiced when her husband went on a Crusade! She was too afraid. Is it any wonder, then, that Elizabeth was terrified when she learned that Louis was going on a Crusade?

Not only terrified—she was so overcome that she fainted. Sick with sorrow, Louis revived her, only to hear the pleading words, "Don't go. Don't leave us, Louis. You might never return!"

Painful though the task was, Louis tried to show Elizabeth why he *must* go. It was God's will, he said. Of course it hurt him to leave her and their children. But it was a sacrifice which God wished them to make. He was convinced of that.

Tears in her eyes, Elizabeth bowed her head in submission. She would not go against the will of God.

It was a sad parting, but a courageous one—smiles and tears. "Chin up!" Louis' kind eyes smiled down from beneath his vizor. The huge warhorse pranced, eager to be off.

Elizabeth smiled weakly, and raised her hand in a salute of farewell. A few moments later, and the little band of horsemen were out of sight, off to join the great army.

The long months of waiting began. Wait for one letter . . . wait for the next. . . . Then the horrible news . . . the Plague . . . Louis dead . . . dead! She had feared it, but she couldn't believe it. Louis gone!

"Dear God," she prayed, "give me the strength to bear this sorrow. It's the worst that could have happened. But Your will be done. I offer You this suffering with my love, and for Louis' speedy entrance into Heaven!"

She was a widow at twenty. Her son Herman, just a small boy was supposed to become the next duke. Until he was old enough, his uncle Henry, Louis' brother, would rule the land. At least, that was how it was supposed to be. The power-hungry Henry seized the throne, and on a cold winter day drove Elizabeth, her four children, and two maids out of the palace!

He was cruel, that Henry. He was one of those who had laughed at the kind little princess years before. Now he warned the townspeople not to take the royal refugees into their homes, nor to give them anything to eat!

Even though Elizabeth had given them so much help in years gone by, the people were too afraid of the new duke to help her.

Evening found the women and children taking shelter in a small, smelly building where pigs had been kept. There they spent the night. Toward morning, Elizabeth waked the others, and they made their way to a nearby Franciscan monastery where they asked the monks to sing a hymn of thanksgiving to God for them!

Elizabeth was now one of the poorest of the poor. Daily she walked the streets, begging scraps for her family to eat, and very often they had to go hungry. What torment it must have been to the mother to see those little children nearly starving! Nevertheless, they always managed to find a place to sleep, no matter how cold and shabby the place might be.

In spite of all her misfortunes, Elizabeth did not fail to thank God. She thanked Him for the chance to experience some of the poverty in which He had lived, for the chance to suffer as He had.

Finally the news of what had happened reached some of Elizabeth's relatives. They immediately sent for her to live with them. And then,

another stroke of good fortune came. Louis'
knights returned from the Crusade, and they forced
Henry to return the dukedom to little Herman.

Elizabeth did not live much longer after this
turn of events. She had been purified, and was
ready for Heaven. A fatal illness seized her, and
consumed by a raging fever, she became weaker
and weaker. Joyfully, she received the Last Sacraments. Her eyes shone with happiness; after a hard
and sorrowful life she was going Home—to Heaven!
Around midnight on November 19, 1231, she died.
So many miracles were wrought through her intercession, that in less than four years Elizabeth was
made a canonized saint of the Church.

*Generosity is a virtue which God loves very
much. We can practice it by sharing our things with
our brothers and sisters and by helping our mother
with the housework.*

Saint Peregrine

Patron of the Cancer-Stricken

The scene was Italy, in the troubled thirteenth
century. The city of Forli had rebelled against the
supreme authority of the Pope, and had been placed
under an interdict.

It was as if the city had suffered a spiritual
death. Church bells could not ring; church doors

would not open. No longer did the faithful assist at holy Mass or receive the Sacraments; no longer did admonishing or consoling voices ring from the pulpits.

The good people suffered very much. But, in Forli there were not very many good people!

Most of the citizens were wicked and rebellious. The Holy See's interdict did not bother them at all; rather, they gathered in the streets, laughing and mocking, saddening the hearts of the honest citizens.

Was Forli, then, a lost city? Had God decided to abandon it forever?

No. Even though the city was rebellious, Pope Martin IV wished it to have a chance to convert itself. There was a holy Servite monk, named Philip Benizi, who had traveled through the Italian peninsula bringing peace to warring cities and calm to troubled souls; this monk, the Holy Father decided, should go also to Forli.

Father Philip Benizi was no longer young, and his health was rather poor, but he was more than willing to do God's will. He set out for Forli. The season was spring and all nature gave promise; did it promise success for his mission, too?

The people were waiting for him eagerly. Their curiosity had gotten the best of them! In a large public square opposite a church they had built a platform from which Philip Benizi was to speak. He would certainly have a new-style pulpit and a very strange congregation!

It seemed that the stern and humble priest, with his modest black robe, white head and shining eyes, already had some sort of power over the mob. A great silence gripped the multitude in the square, while the anxious eyes of the *good* citizens peered down from the surrounding windows and balconies.

Philip Benizi held a crucifix in his right hand. He raised it heavenward, while his lips moved in a quick, silent prayer. Then he began to speak, gently inviting the people to repentance.

The holy priest's heart was trembling; would God work the miracle of a mass conversion?

But then a disturbance began at the other end of the square; there was a group of late arrivals. A young voice hurled an insult, and the spell was broken. From every point in the square rang out new voices, new outrages. The mob stirred. While the good fled, the others moved threateningly toward the preacher. In their lead was a young man, probably no more than eighteen.

Father Philip stood erect, holding the crucifix, his gaze directed toward heaven.

The leader of the young men bounded up the steps of the platform and said something vulgar to the holy priest. Father Philip remained silent. The youth raised his fist and struck him a blow on the cheek!

The square was in a uproar. Insult after insult rained down upon the priest. He was buffeted about, yet always he kept the crucifix clutched tightly in his hand, while his eyes silently spoke forgiveness.

Relentlessly the mob drove the saint from the city. The drawbridge leading to the countryside was lifted behind him, and the walled city of Forli retreated within itself.

Father Philip found himself walking beside a little brook which wound its way through the countryside. The soft murmur of the waters formed a perfect background for his prayer. Battered and beaten as his body was, the priest's soul was as calm as ever.

"Father, forgive them," he prayed. "They are blind!"

He thought of the youth who had struck him, recalling the features hardened by anger and corruption; he saw again the raised hand. . . .

"Father, convert him; he's a poor, blind boy!"

He walked on in the evening stillness.

All at once it seemed to Father Philip that he heard running footsteps. Could someone else be coming to attack him? Perhaps it was only his imagination. . . .

But, no. Now he heard the footsteps clearly. Now he saw the shadow of the runner and heard his voice calling, "Father! Father!"

The elderly man turned to face the boy who ran toward him with his arms outstretched as if in desperation and who threw himself to the ground at his feet, kissing the hem of his robe again and again and begging, "Pardon, Father, pardon!"

The saint understood everything. He bent down and raised the young man to his feet, pressing him to his heart as a father would his child.

The face of the boy who had struck him was no longer hardened by anger and corruption. Tears had purified it and made it young again. The boy's eyes were soft and glowed with a new light. "Pardon, pardon!" he repeated. "I am so sorry for my horrible sin!"

"I know it; I see it," replied Father Philip gently.

"I want to change my life. I want to spend it doing good," the young man blurted out. "God is calling me, and I can feel that a great change must take place in me. I don't know what He wants me to do or where I should go, but . . . I do know that everything that attracted me before repels me now."

Father Philip consoled him and gave him some important advice. "Return home and rid yourself of your vices and defects. Practise honesty and humility. Listen to the voice of your conscience, and do what God will direct you to do. Perhaps someday you will do some great work for Him." He paused. "What's your name, son?"

"Peregrine Laziosi."

Surely Divine Providence had planned this meeting between a great saint and a young man who would one day be a great saint!

Peregrine retraced his steps to the city, where he abandoned his former companions and devoted himself to solitude and meditation. He was annoyed by anything distracting. Worldly companions, amusements, games and debates all repelled him now. The new joy that had taken possession of

Peregrine's heart was to please Jesus and His Heavenly Mother. Nothing else mattered.

Peregrine's companions were amazed at the change. But they figured that it wouldn't last, so they hounded him, dogging his footsteps and trying to win him back. After all, hadn't he been the liveliest, the quickest-witted, the most daring of them all?

"Come back to life!" they urged. But Peregrine would have none of it. He had begun to live, yes, but it was the true life, that which he had found when he met Father Philip and the life of God's grace flowed into his soul.

The days passed. Peregrine felt himself drawing closer and closer to God. He was cultivating, as the holy monk had urged him to do, a trusting, childlike confidence in the Blessed Mother. He prayed to her long and devotedly. Then, one day, while praying in the shadows of the darkened cathedral, the youth actually *saw* his Heavenly Mother, ringed about by a crown of angels.

Peregrine felt a trembling in his heart; his whole being was caught up in admiration of the heavenly vision. The Madonna spoke.

"I am the Mother of Him Whom you adore on the cross. . . . In Siena is a monastery of my servants, Servites; go to Siena, for that is where you belong."

The vision disappeared and Peregrine hurried home, with only one thought in mind—to obey the wonderful invitation of the Queen of Heaven. In the silence of the night, he slipped out of the darkened house and set out into the countryside.

It would be a hard journey, he knew. Four days and four nights it would take him to cross the Appenine Mountains. It would be a lonely trek. . . . But no. God soon provided Peregrine with a traveling companion, a winsome youth whose sparkling and holy conversation made the hours and the miles speed by. When they were in sight of Siena, the stranger suddenly vanished, and Peregrine then realized that an Angel of the Lord had accompanied him.

At last he was knocking at the monastery gate. What a joyous moment it was! He was admitted; he told the monks of his great desire, confessed his past sins publicly, and asked to be accepted into the community. Smiling joyfully, the superior, who was none other than Father Philip Benizi, received him into the Servites.

In the years which followed, Peregrine applied himself to his studies for the priesthood. He showed great humility, recollection, apostolic zeal, spirit of penance and self-sacrifice. After his ordination, he was seized by an ardent desire to return to Forli, where he had spent the wild days of his youth, so that he might dedicate himself to doing good.

Permission was granted, and the young priest retraced his steps across the mountains to the city of his birth.

The rebellious city welcomed her holy son, opening wide to him the doors of homes filled with misery. The people showed him their sick; Father Peregrine cured them. They told him their needs, their troubles, their hopes and desires, and he urged and consoled them. His favorite places were the hospitals, prisons and homes of sinners; he circulated through the city continually, seeking to visit and comfort, by his presence, his words and his deeds, all those who sought his help.

His nights were spent in prayer, and if he fell asleep through exhaustion and toppled to the floor, he picked himself up and began to pray again.

Very early in the morning he celebrated holy Mass, preparing himself each day by going to confession. No wonder this saint worked so many miracles!

At one time, a band of outlaws was roaming through the countryside, attacking and robbing everyone whom they found traveling on the lonely roads winding through the forests and hills. The city officials and police could find no way of stopping them. Then Father Peregrine decided to act.

Armed with only a crucifix, the holy priest entered the forest where the robbers were known to be hiding out. In a short time he found himself confronted by the wicked band. They were armed to the teeth; if they wished, they could have given him a lesson he would not forget, so that he would know that he was only a poor miserable monk. They *could* have done this, but something held them back. The priest was calling many of them by name, and their thoughts turned back to the days of their youth, when they had been Peregrine's own comrades! Now he was looking at them with a gaze that would have touched the hardest heart. They did not raise a hand against him, but let him speak.

And what did he tell them? No one knows. Perhaps he spoke of the reward of Heaven, which awaits the penitent. At any rate, from that day on the country roads were free from robbers, and the story goes that most of that once-wicked band entered monasteries and passed the rest of their lives in prayer and penance.

Father Peregrine was by now quite old. The hard life of poverty and penance which he had led was leaving its mark. Long hours of being continuously on his feet had caused an ugly sore to form on one of his legs, and now it had turned cancerous. The doctors said that the leg must be amputated.

In the solitude of the night, Father Peregrine begged God, "How can I serve You, my Lord, if I can no longer walk? How will I be able to reach all those people who are waiting for me, expecting me to tell them about You and about Your infinite goodness?"

His heart was full of fear. Suddenly, the figure on the crucifix above him began to move! Jesus came down and touched the painful sore, and then disappeared. Father Peregrine wondered whether or not he was dreaming. Dazed, he struggled to his feet, and discovered that his leg was whole and sound once more! Overcome with joy, he flung himself down in front of the crucifix to pour out his gratitude.

The humble priest's life had now almost ended. He was old and ill. At last, he was no longer able to be up and about.

Peregrine knew that the beautiful Queen of Heaven was waiting for him as a mother waits for her dearly-loved child. His soul left the world with complete calm and faith in her.

Father Peregrine was dead! A great crowd of people who had known and loved him, gathered around the body to cry their grief at losing him, for they knew that he had been: "A saint! A saint!"

It was hard for Peregrine to break his bad habits and take up good ones. His love for the Blessed Mother helped him to make the change. We, too, should pray to Mary, especially when we are in difficulty.

Saint Gertrude

Herald of Divine Love

She was born on the Feast of the Epiphany, and that was fitting, for that feast commemorates Jesus' manifestation, and Gertrude would manifest His love by her writings. When only five years old, the little girl was placed in a convent to receive an education. She was bright and active, a quick learner. She studied Latin, philosophy and theology, and became skilled at copying manuscripts and decorating them. All the while she was growing in love for God. When she was old enough, she became a nun.

God had given Gertrude many gifts, including a keen intellect and an ability to give wise advice. She realized that these were not of her own making, but gifts from God. Regarding herself as nothing, she did the best she could to use the gifts for God's glory, saying to herself, "Even if I should later suffer in hell, I would rejoice to see God's gifts to me bearing fruit in others."

Imitating Jesus and doing His will were her only concerns, so much so that her heart was attached to no persons or objects, nor to her own comfort. Ready at once to do whatever was commanded or suggested to her, she passed quickly from task to task, performing each perfectly and with deep love. No matter what she was doing, she offered it to God in praise of His glory.

She loved to pray, but knowing that we are placed on earth to serve God, as well as to know and love Him, she would leave her prayers at once to help any of the sisters who were in need. She tried always to give good example to everyone, so that those around her would grow in holiness.

Sometimes Gertrude seemed to desire the good of her neighbor almost too strongly. She wanted everyone to become perfect, and she spoke sharply to her companions when they committed faults. It was a failing that Gertrude worked hard to overcome, not because it made her unpopular, but because she knew God wanted her to be gentle. When sisters seemed not to like her, she did not mind, because whatever she did was to win God's approval, not theirs.

Gertrude had a great love for Jesus and a sincere desire to imitate His virtues. In every trouble she asked His advice; she was grateful for every favor received from Him; whenever she had not corresponded well to one of His graces, she begged His forgiveness and did penance in reparation.

Some of the graces Gertrude received were extraordinary, and came in the form of visions. However, they were not the source of her holiness, which flowed from her faithful correspondence to the graces of the Liturgy and Sacraments which are available to all of us. The visions were intended as much for other people as for herself, and Jesus had her write an account of them.

"In learning about the favors bestowed on you," He told Gertrude, "many will desire similar graces and will make efforts to lead better lives."

She, however, did not wish to write. It would be so hard to find the proper words! So many of the things she had to tell could easily be misunderstood. ... She hesitated for months, she who had always been so prompt in doing God's will. Then Jesus told her, "Know this—your soul shall not be released from your body until you have completely written this account."

And so Gertrude wrote. The book about her visions was called the *Herald of Divine Love*, for Gertrude was a herald—a messenger—from the Sacred Heart of Jesus to mankind. She also wrote *The Book of Special Grace*, which told the favors God had granted one of the other sisters, St. Mechtilde.

She composed a series of *Exercises* to inspire devotion in others, and wrote many beautiful prayers as well.

The visions did not alter Gertrude's humility. She was very much aware of her faults. There was one fault in particular which she begged God to keep her from committing. At last Jesus told her, "You gain a reward each time you recognize a fault and make a resolution never to commit it again. Even if you fail time and time again, you show Me as much loyalty and honor by your resolutions as a soldier shows his captain by conquering an enemy in battle."

Another time Jesus appeared and said, "Behold, my daughter, in one hand I hold health, and in the other, illness. Choose the one you prefer."

Gertrude threw herself at His feet and cried, "Lord, do not consider my will, but only Yours. Do whatever You wish with me."

Jesus was very pleased. "Let all those who wish to keep Me with them, give Me their wills and never take them back."

Another truth which Jesus taught Gertrude was the value of praying for others. Even when the grace asked for was not granted, another grace was given in its place—a grace which would make the person more Christlike.

Gertrude had a tender devotion to Our Lord in His Passion. She seemed to hear Him saying from the crucifix, "See how—because I loved you—I have been fastened to the cross, despised and torn, covered with wounds, bones wrenched from their sockets. Yet if it were necessary for your salvation, I would suffer again everything that I suffered for the whole world—just for you alone."

Jesus told Gertrude that devotion to His Passion is very good, but that it becomes much more meritorious when someone sincerely tries to imitate the examples He gave when suffering:

"If anyone gives in to another's opinion, he makes reparation for the injuries I received during the first hours of My Passion.

"One who admits his faults atones for the false charges made against Me and for My condemnation to death.

"One who refrains from pleasing his senses repays Me for My cruel scourging. One who obeys those who are hard to please consoles Me for the pain of the crown of thorns.

"If someone apologizes in an argument, he helps Me to carry My cross. If he exerts himself to do more good than he is obliged to do, he repays Me for what I suffered when My muscles were stretched on the Cross and My bones dislocated.

"One who goes to any length to keep another from sinning makes up to Me for My death for man's salvation. One who treats his neighbor with respect and kindness places Me reverently in the tomb."

Gertrude was never strong enough to practice severe penances, but by imitating Our Lord in this way and by keeping her will united to His, she became a great saint.

❀ ❀ ❀

Knowing that Gertrude longed to die and go to Heaven, Jesus gave her a choice: "Choose what you prefer, either to die now, or to earn more merits by a long illness."

"My Lord," replied Gertrude, "may Your holy will be done!" She would not choose for herself.

"You do well to leave the choice to Me," replied Jesus. And he sent her an illness of several months' duration which gave her the opportunity of offering her sufferings to Him to earn many more merits. Then He called her to a royal welcome in the Heavenly City of the Saints.

St. Gertrude always tried to do what God wished her to do. The deeds which God expects of us are those which our parents and our teachers tell us to do.

Saint Catherine of Siena

Ambassador of God

Catherine Benincasa was born in Siena, Italy, in 1347, the youngest of twenty-five children.

She was prayerful from the very beginning. By the time she was five years old, she had the habit of climbing stairs on her knees, saying a "Hail Mary" on each step. It was an early sign of her love for penance.

One day when Catherine was six, she was walking along with her brother Stephen when suddenly she stopped stock still, and stared intently at the sky. There among the rosy clouds was a magnificent throne, and on it sat a kingly figure in papal robes, a crown upon His head. It was Our Lord Himself! With Him, surrounded by halos of light, were St. Peter, St. Paul and the Apostle John.

Catherine gazed up at Jesus, Who was smiling and calling her to Himself. He raised His hand in blessing; then the vision vanished. From then on, Catherine's soul was on fire with love for God.

She had stopped still while looking at the vision. Stephen, too, had stopped and was staring curiously at the sky, but, seeing nothing, he said at last, "Hey, Catherine, why aren't you moving?"

"Oh, Stephen," she breathed. "If only you had seen what I saw just now!"

The boy could not know about the great desire which his sister now had to flee the world and seek refuge in God alone. From then on, Catherine longed for a life of solitude, prayer and penance.

When she was seven, she made a vow of virginity.

One day, Catherine set out for the country, carrying a loaf of bread. That loaf, she thought, would be enough to feed someone as small as she for several days. She was going to seek that peace and solitude she had dreamed of. Siena was far behind her when she stopped in a sheltered country spot.

But a strange feeling came over her. She understood that Jesus was telling her to wait, that she was too young, and must return to her family.

Sad, but obedient, little Catherine started back toward the city. Only then did she realize how far she had come! Fear gripped her.

But what was happening? Suddenly Catherine felt lighter; looking down, she saw the road speeding by beneath her unmoving feet; she was being carried toward the city by a mysterious force. A short distance from her own home, the unknown power set her down on the ground again.

Back home, Catherine began to make new penances for the love of Jesus. She began to eat less and less, and to sleep less and less. She spent her nights praying fervently, kneeling up straight on the hard floor.

Catherine's parents and relatives were puzzled. Why was she such a strange girl? Why didn't she like fine clothes as the other girls did? Why didn't she want to be admired? Why didn't she like boys? She was entering her teens, and since she was charming and had a winning personality, her relatives thought it was time for her to be married.

But Catherine had vowed her virginity to God at the age of seven; she wished to be only His, and refused to listen to talk of boy friends and marriage.

"Let us put her to doing the housework," her parents decided. "Then she won't be able to spend all her time praying."

So Catherine took care of the house, doing each and every duty well. She was serving God with her hands, while she kept Him in her thoughts and in her heart. Instead of lessening, her love for Him and union with Him grew. A great resolve was forming within her: she wanted to become a sister.

When her parents found out her hopes, they said, "No." But Catherine did not let that stop her. She kept on begging her mother to let her enter the Dominicans, and paid no attention at all when friends told her mother, "Catherine is too pretty to be a sister!"

Too pretty? Would such a human motive come between Catherine and her spiritual desire? "Send me a sickness, my Lord," the girl prayed. Make me ugly, but grant my great desire."

The sickness came, and Catherine's beauty faded. At last she was permitted to enter the Third Order of St. Dominic. As a religious, she continued to live in the world, and went about doing good. Her father let her spend part of the family's income in helping the poor.

On fire with charity, Catherine longed to help everyone in need. One day, while she was praying in the Dominican church, a beggar came up to her. Holding out his hand, he said, "Please do an act of charity."

Of course, Catherine wanted to help him, but she had no money, nor even a piece of bread.

"I'd like to do it," she told the beggar, "but I have nothing with me."

He looked at her trustingly and remained where he was.

Then Catherine remembered that her rosary had a tiny cross made of silver. Joyfully, she detached this and gave it to the poor man. "Here, take it!"

He accepted the offering and left.

That night, Catherine saw Jesus, and He said to her, "My daughter, you have given Me this silver crucifix, which will be presented for your greater joy on Judgment Day."

How happy Catherine was!

Then there was the incident of the flour.

Times were hard; people were poor and food was extra scarce. All were in need.

Catherine, who was visiting a friend, learned that her flour was spoiling.

"Spoiling?" she asked. "But surely it can be used to make bread for the poor."

"Impossible," the friend replied. "It's too far gone!"

But Catherine, glowing with enthusiasm, began to make dough and to knead it thoroughly. Under the pressure of her fingers, the dough lost its original bad smell and took on a sweet, fresh odor. From it Catherine shaped many little loaves of bread, which were baked and given to the poor. Wonder of wonders! The loaves multiplied as she gave them out!

Another time, there was a woman dying of leprosy. She was in the hospital but no one came to see her; no one wanted to have anything to do with her. That was understandable, because leprosy was a dreadful disease.

Only one person did not avoid the sick woman, and that person, of course, was Catherine. Fearlessly, lovingly and humbly she began to care for the leper. It was not long before the woman started to take advantage of Catherine's kindness. She scolded her and ordered her about. Catherine just took it; she didn't answer back even once, but continued to care for the woman as tenderly as she could.

And when we stop and think of it, what was that poor leper to her? Nothing more than a stranger. . . . But wait! That was not the way Catherine saw her; instead, in that suffering woman, and in *all* who were suffering, she saw Jesus. In trying to ease their pain, she was trying to ease His.

After a while, a large sore began to form on Catherine's hand. But she ignored it, and kept on caring for the sick woman. When the leper died, she prepared the pitiful corpse for burial and went with it to the tomb. And then the miracle happened: the skin of Catherine's hand became pale and smooth again!

A young soldier from a nearby city had been taken prisoner during a dispute and condemned to death. Since he had not committed any crime, the young man felt very bitter about having to die. He uttered some horrible blasphemies.

Catherine went to him and talked to him. She persuaded him to accept the death that awaited him. She told him of the great gladness he would know in Heaven. The young man repented, and died saying the name of Jesus.

Catherine had had very little education, but she was filled with a God-given knowledge which made her able to talk with even the most highly-educated people.

She became an ambassador, a bringer of peace to the Italian cities which were fighting among themselves. Sometimes she was sweet and encouraging; sometimes sharp and firm. She undertook hard, tiring journeys.

One mission took her to the city of Pisa, where, while praying in the church of St. Christina, she said, "Make me suffer as You did, my Lord!"

And God answered her prayer; He gave her the stigmata; that is, the wounds which He Himself had borne. They were not visible, but the pain was there, and tormented her terribly. Her disciples, who could not help but see the effect of the sufferings upon her, prayed to God to ease the pain—and He did so. This displeased Catherine, who knew that suffering is a way to reach greater heights of holiness.

* * *

At that time, the Pope was living on lands which he owned in France. His influence throughout the whole world had fallen low, because he was not ruling from Rome, the center of the Church. For that reason, and also to bring peace back to the warring cities in Italy, Catherine wrote many letters to the Pope, urging him to return to Rome. Then she went to France in person.

When Catherine spoke to the Holy Father, her words were so convincing that he was amazed. But the French bishops tried to tell him that she was not as brilliant as she seemed. They called her before them and asked all sorts of theological questions. She answered correctly each time, because God's grace told her the answers to all those big questions she had never studied about. In fact, Catherine knew more about theology than those who had studied the subject for years!

At last, because of Catherine's urging, the Pope returned to Rome—and what great rejoicing there on his arrival in the Holy City!

Catherine's full life, rich in sacrifice, suffering and merits, drew to a close when she was only thirty-three. Her joyful soul sped heavenward to the Spouse Who had looked down upon her and blessed her as a child.

St. Catherine loved Jesus so much that she wanted to be like Him. So she wanted to suffer. We can show God we love Him by not complaining when we are hot or tired or uncomfortable.

Saint Bernardine of Siena

Messenger of Peace

Little more than ten years after the great St. Catherine died, an orphan boy arrived in her city of Siena, to be the guest of his uncle and aunt. He was Bernardine, son of "Tollo" of the Albizzeschi.

Little by little, Bernardine came to know that city which was to become "his" city. "Our Cathedral is dedicated to the Blessed Virgin assumed into Heaven," his uncle told him one day.

"And I too was consecrated to the Madonna when I was small," replied the boy.

"Study hard, Bernardine," his teacher used to say. "Perhaps you too will one day be the glory of Siena, which has always boasted men of heroic virtue." And the lad would apply himself lovingly to his studies.

Right from the start, Bernardine was of good influence on his friends.

"I tell you its my turn, you devil!" a boy yelled on one occasion.

"Hey, watch what you say! Bernardine's coming!" hissed another boy.

Even the poor of his neighborhood came to know Bernardine, because he was always interceding for them. He would say "I beg you, give alms to the poor, for the love of God." And people listened to him and gave.

The years passed. When Bernardine was sixteen, he, as was the medieval custom of boys of his

"Study hard,
Bernardine!"

age in Siena, offered a large candle to the Blessed
Mother on the Eve of the Assumption. "May he
continue to be as pure and brave as he has always
been," said his aunt and uncle.

That night, Bernardine was in the garden behind his house still full of the wonderful feelings of
the day. Suddenly he seemed to hear a voice.
"What's up? Someone's calling for help! Who could
it be?"

Yes, someone *was* calling for help, no doubt
about it. Bernardine's generous heart urged him to
waste no time in hurrying to the rescue. "The gate
is locked! I'll jump over the wall!" No sooner said
than done.

In the dim street, Bernardine saw a gang of
rich noblemen's sons bullying a good boy, who had
been with him in the procession in honor of the
Blessed Mother. Running toward them, he shouted,
"Shame on you!"

Seeing him, the drunken youths began to make
fun of him, "Here comes another sissy! Hit him! Give
it to him, too!"

"I'm not afraid of you," Bernardine shouted,
facing them fearlessly. "Get behind me, Jacob," he
said to the other young boy.

After a few minutes, Bernardine, seeing that he
was being overpowered by the superior number of
his opponents, sent up a quick fervent prayer to the
Queen of Heaven. It was answered at once. Bernardine heard voices a short distance away. Recog-
nizing them, he called "Bert! Bill! Fellows, come
and help me! Hurry!"

"Shhhhh!"

The gang of bullies took to their heels when they saw Bernardine's friends running toward them. "Thanks, fellows, you're real friends," said Bernardine. Then he added, in a determined tone, "We've got to unite ourselves, to make the boys of Siena the glory, not the disgrace of the city!"

Then he took them to see the "Lady of his heart," a beautiful image of the Blessed Mother. Some bystanders, watching Bernardine, remarked, "Oh, he's crazy!" While others said, "Wait and see! I tell you he'll be our saint!"

Now we come to the year 1400, the year of the solemn Universal Jubilee. Bernardine joined the "Company of the Disciplined of Mary," a confraternity which worked in the hospitals to relieve the suffering of the sick.

On one eventful day, which was to mark the start of a lifetime of heroism, Bernardine was out enjoying the fresh air, when he suddenly saw something that made him exclaim: "A pilgrim. . . . But something is the matter with him! He needs help!"

Bernardine ran towards the man, who had fallen to the ground by then. To his surprise the man pushed him back with a violent gesture, crying out in a terrible voice, "Go away! Go away!" On his face the unknown traveller bore the marks of a horrible disease: the plague.

The plague, a dreadful sickness, had again put in its appearance as a result of the thousands of pilgrims who had gone to Rome. Heedless of the

To the rescue!

danger to himself, Bernardine lifted the sick man into his arms and carried him to the hospital.

The contagion spread quickly in just a few days. Bernardine was everywhere, helping the stricken, comforting the dying. "Courage, fellow! Have faith!" His sweet words were directed to all those who turned to him.

Terror-stricken, the people of Siena fled the city, taking time only to pick up a few provisions. Meanwhile, in the hospital there remained no helpers and no nurses. The sick were streaming in from every section of the city.

It was then that Bernardine called ten of his closest friends and said to them, "In the Gospel it says that God will not fail to reward us for all the good we do. Do you want to help me, brothers?"

"We're with you!" they answered in one voice, and set themselves to work at once with a fervent and holy will.

The sick continued to arrive. Bernardine did all he could for them, even the lowliest tasks, and tried to cheer them. "Come on," he'd say, "those of you who can, sing with me." And he would begin a lovely, consoling hymn to the Blessed Mother.

Finally the terrible plague died out. But Bernardine, completely worn out by his efforts, fell sick. To one of his relatives who kept saying, "It's really a shame that you should become sick now that everyone is well again," Bernardine replied, "My cousin, the Lord knows what He is doing."

The plague!

During his long illness, Bernardine brought to maturity one great desire. Just as soon as he was cured, he said to the woman who had nursed him. "Dear cousin, you have been a real Mother to me. I've got something to tell you. I think the Lord has called me; I must do something for Him."

Not long after, the noble Bernardine of the Albizzeschi gave up all his possessions and put on the humble robe of a son of St. Francis. He was twenty-two when he became a Franciscan.

He went to a small monastery, where lived a few humble friars who could not even read or write.

"We have only a little bread and some cooked greens," they told him. "We are poor."

"No, brothers, we are rich!" replied Bernardine, for he meant that anyone close to God is rich.

The Lord wanted even more from Bernardine. Two years after his ordination to the priesthood, he made up his mind to build a humble monastery.

"We'll build a little nest of strict observance to our holy rule," he said happily.

But how many struggles he had to sustain! Not all of his relatives understood him. Upon meeting Bernardine one day, one of them said scornfully, "You're nothing but a crazy beggar! I'm ashamed to be an Albizzeschi, related to you!"

"We'll see if I'm the honor or the disgrace of my family," was Bernardine's calm reply.

* * *

At that time, fierce, bitter battles raged all over Italy between various families. The wealthy nobles

were arrogant and cruel; they fought among themselves over trifles. One bloody fight followed another endlessly with undying hatred on both sides. The
people suffered from all these bitter feuds and from
the cruel oppression of the rich.

Persecuted and abandoned, the poor became
lawless and evil. . . . All these things caused Bernardine great sorrow. What could he do about it?
He sought to bring the word of God to all—to the
powerful nobles and to the humble poor. So, with
two brothers, he set out on his mission of bringing
peace throughout Italy.

And he preached from village to village, from
city to city, in the squares, in the churches. Everywhere Bernardine's words brought comfort to all.
He was truly God's envoy. He preached brotherly
love, peace with neighbor and with God. He was
truly a messenger of peace!

Bernardine went throughout Liguria, Lom-
bardy, Venice, Umbria, and Tuscany on foot,
preaching of Jesus with an ardent love; and the
faithful grew from a few handfuls to a crowd, to a
multitude. . . . As the years went by, Bernardine
harvested fields of faith.

Now in the public squares of the great cities
burned the "bonfires of vanity," into which people
threw their luxurious clothes and adornments—the
trappings of vice and sin. Bernardine would stand
by, urging them on. "Rid yourselves of all these
foolish things—give them up!"

A few powerful men were against Bernardine,
however, and when they saw an unusual mono-

gram of the Holy Name of Jesus, which Bernardine showed to the faithful for them to venerate, they murmured: "Do you see that queer emblem the friar holds up after he preaches? I tell you it must be a sacrilegious insignia!" And they laid their plots.

Bernardine was preaching at Viterbo when a very important envoy arrived at the monastery where he was staying. A message for Bernardine the friar from His Holiness, the Pope!

What did that message contain? And why had the Pope himself deigned to send it to the humble friar?

It was a call to Rome and Bernardine understood at once that his enemies must have made a very serious accusation against him. Yet he made his preparations to leave with his usual serenity. "Don't worry," he told the Brothers. "No matter how things will go, we'll meet again in Heaven!"

Bernardine put all his trust in God, and God did not disappoint him. In a short while, his innocence was clearly established and in Rome itself, in obedience to the Pope's wishes, he began to preach again. It was Bernardine's hour of triumph and in his preaching, he glorified the Holy Name of God.

He did his best to keep peace between the warring families, to unite them all in the love of Jesus, saying: "Put *His* Holy Name on your banners, on the flags of your ships. Write it everywhere!"

God, Who had called Bernardine, now began to work miracles through him. One day, while

Bernardine was preaching in a public square, a mad bull came charging into his crowd of listeners and killed a young man.

"It is the devil from hell trying to stop the work of God!" declared Bernardine. Then he added, "Have faith and through God's mercy, this boy will be saved!" And he made the Sign of the Cross over him.

The young man arose immediately, asking, "Who called me?"

"A miracle! a miracle!" shouted the crowd.

"Take him home and venerate the Name of the Lord," Bernardine said simply.

Working miracles and inflaming the crowds with his own great love for Jesus Christ, the saint reached Milan, where he intended to preach. But Duke Philip Visconte whom he had reproached in public called the saint to his palace and warned him, "Brother, if you don't stop preaching, I'll have you tortured horribly!"

"I shall be happy to suffer for the love of Christ," replied Bernardine. The duke was about to insult him for that answer when one of his courtiers whispered something in his ear. Then the wicked duke said in a false, oily tone, "Pardon me if I have offended you. Please accept this money for your monastery."

If Bernardine would have taken that money then the people would believe that he who preached against riches himself accepted gold. But Bernardine was too wise for the duke's tricks. "We don't need money," he said, "but if you force me to accept it, then allow me to bring it where I shall go."

Followed by the duke's men, Bernardine went directly to the prison, where with that gold, he bought the freedom of poor political prisoners, as was customary at the time, saying to them: "Go home free, in the name of Jesus Christ!"

If the money should not have been enough, Bernardine would have offered to take someone's place in prison. But there was enough money. How many hearts were made happy on that day! "Thank you, thank you, Friar Bernardine!" cried the poor prisoners, kneeling at his feet. "Thank you so much!"

The saint continued his travels, always on foot. He journeyed to the most out-of-the-way places and in the worst weather. "Courage!" he would say to his companions, "we'll see a light glowing pretty soon and find shelter. There's always a little light, even in the darkest night."

Wherever he went, Bernardine was like a flame of love that purified souls and brought peace to men. Those who had quarreled with their friends or relatives went in search of them to tell them, "Come back home with me! Let's give each other the hand of friendship!"

Men who had stolen animals, touched by Bernardine's preaching, repented and returned the stolen property to the owner with these words, "Here, I give you back what is yours. Forgive me in the name of Christ!"

Bernardine thus brought peace and concord among many cities and among many families. At this time there arrived in Siena, Sigismund, the son of Charles IV. He had come to Italy for the purpose of being crowned emperor.

Even Bernardine was in Siena and, although he had severely criticized Sigismund, he went to see him and courageously told him: "The Pope and the emperor must work together for the earthly city willed by God. I have come to talk to you."

After several months, the negotiations bet een the Pope and Sigismund were completed and the latter set off for Rome to be crowned. At his side there was Bernardine who said to himself: "I bring Caesar to kneel at the foot of the Vicar of Christ!"

In this manner Bernardine, old and worn out by his hard life of sacrifice and penance, kept on preaching and working marvelous miracles for the people of one city after another. It is the year 1344, the city of Aquila was awaiting his arrival.

One of the brothers asked him while they paused to rest, "Do you remember, Father, the time many years ago, when you preached in this area on Assumption Day?" "Yes," Bernardine replied, "I do remember," and he seemed to be living again that moment when. . .

. . . during the course of his preaching he had said, "Clear, precious and beautiful as a star is our most pure Virgin Mary!" And the crowd had suddenly begun to shout. "Look up at the sky! The star!" Sure enough, in broad daylight a most marvelous brilliant star had appeared in the sky. . . .

The memory of this soul-stirring moment was too much for the poor heart of God's weary traveller and Bernardine sank to the ground murmuring, "Most Holy Virgin, My sweet Mother..." Frightened, his brothers tried to help him.

The people of Aquila who had come out to meet the beloved preacher had to return with him in a sorrowful procession. For three days, they waited in suspense, hoping that he would regain his strength. . . .

But on Ascension Day, the bells announced Bernardine's last great journey. From everywhere, people gathered to give honor to the mortal remains of the saint.

Yet, though they gathered for such a holy purpose, there was fighting between the common people and the wealthy.

"Get out of my way, you ignorant fool!" a nobleman yelled at a peasant.

"We've had enough of your arrogance!" was the farmer's defiant reply. "Friends, gather round me!" The furious battle was on.

Swords and clubs were being threateningly waved when someone shrieked, "Stop! Look! Look towards the church!" Terror-stricken, openmouthed, they all turned to see. What was it?

From the pale, waxen face of St. Bernardine, whose body had been laid out in the church, blood began to flow—so much blood, in fact, that it was streaming out of the church onto the square in front!

"He said it," admonished a brother. "He had said: 'I would give all my blood to put an end to fighting and hatred!' " Then all the men began to shout, "Peace, friends! Peace, brothers!"

Numberless miracles occurred after the saint's death but the greatest miracle was his life and his mission as "Messenger of Peace."

Sometimes we, too, can be peacemakers. We can do it by keeping calm when our friends are arguing. If we keep calm we can think of something nice to say to bring peace.

Saint Frances of Rome

Friend of the Poor

"It's a disgrace!" the aunt spluttered wildly. "A disgrace and a scandal! I've never seen the like. What must people be saying about us—you taking little Frances into those horrid alleys and hovels, exposing the child to filth and disease and—and—goodness knows what!"

Frances and her mother listened silently. The little girl felt like quoting the Gospel, "As long as you did it to the least of My brethren you did it to Me," but instead she bit her tongue and withdrew into a corner.

Her mother was calmer, for she was used to such talk. Never did she let it keep her from paying daily visits to the riverside hovels of the poor, with little Frances pattering along beside her. In those days, no orders of sisters had been founded to care for unfortunate people, so they depended entirely upon kind, wealthy families like that of Frances.

Frances was an impetuous child, with a stubborn streak, but she had a great love for God. Even when singing and skipping happily, she betrayed the deep silence in her soul by the earnestness of her glance. Frances was a child united with God.

She liked to read about the saints, especially about hermits in the Egyptian desert. She wanted to imitate their strict penances, and, when her mother said she was going too far, she objected, "Mother, you said we should do penance!"

"Yes, dear, that is true, but not the severe penance of a desert hermit. The past is gone, and we must imitate our Crucified Lord in the fourteenth century, not in the third."

"Offer everything you do, no matter how small, to God," Frances' confessor told her. "Renew the offering often. Then some day you will have a great sacrifice to make to God. You will sacrifice your own will." Frances pondered the words often without understanding their meaning.

By the time she was eleven, she had developed a strong desire to consecrate herself to God. At Christmastime of that year, before the midnight Mass, Frances offered herself to Him as a victim to destroy the evils which troubled the Church at that time. After returning home, she spent the whole night in prayer.

Had God accepted her offering? Yes—she would become a victim sooner than she expected!

On a sunny day the following spring, Frances approached her parents as they were resting in their garden and asked, "Mother and Dad, may I have your permission to enter religious life?"

Her parents looked neither surprised nor happy. A few uneasy seconds crept by, and then her father cleared his throat and said, "No, Frances, we cannot permit you to do so. In fact, I have promised you in marriage to Lawrence, the second son of Andrew Ponziani!"

Frances felt as if her heart had leaped into her throat and was about to choke her. She had been so sure they would say, yes. And instead, they were determined to say, no. For a moment the girl could say nothing, then she murmured some excuse—she hardly knew what—and fled—fled to find her confessor.

While on the way, she began to think, "Is this the sacrifice God wants—the great sacrifice of my will? But not this! This will tear me away from Him! Not this!"

And yet . . . if this were His will must not she obey? Deeply worried, she told the holy priest everything. He listened gravely, then replied, as she had feared, "If your father is determined, then God wants you to marry. You will still be able to serve Him. Your role in life will be to suffer and to obey."

And so Frances accepted it. She prayed to Mary for strength, and began the long walk home.

After all, she reflected, it is a great and noble thing to be a wife and a mother. One serves God in one's partner and one's children. One serves Him by responding generously to the demands of each moment. One finds God while doing household tasks.

"I am sorry if I have caused you pain," she told her parents that evening. "The suddenness of this news startled me. I am sure your decision has been wise." She said it gently, and her happy parents had no inkling of the ache in her heart. The sacrifice had begun.

Lawrence belonged to a very wealthy family. He was a few years older than Frances, a rugged young man, slightly shy and very kind. Their wedding was a splendid affair and at its conclusion Frances felt the grace of the Sacrament flowing through her—the grace on which all married couples depend to perform all their new duties well and faithfully, forever.

The family circle she entered was a pleasant one. There were two other couples and many servants, all living in one magnificent house. Lawrence's parents were very kind to Frances, and so was his brother, Paul. Paul's wife, Vanessa, was a holy and pious girl whom Frances liked immediately. It was Vanessa who showed Frances how she could continue her fasts, mortifications, and prayers without letting the curious eyes of friends know what was going on. At social activities Vanessa and Frances dressed beautifully and flitted about as good hostesses; no one knew that they wore coarse, rasping hairshirts underneath their fine gowns!

Frances continued her kindnesses to the poor, and soon everyone in the neighborhood knew of her generosity. Each day she visited the Hospital of the

Holy Spirit to tend the patients who were danger-ously ill. Often she and Vanessa asked city officials to free debtors from prison. Such good example led other wealthy Roman women to do similar works of charity instead of spending twenty-four hours a day enjoying themselves.

Whenever Frances committed the slightest fault, she became aware of the presence of her Guardian Angel. Sometimes she knew that he was standing nearby, disapproving. At other times she felt him slap her cheek! From this she learned that God does not want those whom He loves to commit even the slightest fault!

Frances and Lawrence prayed to have children, but their first three babies died right after birth, to the great sorrow of the young couple. Then their fourth child was born. It was a little boy, whom they named Baptista for St. John the Baptist. As he grew up he became very much like his father. The next boy was named Evangelista, after St. John the Evangelist. He was quiet, like Frances, and always thinking of God. Agnes came later, and resembled Evangelista.

Frances was careful not to spoil any of her children. She taught them the evil of sin and scolded them whenever they committed a fault. Yet when they were truly sorry for having offended God, she was gentle and forgiving—as God Himself would have been.

❋ ❋ ❋

Once a great flood swept through Rome, ruin-ing homes and leaving hundreds of people without shelter. Right after that came an epidemic and then a famine. The city was full of sick and dying.

"We must do everything we can to help them," Frances told the servants. "We have an abundance. Give food and clothing to all who ask it."

She herself went to help those who were too ill to come begging at her door. She and Vanessa passed from filthy hut to filthy hut, giving grain and oil to the sufferers.

"We shall have nothing left for ourselves and the servants!" exclaimed Lawrence's father. "Vanessa and Frances, give me back the storeroom key. From now on, no more food to those beggars!"

Yet the poor were clamoring at the gate. They lay dying in their hovels! Frances could not bear to see such misery. She went to an empty grain bin and began to pray fervently. In a matter of seconds it was full again, and Frances began to distribute the grain. This happened several times!

How selfish I have been, thought Lawrence's father, his eyes bright with tears. "My child," he told Frances, "you have discovered the secret of true happiness which is generosity and a love that grows the more that it is shared. Please pray that I will learn to be unselfish like you!" He returned the storeroom keys to his grateful daughter-in-law.

❊ ❊ ❊

Crosses are always found in the lives of those whom God loves the most–because they know how to use the crosses best. They offer their sufferings to Our Lord for the conversion of many sinners so that a great multitude of souls will spend eternity rejoicing and praising God in Heaven.

Frances had many crosses. One of the first came shortly after the outbreak of a war between rival nobles. Lawrence had become an officer in one of the armies and had ridden off to fight. As all wives do, Frances worried and prayed, especially when she got word that a battle was raging. And then a messenger came running up the street and rang the bell at the big front door. As he blurted out his tale, the young woman froze in anguish, for the message was: "Lawrence Ponziani was stabbed on the battlefield, and may be mortally wounded. They are bringing him here, now."

Stunned though she was, Frances quickly sent messengers to call the nearest priest and doctor. Then, holding her breath as it seemed, she awaited the arrival of the stretcher-bearers.

They carried Lawrence in, eased him down, and stood about anxiously while Frances unstrapped the heavy armor. She felt for a pulse beat. Yes—it was there, although the hand was icy! Lawrence's eyes were closed, but Frances whispered the act of contrition in his ear.

The wound beneath his heart was deep, and blood continued to ooze from it. Frances applied cloth after cloth, prayer after prayer.

The hours merged into days and the days into weeks as Frances nursed her feverish husband back to health. At last he was well enough to say, "The poor need you, Frances. If you go out to help them, I shall be careful not to strain myself."

Frances agreed. Her sister-in-law Vanessa had continued her errands of mercy during the past few months, begging food and clothing for the poor, treating the plague-stricken, burying the dead. During this time Vanessa had lived in a dirty shack, its floor made of clay and bones, sleeping on a mound of straw infested by vermin. Such was the heroism of Frances' beloved companion.

Frances and Vanessa set up a food center where the poor could come daily to obtain something to eat and drink. They cared for the sick and the imprisoned, and taught catechism to children, for there was no other place they could learn catechism in that time of war and plague.

And then–Lawrence's brother Paul, Vanessa's husband, was kidnapped by the enemy! Frances received a message, "I want Lawrence Ponziani's son as hostage or else I will kill my prisoner!"

They had Paul, and now they wanted little Baptista! Frances cringed at the thought of that innocent child in the hands of such unscrupulous men. She *could not* hand him over to them—and yet she could not let them kill Paul. Frances hastened to the chapel where she spent the whole night weeping and praying. The next day, she took Baptista to the enemy.

"Place the boy on your horse and take him with you," the cruel noble ordered one of his officers. The soldier helped Baptista to mount, but once he had done so, the horse would not budge.

"Here, mount him on mine," offered another soldier. Again, this horse would not move.

They tried again and again, but with no success! Trembling with something which seemed more fear than rage, the leader ordered, "Enough! Release the boy!" And they brought Baptista to his mother.

* * *

Lawrence's life, too, was in danger, so friends helped him to escape from Rome and go into hiding. They were wise in doing so, for one day a band of horsemen thundered up before the house.

"Quick!" exclaimed Frances as she heard the men shouting and milling about outside, "Take the children, Vanessa, and hide!"

"Not I, Mother," said Baptista. "I'll stay with you!"

Hastily Frances closed Vanessa and the two little ones in a secret hiding place. Then she and Baptista stood clinging to one another while the angry soldiers stormed about searching for Lawrence. Full of rage at not finding him, they began to destroy the beautiful furnishings, slamming and shattering and burning. Then they snatched Baptista from his mother and thundered off down the street.

* * *

Consoling news—that family friends had helped Baptista escape to join Lawrence in his hiding place —was followed at once by more sorrow. Evangelista fell sick with the plague and died. His last words were, "I see the Angels coming to take me to Heaven." His death was followed by that of Agnes a few months later.

There was no time for sorrow. Daily Frances and Vanessa drove a wagon through the city streets, gathering the bodies of the plague victims and taking them away to be buried. They comforted the dying and encouraged them to repent of their sins. They tended the sick. They went from door to door, begging bread for the poor. By now they themselves were so poor that in summertime they went into the country, and learned how to swing a scythe to harvest grain.

When peace was made at last, Lawrence returned from his exile. He was thin and worn. With him was his brother Paul; he, once so sensitive, was now a shell of a man with vacant, staring eyes. Baptista returned, too, no longer a plucky ten-year-old, but a strong young man of seventeen.

Like the tireless spiders who build and rebuild, the family and its servants put hands to the task and began to repair what had been destroyed. In a little over a year, they had a new home—plain and simple compared with the first one, but having at least a roof to keep out the cold.

* * *

Needless to say, Frances continued her works of charity. Times were better now, but there were always the poor, always the sick. Later she founded a religious community—the Benedictine Oblates—composed of young women and widows.

One by one, Paul, Vanessa, and Lawrence went to God, and Frances was left alone. She mourned but little, for her dear ones were enjoying eternal happiness. She too had not much longer to live. She entered the little community she had founded, determined to pass her last years there.

Frances had led a life of continuous self-denial. Not only had she denied herself food and rest and comfort and finery; she had quenched impulsiveness and obstinacy, pride and resentment over injustice. She had truly conquered herself.

When Frances died, at the age of fifty-six, her last words were those of her son, Evangelista: "The Heavens are opening and the Angels are coming to meet me."

Just as St. Frances was kind to people who had nothing to eat, so can we be extra kind to the boys and girls who do not seem to have many friends and good times.

Saint Rita of Cascia

Patron of the Desperate

It was the evening of May 22, 1457. In the Augustinian Convent in the pleasant little city of Cascia, Sister Rita was living her last earthly moments.

She was a small sister, seventy-six years old, who had lived a sorrowful life,weighted with anxieties, shot through with pain, ennobled by prayer, and enriched by penance.

The days, months and years had passed with a succession of great sorrows and wonderful joys; Rita had accepted both smilingly, in the spirit of holy obedience, happy to serve her Jesus. Now the final moment had come; Rita had so suffered, waited and hoped for it, and now Paradise was at last only a few breaths away. In the hands which had worked so much good, which had so often been joined in prayer, a Crucifix was held tightly. He Who had suffered so much more, He would help!

As the little sister lay on the small bed, her gaze moved upward . . . then she became still: Rita had expired!

But what was happening? All the bells of Cascia began to ring spontaneously! It was a gay sound with no note of sadness in it, and the people of the little city, awakening with a start, asked one another what could be so important that it made the bells ring at that strange hour.

A saint had died; a saint had gone to Heaven!

✿   ✿   ✿

Rita's childhood had been a happy one. Her parents were pious, and they taught their little one to pray, to have devotion to the Passion of Jesus, and to be kind to everyone, especially to the poor.

As Rita entered her teens, her love for Christ's Passion grew, and she spent hours praying in her little room. She longed to enter a convent and to consecrate herself forever to God.

Imagine the young girl's sorrow, then, when her parents told her that they wished her to marry

a certain young man who had asked for her hand—
Paul di Ferdinando.

Paul di Ferdinando! He was a stormy man
known far and wide for his furious temper. It was
difficult to picture the sweet and gentle Rita married
to such a person.

It was a real cross, Rita thought to herself. I
wish to become a nun and belong only to Christ,
yet I see that God's will is otherwise. This is the
cross He has prepared for me, and I must accept it,
however against my inclinations it is!

So Rita and Paul were married, and Rita's trials
began. Although she was always serene and gentle,
she was shouted at and beaten frequently by the
fiery Paul. He took out on her all the unpleasant
things that happened to him during the day. But
never did Rita argue or protest; she was meek and
gentle and kind.

As the years passed, Paul began to wonder at
the loving patience of his wife. He tried to check
his anger when it rose within him; he began to go
for walks in order to "cool off." He began to admire
Rita and to do little things to please her. A lion was
changing into a lamb!

The couple had two sons, James and Paul. They
inherited their father's fiery nature, but Rita was
careful to check those tendencies, and Paul himself
tried to avoid giving them the bad example of losing
his temper before them. Due to his wife's example
and prayers, Paul was slowly becoming a good
Christian. People marveled at the change.

But not everyone appreciated the new Paul. During his lifetime that stormy man had made many enemies–and one evening, as he was walking home from the village, Paul was attacked and murdered by a gang of cutthroats such as he himself had once been!

In sorrow Rita gave Paul a Christian burial. She prayed earnestly for the repose of his soul, and performed many penances. She also turned a watchful eye on her teenage sons, knowing full well that in those times of crime and violence they might decide to take revenge on their father's slayers.

Sure enough! James and Paul grew more rebellious day by day, until Rita knew that her words and example had lost all power over them.

"Dear God, conserve them in the state of grace," she prayed. "Do not let them become wicked and lose their souls!"

She begged God daily for that grace–and He answered her prayer. Both boys became seriously ill. Rita nursed them devotedly through long, watchful nights, gently reminding them of the nearness of eternity and the need of sorrow for sin. The boys became less rebellious; they repented of their fits of anger and desires for revenge; they passed away peacefully, within a year of their father's own death.

After the death of her husband and sons, Rita dedicated her time to the poor, the unfortunate and the sick. The village of Roccaporena was small, and everyone knew and relied on Rita; in her goodness and inspired charity she was a true consolation.

The world held no attraction for her; she felt a great desire to dedicate herself completely to God; she wished to become the spouse of Jesus.

She resolved to prepare for this carefully, devoting hours to prayer and penance in a lonely country spot, from which she could see the little city of Cascia and the convent of the Augustinian Sisters, where she yearned to be.

One day Rita decided that she had waited long enough. She set out for Cascia, determined to ask admission to the convent.

Her heart beat wildly; what would be the response?

Having arrived at the convent, she told the Abbess her burning desire.

"Daughter," was the reply, "this is a home for those who have never known the world. You have been an earthly wife and mother; this place is not for you."

The gates were shut upon poor Rita, who returned to her life of prayer, seeking always more austere penances. From her secluded spot she gazed down upon Cascia, the city which was calling to her!

At last, she felt that she *must* heed that call. Heart pounding, she once more knocked at the gate of the convent. The Abbess recognized her, but once again she had to say "No," although her own heart was bleeding.

Rita did not let herself become discouraged. She returned to her house and prayed more fervently than ever. And at last her perseverance was rewarded; Rita was admitted into the Augustinian convent! With great joy she took her place among the members of the community, and soon was edifying them by her saintly example.

Her faith could have moved mountains; her humility was greater than one could possibly imagine, and her obedience had no limits. She was careful to avoid even the smallest infraction of the rule.

Finally came the day of the indissoluble solemn vows. Rita was so happy. Now she would be a spouse of Jesus forever!

She was so happy that she could not even look at her sisters, and retreated into a corner of the garden to think about what had happened. A very sweet sensation spread through her, completely detaching her from the world. She did not slumber; no, Rita was in an ecstasy, a heavenly transport.

She saw a beautiful ladder, which seemed to be of crystal, rising from her feet and ending in Heaven. How infinitely long it was! How many, many steps! The ladder shone with a celestial light and myriads of Angels were ascending and decending it in a marvelous order. At the top was Our Lord, Who looked down and signed to the sister to climb towards Him!

What an irresistable invitation!

This, then, became her program: Rita determined to progress continually—to climb a little each day, to strive always for perfection, always for sanctity.

In her little cell, the poorest and meanest in the whole convent, she prayed unceasingly and made penances and mortifications without number.

She also deprived herself of some of her daily portion of food, in order to give it to the poor who came begging at the convent gate. Whenever it was permitted, she went to the homes of the sick and the aged to care for them.

Of course, Rita's troubles did not end when she entered the convent! The devil always tempts souls who are favored by God, and he put the thought into Rita's mind that she was not meant to be a nun and that she should return to the world. But Rita was too smart for him. She knew that the fact that she had been permitted to make her vows meant that God wanted her to be a sister for the rest of her life. She ignored the temptation, and prayed harder.

Then she had temptations against purity. She pushed them out of her mind and made more mortifications of her senses.

So then the devil tried to flatter Rita, and put it into her head that she was really holy because she had overcome all those temptations. However, Rita realized that this was a temptation, too—a temptation to sins of pride—so she prayed earnestly to become humble.

The sisters had not been long in realizing who it was that had come among them; they regarded her as one favored by Heaven.

Sister Rita was a model of obedience; when told to do anything, she would have done it even at the cost of her life. "I will test her!" thought the Abbess, one day. Taking a dry dead stick, she stuck it in the earth, upright and called for Sister Rita.

"Every day," she said, "you will water this."

Many people would have said, "How silly!" or something even worse. Water a dead stick? What for?

But Sister Rita didn't think anything like that; she just obeyed, simply and happily.

Every day she could be seen with her little sprinkling can, watering the dead stick. The sisters watched her with admiration, and perhaps a little amusement, too.

"What faith!" they exclaimed. "What obedience!"

"She is an example."

"But to obey so blindly...?"

But Rita knew that obedience in everything except sin is a source of tremendous merit–especially when a person has great love of God, and obeys for love of Him. She felt that such things were small in comparison with Jesus' obedience to His Father on the Cross. How much more Rita wished to be able to do for Him!

One day, after listening to a certain sermon, she entered the community chapel and knelt before its large crucifix; extending her arms she offered her entire being to the Divine Sufferer.

"Jesus, make me suffer with you."

As she was begging Him to share His torment with her, she felt a sharp stab in her forehead. It felt like a thorn! She believed she would faint from the pain as a stream of blood trickled down her pale face. "O my God," she exclaimed, "this suffering is very great, but my love for You is far greater!"

The wound was deep, and did not heal as the days passed. From it began to issue a horrible smell, which made everyone keep away from the suffering sister.

"It has such an odor!" the sisters whispered to one another. "Surely it must be contagious!"

Rita moved into a lonely cell as far as possible from those of her sisters, and there she passed the greater part of every day. Sometimes the sisters, overcoming their distaste, would come to see and comfort her, but Rita did not wish them to do this, for she did not like anyone to suffer on her account.

When she approached the Altar to receive Communion, she showed her unhappiness at inconveniencing the sisters.

"Excuse me," she would beg. As soon as she could, she hastily retired again to her hermitage.

For fifteen years Rita suffered from the horrid wound. It grew more painful as time passed, until she felt it even when she was sleeping. Yet through all the pain, Rita remained serene. She was still grateful to God for having permitted her to suffer out of love for Him. It was a long, drawn-out martyrdom.

Rita's final illness brought her three years of unspeakable pain, but though her body was in torment, her soul was full of peace and joy. At last a bright light flooded a corner of her poor cell, and she saw Jesus and Mary, Who told her that she would be in Heaven with them within three days.

It came to pass, and as we have seen, the bells of Cascia began to ring spontaneously when she died, to signify that a bright new star was shining in the firmament of the saints!

We can be patient, as was St. Rita, by trying to understand people who are angry and upset, and by excusing them no matter what they say.

Saint Joan of Arc

Warrior Maid

Joan was a strong, lively girl. She liked to play with the other village children, to run races with them, to dance and picnic during the village festivals. She was quick to do any job that was needed—anything from spinning and cooking, to weeding and digging, to tending cows in the riverside meadows.

She had never gone to school, but what need was there of that in those days? She knew her prayers and little stories about the saints—that was the important thing. Her favorite spot was a little woodland chapel dedicated to Our Lady, which she visited often.

Although she herself was happy and secure, raids and battles between the people of her village and neighboring towns kept Joan aware of the fact that she was living in the midst of war.

In history books that bloody struggle would be called the Hundred Years' War. It was fought between France and England–and the English were winning steadily, because of their better fighting methods.

France needed good leaders. Charles, the dauphin or prince, who claimed to be the country's true ruler, lacked knowledge of warfare. The nobles who led the soldiers were proud of their old method of fighting on horseback in armor, and would not admit how much better it was to stay on foot and use bows and arrows as the English did.

In battle after battle, swift arrows from English longbows picked the French knights off their galloping chargers. Still the French failed to learn the lesson!

Of course, Joan did not know about all these things. She had been told about small woodland skirmishes that took place near her home, but she knew nothing of great battles, such as Agincourt, where thousands of French lives had been lost.

She was a sturdy twelve-year-old, calmly tending her garden one hot summer noon, when a strange voice caused her to look up. A bright light was hovering between her and the village church. What could it be? The girl remained frozen to the spot.

"Joan, daughter of God, go to church often. Be good and virtuous. God demands it."

The light disappeared. In spite of the hot summer sun, Joan shivered. What was this all about?

She pondered. God must wish something special of her. Be virtuous... "My God," she whispered,

"I promise You I shall go to church very often, and I shall remain a virgin as long as it shall please You!"

Soon afterward the voice spoke to her again. And again on another day. This time, in the bright light, she saw a splendid Being whom she knew was the Archangel Michael! Around him were many other Angels. They were so beautiful! When they disappeared, Joan started to cry, so much did she wish to go with them!

Soon the girl had heavenly visits from St. Catherine of Alexandria and St. Margaret of Antioch. Both of them had been martyrs. People of that time had a great devotion to those two saints and to St. Michael, who was a special patron of the French Royal Family.

"Joan the maid, daughter of God," the saints said to her often, "you must leave this village. You must lead the dauphin to Rheims, where he will be crowned." They told her that she would go into battle and drive the English army from the city of Orleans.

All of this puzzled the little peasant. "I'm only a young girl!" she protested. "I cannot fight!"

"Go, daughter of God!" was the reply. But as yet Joan did not know how to begin. Four years passed by, during which the voices spoke to her often. At last they said, "Go to Robert de Baudricourt in the town of Vancouleurs, and he will give you men to take you to the dauphin."

Robert de Baudricourt was a noble who fought on the dauphin's side. Joan and her brother-in-law, Durand Laxart, went to his fortress to see him.

"Your Lordship," began Joan, "I have a message for you. The dauphin must remain ready to fight, but he should not enter battle. This kingdom does not belong to the dauphin, but my Lord wishes him to become king and hold the land in His name. The dauphin will be made king in spite of his enemies, and I myself will lead him to be anointed and crowned."

"Who is this Lord you speak of, and what right has he to give orders to the king?" growled Sir Robert.

"The Lord of Heaven," Joan replied.

But Robert de Baudricourt did not believe her, and Joan had to return home.

The next year, when she was seventeen, Joan returned to Sir Robert, again to ask his help. This time he was more willing to listen, since the French had been suffering many defeats. After a few weeks he sent her to the dauphin. She was dressed as a boy and had her hair cut short like a soldier's. She had always been a good rider, and sat her plunging steed with ease.

Joan sent word ahead that she was coming, and so the dauphin was waiting for her arrival. But he was not seated on his throne! He wanted to test her and make sure that she really came from God, so he stood among the nobles, trying to look like just another one of them. Joan went straight up to him and introduced herself, then told him a secret which only he had known, so that he would be sure she was God's agent.

Dauphin Charles had a suit of armor made for Joan and a beautiful flag, which pictured the King of Heaven with Angels on either side of Him, bearing the names of Jesus and Mary. Now she was ready to drive the English from Orleans.

Orleans had been under seige for months. The English had built forts around it, and choked off the flow of food and other supplies into the city. One dark night, Joan and a few soldiers slipped past the enemy forts and entered the city. How eagerly the people greeted her! They waved and cheered, while their torches flickered wildly.

A few days later, Joan rode into battle. Some of her soldiers went first, and attacked one of the forts. The fort put up a good defense, so nothing happened until Joan thundered up on her big warhorse, banner whipping in the wind, and cried to the French to attack. Her troops sprang into action at once. They had heard the ring of authority in her voice and were certain that she was sent by God. They stormed the fort and took it!

The next day was Ascension Day, and Joan gave orders that there should be no fighting. But the day after, she and a band of fighting men stormed another English fort. Again, success!

And the following day? They attacked a larger English fort. While arrows rained down upon them, the French placed ladders against the strong wall and started to climb. Then an arrow came whistling down from the battlement and drove into Joan's shoulder!

Breathlessly, everyone crowded about her. Would she be all right? Joan herself wrenched the arrow free, and said, "The wound is not deep, but I should like to go to confession. Please call the chaplain!" After confessing herself, she returned to the battle.

They fought on until evening. "We may as well retreat," said the French commander at last. "We're getting nowhere."

"Not so," the maid replied. "It will not be long before you take the fort." And sure enough, that same evening the French soldiers fought their way up the walls to victory!

On the following day, the English army retreated, and left Orleans in peace. Thus was accomplished the first part of Joan's mission.

Orleans was a "turning point." In the years to come, the English would be driven back, back to the coast from which they had come. For now they were fighting a nation who knew that God was on their side.

And why was God on their side? Why had He bothered to interfere in the petty affairs of men? Had we lived in Joan's time we would have found no answer, but looking back over the centuries we can make a guess as to the reason. About a hundred years after the Battle of Orleans, England left the Catholic Church. Now, if England had conquered France, France, too, would have lost the Faith, and perhaps other nations would have, also.

Now Joan returned to the dauphin and urged him to go to Rheims to receive his crown. He, however, was afraid to travel, for fear that the English would capture him. "We shall clear the route for you," promised Joan. She and her army set out with hopeful hearts, and drove the enemy away from the route to Rheims so that Charles could travel in safety.

On July 17, 1429, Charles and Joan marched down the broad aisle of the Rheims cathedral. The archbishop anointed the dauphin with great solemnity, and proclaimed him king. Joan, who stood nearby holding her beautiful standard, now knelt at the king's feet, weeping for joy.

✿ ✿ ✿

What was to happen next? "Continue to fight," the Voices told Joan. "But, daughter of God, be prepared, for you will be taken by the enemy!" And so it came to pass, about ten months later when Joan was cut off from her men during a small battle. She was surrounded; someone grabbed the bridle of her horse; she was taken. Then began the most dreadful part of her life!

Joan was put on trial by some English churchmen and some French churchmen who were their allies, and charged with being a heretic! For several weeks she was questioned, many hours a day. They were cruel questions, intended to confuse her. The purpose was to show that Joan was not sent by God, so that the French would lose confidence in their king and the English would win the war.

Joan was sentenced to be burned at the stake on Wednesday, May 30, 1431. When she was taken out before the people that morning, she said to them,

"I beg all of you standing here to forgive any harm I have done, as I forgive you the harm you have done me. I beg you to pray for me." She fell silent, and remained in an attitude of prayer for some time, then, "Does anyone have a cross?" An English soldier hastily bound two bits of wood together and handed it to her. Joan slipped it inside her dress.

Then they led her to the stake and bound her to it with heavy chains. Someone held up a crucifix so that she could gaze at it. "St. Michael," the maid whispered, "help me to die a good death." The wood was on fire now. She could hear it snapping and crackling, she could feel the heat. Orange tongues of flame were licking about her. Pungent smoke filled her nostrils. A tremor ran through her as the flames found her clothing, and roared through it. Pain, hot, searing pain. . .

"Jesus," called Joan softly. She continued to call Him until she died.

At the moment of Joan's death, many of those who had guarded and condemned her realized that they had burned a saint. Until then, their eyes had been blinded, but now they knew. And, as a little sign from God, Joan's heart had not burned.

St. Joan obeyed the Voices, even when other people thought she was foolish. Let us always obey our parents and teachers, no matter what other boys and girls may say.

In the midst of the fun

Saint Francis Xavier

Apostle of the Indies

Francis was the son of a noble Spanish family. Although he was a quick, lively boy, fond of sports, he did not choose a military career as most young nobles would have done. Instead, when in his late teens, Francis went to Paris to study at the College of St. Barbara.

Parisian students led a carefree, active life, and Francis was always in the midst of their good times. He kept up his studies, too, for he saw a university degree as a means to fame and fortune. Although he had no definite plans for his future, he knew he wanted to do something great with it.

An especially close friend of Francis was his roommate, Peter Favre. One day Peter said to Francis, "Have you seen the new student? He is Spanish as you are. His name is Ignatius Loyola."

The name did not mean much to Francis. Nor was he impressed by Ignatius' appearance when first he met him. Ignatius was an older man than he, and he dressed very plainly, whereas Francis wore finery befitting his noble rank. But Ignatius had an interesting story behind him. He had been a captain in the army, and now he was a soldier of Christ.

It had come about in this way: During a war in Spain, Ignatius had been injured. While waiting to get back on his feet, he looked for a way to pass the time. One so active as he, couldn't sit still for long hours doing nothing! "Bring me something to read!" he ordered.

The only books they could find for him were the life of Christ and the lives of the saints—strange reading indeed for a worldly person like Ignatius. Nevertheless, he decided to make the best of it. He read, and read, and the grace of God stirred in his soul.

When Ignatius' leg was healed, he did not return to the army. He had seen that the true heroes have always been heroes of virtue, like Augustine, Francis, Dominic. . . . "If they could do it, why can't I?" he asked himself. And so, he began a long pilgrimage.

He walked from monastery to monastery, shrine to shrine, begging for alms in order to have a bit of bread to eat. He journeyed from Spain to Italy, where he boarded a ship bound for the Holy Land. Ignatius remained long and thoughtfully in the hallowed places where Jesus Himself had lived and walked. God was calling him to a special mission. He returned to Spain to study.

There were many things he had to learn. First came Latin, for priests must know Latin. How hard it must have been for Ignatius, a man of thirty-three, to sit in the midst of a classroom of jeering and taunting little boys who laughed every time he stumbled over the tense of a verb! But this was God's will for him. With determination he set about learning all the endings of the strange Latin words, and whenever he made a mistake and the boys began to mock him, he just smiled.

Ignatius

Ignatius' mind was so fixed on God by this time, that when he had to conjugate the Latin verb *amo*, to love, he would say to himself, "I love God, I am loved by God . . ." and then he would stop and reflect on this wonderful truth!

Logic and theology were next in Ignatius' program, and after these came philosophy at the College of St. Barbara in Paris. That was where he met Peter and Francis.

Peter began to tutor Ignatius, to help him out, and Francis teased his friend about this. One day he was making fun of them at the dinner table, when Ignatius asked with a smile, "Tell me, Francis, 'what does it profit a man to gain the whole world and suffer the loss of his soul?'"

"I didn't ask you to preach!" Francis snapped.

But, although the young Spanish nobleman was rebelling, God's grace was at work in his soul. Many young men had begun to seek out Ignatius, to talk to him about religion and philosophy, and Francis was curious about the attraction this former soldier had for his comrades. He began to join in their informal gatherings. Then, when Peter had to leave the college for a while, Francis began to instruct Ignatius in his place.

He soon found that he was more of a pupil than a teacher. He went with Ignatius to the hospitals, and was edified by his great charity to the sick. He walked with him through the filthiest sections of the city, where misery was stamped on every face, and watched the older man strive to spend and overspend his energies in easing the sufferings of

the poor, the sick, the starving. Ignatius thirsted for sacrifice. Francis' own uneventful existence seemed pointless in the face of that burning Ignatian ideal.

And so grace triumphed over comfort-loving nature. Francis decided to join the community of religious which Ignatius was forming!

That little band of Christ's soldiers took the name Company of Jesus; today they are known as the Jesuits. They made their first vows on the Feast of the Assumption, 1534. Four years later their rule was approved by Pope Paul III, and three years after that Father Francis Xavier stepped aboard the ship *St. James*, bound for India.

He had changed greatly in those seven years. Correspondence to his first call had paved the way for one grace after another. Following the *Spiritual Exercises* of Ignatius, he had dedicated himself totally to Christ, and in reparation for the pride and vanity of his past life, had fasted severely, bound his swift legs with cords, joyfully tended the incurably sick—and made every sacrifice he could think of. His love for Christ grew by leaps and bounds until he longed to bring the whole world to know and love its Lord.

He was well on his way to holiness. He still was tempted, still yielded to his pride, still felt his hot temper welling up within him—but he was determined to overcome these faults, and he longed to pour out every ounce of his energy in God's service.

Father Francis Xavier would never see his homeland again. He would travel up and down the Orient until the day of his death, and would become the greatest apostle since the days of Saints Peter and Paul. Often he had dreamed that he was carrying an Indian on his shoulders. Now the dream would be fulfilled, as he carried thousands of Indians to eternal life.

The *St. James* plowed through the blue Atlantic, rounded the tip of Africa, put into port at Mozambique, and crossed the Arabian Sea to Goa, on India's southwest coast. It was a year-long voyage, in an unhealthy climate with poor food, and—as always happened—many of the passengers became sick and died. Seasick himself, Father Xavier was always among the passengers, washing and feeding the sick, giving them medicine, preaching sermons, and preparing the dying for a holy death. He was a real inspiration to the rough sailors, whose confidence he won with his sincere friendliness. They soon found that the priest was truly interested in them, and at his gentle urging they began to drop their bad habits and lead worthy Christian lives.

Everyone who met Father Xavier noticed how friendly he was, and how cheerful. He seemed to draw souls to himself like a magnet. And having drawn them to himself, he turned their thoughts to Christ, Who had loved them with such infinite love that He had shed His last drop of Blood for them. How many souls became kind and considerate of others because of this zealous missionary's kindness to them!

Goa was an Indian seaport which the Portuguese had conquered not long before. Many of the natives had been slaughtered or mistreated, and the

Portuguese Christian settlers had taken to leading lives as bad as those of the infidels. Father Xavier found conditions so bad that once he wrote, "It would be far better for me to be massacred by those who hate our holy religion, than it would be for me to live on as a powerless onlooker to all the outrages which are committed daily against God despite all our efforts to prevent them. Nothing saddens me so much as my inability to control the terrible scandals given by certain important persons."

Yet the poor were not beyond his reach. It was to the poorer Portuguese and to the half-castes that Father Xavier directed his first pleas.

Each morning he would walk through the streets, ringing a bell, calling out, "Faithful Christians, friends of Jesus Christ, send your sons, your daughters, and your slaves, to Christian doctrine classes, for the love of God!" This was a novelty. People would crowd around the good priest, who then led them into a church. He recited each lesson in rhyme and encouraged the people to sing it, so that the Creed and the Commandments were soon being sung by people everywhere—in the streets, on the ships, in the fields. Other priests began to follow Father Xavier's method.

The sick, the dying, slaves, sinners of all types— these came swarming to Father Xavier in order to receive the sacraments. They knew he loved them; they could sense that he desired the eternal happiness of their souls. To those who could not approach him—namely, the lepers—Father Xavier went personally. Each Sunday he said Mass for them and administered the sacraments.

How difficult it was to show these people that they were all brothers in Christ. The caste system was in full swing in India. Each social class had to keep away from members of other classes. Maharajahs with fabulous jewels looked down on soldiers who rode to war on elephants, and these in turn turned up their noses at the ragged beggars who whined in the streets for a bit of bread. Yes, Goa was a challenging field for any missionary.

And other souls were waiting, too. Father Xavier was eager to visit the poor Christian fishermen who lived along India's southeastern coast. As soon as possible he sailed from Goa, and voyaged the six hundred miles to Cape Cormorin, the southern tip of India. He was to make that passage twelve more times during his mission in the East.

From the Cape he walked northeast, from coastal village to coastal village, teaching the basic truths of the Faith to the Paravas, or pearl divers. These had been christianized a few years before, but had resumed pagan practices because of lack of instruction. That must not happen again. The priest appointed catechists from among the natives to continue the work he was beginning.

Father Xavier soon became a familiar figure to the simple, warmhearted natives. When they saw the kind priest coming they knew that the "Black Man", as they called him because of his black robe, was coming to help them build little chapels out of sticks and mud, to cure their sick, and to pray with them to the one, powerful and merciful God of Heaven.

Upon returning to Goa, Father Xavier found a welcome letter from his spiritual father, Ignatius. It was the first word he had received from him in two years, so slow were the communications!

Back again in the coastal villages, the missionary found trouble in the air. Rumors of raiders flitted from one small community to another. One dark night the townsfolk came running up to Father Xavier screaming, "Save yourself, Father! They will kill you!" A band of outlaws had swarmed into the town, burning and killing.

Father Xavier breathed a quick prayer and with steady courage went out to meet the robbers. "They are human beings, just as we are," he remarked. He held the crucifix before him and seemed not to hear the screams of the women and children who were being slaughtered on all sides.

The outlaws were astonished. What powerful charm was this which the black stranger held in his hand that kept him from fleeing in terror? Why, the natives would tremble just to hear the word "outlaw," and here was this slight man facing their cruel knives quietly, with no sign of fear!

This was too much for them; it was better not to face such powerful magic. Slowly the brigands withdrew into the night. . . .

* * *

News of such great heroism spread fast, and soon reached the Rajah of Travancore. He wel-

What magic
was this?

comed Father Xavier into his territory. There the missionary found people who were eager for instruction. Often as many as six thousand would gather to listen to him, and since the country was flat he found it necessary to climb up into a tree so that everyone could hear. In that part of India alone, Father Xavier baptised thousands of persons and built many small churches.

Meanwhile disturbing news came filtering out of northern Ceylon, where a priest sent by Father Xavier had made many conversions. A crafty rajah who hated Christians had ordered all of them to be killed if they would not renounce the Faith. The new Christians however, remained loyal to the end. They were slain, and their radiant souls sped to Heaven to join the glorious band of martyrs who will sing God's praises forever.

Anxiously Father Xavier followed reports of a struggle taking place between the rajah and another claimant to his throne. If only that cruel ruler could be driven out before he murdered the rest of the people! The revolt failed. Father Xavier heaved a sigh of disappointment and looked to the future; perhaps he should sail to the East, for the remainder of India was still closed to Europeans. . . .

He took a boat going north to the village called St. Thomas of Meliapor, where according to legend the Apostle Thomas had been buried. A priest and a small community of Christians received him happily, and the missionary set about making conversions. One day he sought out a rich man whom he knew had been avoiding him on purpose. The man's name was Jacinto, and he was the object of gossip for miles around, because of the bad life he led.

"Good evening, Jacinto," Father Xavier greeted him. "I trust you will forgive me for taking the liberty of calling upon you at this hour!"

Here it comes! thought Jacinto. He's going to preach to me!

Nevertheless, there was nothing the rich man could do. Father Xavier had arrived at the dinner hour, and the only polite thing to do was to invite him to dinner!

They chatted amiably. Father Xavier joked a good deal, and Jacinto found himself unbending a little and laughing with the missionary. But he was still waiting for the sermon.

At last Father Xavier said, "Thank you very much for your kindness, Jacinto. It has been an enjoyable evening. I should return to my lodgings now."

"It was a pleasure having you, Father; do come again," the rich man mumbled. He watched the slim figure of the priest stride away into the dusk. "Not a word about changing my ways," he marveled. "Has he decided that I am hopeless?"

Jacinto did a lot of thinking that night. He paced from one room of his fine house to another, pausing now and then to stare out into the velvety tropical darkness. "I have gone so far that Father Xavier will not say a word to change me—he who has converted the most hardened of sinners!"

Father Xavier was not at all surprised when the shamefaced Jacinto approached him the next day and blurted out, "Father, I have something to tell you!" Jacinto made a full confession of his sins, and promised to perform all the penances and employ all the remedies Father Xavier prescribed for him. From that day on, he was a new man!

* * *

On the apostle's tomb, Father Xavier prayed earnestly, "My Lord, please show me Your divine will, to which, with the help of Your grace, I shall be faithful no matter what!" And God, Who had given Francis that ardent desire to serve Him, now gave him the answer to his question. Suddenly, deep in his heart, Father Xavier knew that he must go to Malacca. That Maylayan seaport was the crossroad of the East, where merchants from Arabia, Persia and India bartered with those from China, Japan, the Philippines and the Spice Islands. The city was a Portuguese stronghold, having been conquered thirty years before, and its people had fallen victim to the same vices which Father Xavier had found running wild in Goa.

The missionary's fame went before him. As he stepped ashore he was greeted by a large crowd, especially of children, eager to see the famous priest who loved people so much. Father Xavier greeted them warmly, and set about winning their hearts for Christ. He took up residence in the hospital, where he tended the sick by day and prayed by night, allowing himself only two or three hours' sleep as he made penance for the misguided people of Malacca. Often he went into the soldiers' barracks, into the prisons, into the homes of the poor and miserable, becoming a friend and inspiration to all. Malacca became a less wicked town.

Two thousand miles to the East, the Moluccas and Spice Islands began to beckon to him—that maze of islands which lay along the equator between Celebes and New Guinea—22,000 square miles of thick-jungled islets, of rank marshlands and sunken reefs, of treacherous channels where pirates and wreckers lurked, of steaming volcanos and spouting geysers. The heat was torrid; the storms were fierce; the vices of the Portuguese and natives were horrible; it was mission territory, indeed!

And Father Xavier loved it. During all his years in the East he was never happier than he was on his voyage through the Moluccas. He went from island to island—Amboyna, Baranura, Rosalao, Ulate, Ternate, the Iles del Moro where the savages lived on human flesh, on and on—preaching, baptizing, exhausting himself in that climate which drained all energy, always asking his Lord for "More, more; do not take this cross from me unless You give me a heavier one!" Three times he was shipwrecked, but nothing could turn him back. These people had been redeemed by the Blood of Christ and Francis knew that it was his duty to cooperate with his Lord. "Pass before your eyes," he once wrote, "all the things that God has not done, which He would have done had you not placed obstacles in His path."

From the Moluccas, Father Xavier returned to Malacca, where he labored a few more months before sailing for India. He landed in Cochin, and hastened to revisit the fishing villages of the Paravas.

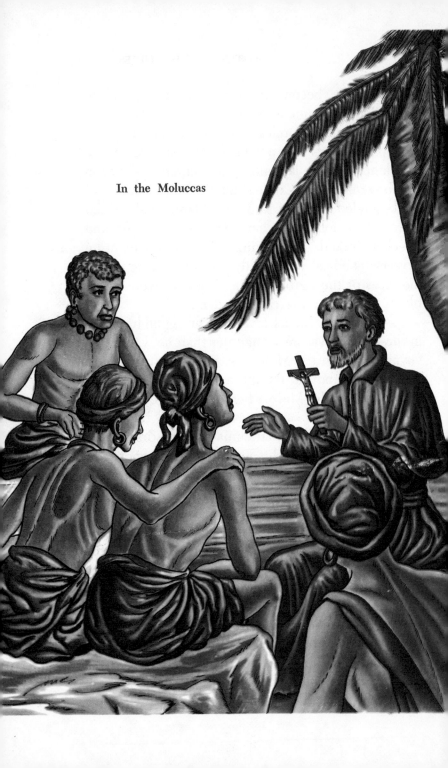

In the Moluccas

Those simple folk were overjoyed to have him again, but he could not tarry long, for he had to make his way to Goa, the seat of his missionary operations. From Goa, he sailed far north to Basein, and returned to Cochin ten weeks later, having sailed over one thousand six hundred miles in that space of time. Again duty called him to Goa and Basein. Settling down at last, he spent the winter in Goa, where he devoted much attention to the College of St. Paul which was training native seminarians for the priesthood. He also made some changes among the little groups of missionaries he had assigned throughout his vast territory, and appointed local superiors. He wished to have everything functioning well without him, for who knew what his next voyage would bring him?

He hoped to go to Japan.

   ❊ ❊ ❊

The "Land of the Rising Sun" had had a strange fascination about it, ever since the thirteenth century when Marco Polo first wrote of a mysterious island empire which lay somewhere east of China. Since that time a few Portuguese traders had set foot on Japanese soil, but they had not ventured inland and could report practically nothing of the land or its people. There was, however, a first-hand source of information in the person of a young Japanese named Yajiro, whom Father Xavier had met in Malacca and whom he had instructed and baptized. Yajiro told Father Xavier of the religion, government, customs, and philosophy which his nation possessed. These people sounded well-disposed to receive the Faith.

"Father, do not go!" urged one of the priest's friends.

"It is too dangerous a journey!" chimed in another. "The voyage is long; pirates infest the waters; storms are frequent and violent!"

"And if anything went wrong there would be no refuge to flee to, for the Chinese will let no westerner enter their harbors!"

Father Xavier just looked from one to the other and smiled.

Seeing that he was having no effect, the first continued, "There are still infidels to be preached to on the small islands near Goa—no need to journey thousands of miles to find them!"

Father Xavier laughed kindly. "Someone else can preach to them," he said.

        ❋   ❋   ❋

Before embarking for Japan Father Xavier had to pay another visit to the Fishery Coast of his beloved Paravas. He who was always searching for new souls to win to Christ could never abandon his concern for those whom he had already won; he was forever writing letters of detailed advice to the priests he had settled in various regions, to make sure that they were caring for their little flocks lovingly and watchfully.

One more quick visit to Goa and Father Xavier was in Cochin once more. He wrote to the Jesuits in Rome: "It is true that we shall find ourselves in the midst of savages. . . but we have only one thing to dread; that is, to offend God. . . . One delightful thought fills us with enthusiasm and strength; it is that God sees and knows our hearts, that He reads in the depths of our souls that our one aim is to make Him known and served, to extend His empire, to procure His glory."

During a stopover at Malacca, Father Xavier wrote another batch of letters to his charges. One of them, a note to a young Jesuit novice, shows clearly his own virtue and spirit of sacrifice: "Whatever you do, whatever the situation, strive always to gain mastery over yourself. Subdue your passions, embrace what is most unpleasant to your senses; above all things repress the natural desire for glory, and give yourself no rest in that regard until you have torn the pride out of your heart by its very roots, and you are content to be considered less than everyone else, even rejoicing to be despised. Without such humility and mortification you can neither grow in virtue, nor be an instrument for saving souls, nor persevere in the Company of Jesus."

Late in June, 1549, Father Xavier set sail for Japan in an unwieldy Chinese junk, skippered by a Chinese pirate. The missionary was accompanied by Father Cosmas de Torres and Brother John Fernandez, and by Yajiro, who had taken Paul as his Christian name. It was a three-thousand-mile voyage, consuming two month's time. On the way, the three Jesuits studied Japanese earnestly.

"What do your people believe, Paul? What sort of religion do they have?"

Paul explained that most of his people worshipped idols. Some believed that the soul was mortal, while others held that when the body died, the soul went into another body. Sometimes they worshipped the sun and moon or kings who had died years before. Some of the Japanese believed that there was no God at all.

The southernmost island, where the missionaries landed, was Kyushu. Father Xavier loved the people at once. They were skillful warriors, daring and chivalrous, like some of the noblemen he had known in Europe.

Eagerly the missionaries began to teach them the Creed, Commandments, and simple prayers which they had translated into Japanese.

The bonzes, or pagan priests, were learned and crafty. They asked Father Xavier questions which would have stumped most Christians, but the studies of years before came to the missionary's aid, and he answered the bonzes' arguments with a thorough grasp of logic and philosophy.

In comparison with other lands, Kyushu gave Father Xavier few converts. But those few were made of the finest steel. They clung to the truths of the Faith, obeyed the Commandments, and continued reciting the prayers Father Xavier taught them—for ten long years, until another missionary returned to be their shepherd. Three hundred years later, after bloody persecutions, a faithful band of Japanese Christians again welcomed missionaries to the shores of Kyushu.

* * *

The largest of the Japanese islands was called Nippon. The four missionaries landed at Yamaguchi, a major seaport, and began a 300-mile trek inland to Miyako, the capital. On their backs the travellers carried a coarse blanket, a few books and a portable altar. Winter was beginning. Sleet pelted the travellers; snow choked the roads; icy winds stung to the bone. By night the missionaries huddled in a little glen or by the side of a lonely pagoda. By day they trudged northeast, their bleeding feet leaving red marks in the snow.

When they reached Miyako they appoached the emperor's palace.

It was Father Xavier's idea to obtain the emperor's conversion—or at least to obtain his permission to preach the Faith throughout Nippon. Praying earnestly for that grace, he approached the palace guards and requested an audience with the emperor the commander of the armies. Little did he know that both rulers were only tools in the hands of powerful feudal lords!

He was not granted admittance, in spite of all his pleading, in spite of all his prayers. For eleven days he waited at the palace gates in the rain and snow, listening to the jeers of the people. Then he realized how futile his attempt was.

"It is not the will of God," he told his companions regretfully, and they returned through the snow to the coast and Yamaguchi.

In Yamaguchi Father Xavier disputed long and skilfully with the bonzes. Twice they became so enraged that they attacked him, beat him, and would have killed him had not a terrible thunderstorm arisen. Yet he was winning converts—not by the thousands as in India and the Moluccas—but by ones and tens until they numbered around a thousand. And those converts were good. They were the precious fruits of Father Xavier's fasts, of his night watches, of a union with God so close that he often repeated the Name of Jesus in his sleep. They were the fruits of Xavier's heroic virtue, and they were faithful to the end.

Having made conversions in several other cities as well, Father Xavier left Brother John Fernandez, a tireless worker, in charge of the Japanese mission. Two and a half years had passed, and it was time to check on conditions in India.

✿ ✿ ✿

On the Island of Sancian, off the China coast, Father Xavier met an old friend, a merchant named James Pereira, who invited the missionary to accompany him back to Malacca. Father Xavier accepted gladly. As the two men stood on the deck of Pereira's *Holy Cross* watching Sancian fade from sight, Pereïra remarked, "I have a problem, Father. Look at this letter I've received."

Francis opened the letter carefully. It had come from a Portuguese merchant imprisoned in China for smuggling goods. Since the Chinese emperor had forbidden all trade, everyone caught smuggling was held in prison and tortured cruelly. Several men were there now, the letter stated, and would remain there until they died, unless some kind of agreement could be made. Would Pereira ask the Portuguese government to appoint him ambassador to the emperor? By means of costly presents, he might be able to obtain the prisoners' freedom and reopen China's ports to trade.

Father Xavier folded the letter slowly. His eyes were glowing.

"Well?" asked Pereira. "What do you think I should do, Father?"

"I think," replied the priest slowly, his eyes on the China coast, "that this is the opportunity we've been waiting for. All China bows before one man—the emperor. If he became a Christian, the entire nation could be converted. And the Japanese, who look up to the Chinese in matters of religion, might soon follow."

"Yes," he continued, "let us try it. You, as ambassador, to beg the prisoners' release and the resumption of trade; I, as your companion, to bring the emperor the treasures of Heaven."

As the sturdy ship plowed her way toward Malacca, the two friends made their political and financial plans. "Our first aim must be to free those wretched prisoners!" Father Xavier exclaimed. "And yet," he added strangely, "I'm afraid the devil will cause our attempt to fail." He repeated that fear several times in the next few days.

Finally Pereira replied, "Surely you are mistaken, Father; we are bound to succeed."

"You will see," murmured Father Xavier uneasily. "You will see."

❁ ❁ ❁

Goa welcomed him joyfully. It watched with admiration as he plunged into a round of administrative duties, reorganizing, encouraging, appointing. One of the appointments was that of a second-in-command who would carry on if anything happened to him. Before departing for Malacca he knelt at his new vicar's feet and renewed his religious profession.

Father Xavier arrived in Malacca before Pereira. He was waiting eagerly when the merchant's sturdy ship hove into view and dropped anchor in the harbor.

Almost at once the blow fell: the governor of Malacca placed an embargo on the *Holy Cross* and had her rudder removed by force so that she could not leave the harbor!

Why did the Portuguese governor deliberately oppose the noble plans of his countrymen? We do not know, but oppose them he did—in the face of pleas from Father Xavier, from mutual friends, from his own brother.

"Let's seize the rudder, and may no man stand in our way!" roared one of Pereira's sailors.

"Aye!" cried his shipmates.

"No!" said Father Xavier firmly. "There must be no bloodshed."

The Lord would repay. Father Xavier had a power which he seldom thought about; he happened to be the Pope's official representative in all the East. That meant that anyone who prevented him from fulfilling his duties—and bringing the Faith to

China was a duty—should be excommunicated. Father Xavier did not want to use that power, but he knew that justice demanded him to do so. He pronounced the sentence.

The governor howled with rage. Excommunication! "Why you. . . ." He burst into a string of insults. Then he ordered, "The embassy to China shall not embark. Pereira and his crew will remain here and a new crew will be placed aboard the *Holy Cross*. The ship may proceed to China, and you—" he glared at Father Xavier—"may sail with her."

* * *

Only two of Father Xavier's old companions were permitted to sail with him—Christopher, a Malabar Indian, and Anthony, a Chinese.

As Father Xavier walked past the governor's house for the last time, he murmured, "I shall meet him at God's tribunal. May God spare and save his soul." Like a man whose heart was breaking, he prayed for his persecutor.

The *Holy Cross* made her way northeastward to Sancian and anchored offshore. It was a barren island, its only inhabitants being Portuguese traders who were trying to smuggle goods in and out of China. Father Xavier approached them at once and asked them to help him reach the mainland.

"Impossible!" they exclaimed. "It means death, or torture in the prisons of Canton. You cannot take the risk, Father, nor can we!"

Father Xavier knew they were right. But China lay before him, its millions of people completely unaware of the Redemption. He could not leave.

For two months the *Holy Cross* lay at anchor off Sancian while Father Xavier awaited his chance. At last it came. A Chinese trader asked for a huge sum of money. Father Xavier had powerful friends; he knew he could borrow the money, it was a bargain.

But when the appointed day came the Chinese trader did not appear. Nor did he come the next day, nor the next. As the hours slipped away the missionary who had labored so tirelessly for years felt his strength ebbing away. Such a fever seized him that his companions took him to the shore and placed him on a rough pallet in one of the trader's little huts. Through its doorway Father Xavier could see the China coast.

The fever made the priest's mind wander, but he prayed almost continually, "Jesus, Son of David, have mercy on me! Mother of God, remember me."

There was no priest to hear his confession, to give him Viaticum, to anoint him with the holy oils. Except for Anthony and Christopher, Father Xavier was entirely alone. What a strange end to his heroic labors for Christ! And yet, what counted apparent failure—or apparent success, for that matter—as long as all of it had been done only for God? "In Thee, O Lord, have I hoped," he exclaimed with some of his old joy. "I shall never be confounded!"

In the small hours of a December morning Father Xavier raised his eyes to the crucifix. "Jesus," he murmured—and his soul passed peacefully from his body.

Word of the heroic missionary's death spread quickly through the Orient. It passed from ship captain to cabin boy, from merchant to townsman, from missionary to humble native. From the far-flung Moluccas to the coast of the Paravas, from Malacca to Goa, the East mourned the passage of its greatest benefactor.

In Goa, where his remains were borne, crowds swarmed to the beach to meet the ship; for days they filed past the body, which showed no sign of corruption. Father Xavier had passed in and out of those people's lives in a few short years, but not even centuries would erase his memory from their hearts.

One burning desire filled St. Francis Xavier's soul—to do something for Christ, who had suffered so willingly for him. We, too, can do something to show Our Lord we love Him. We can do unpleasant duties willingly and offer them all to Jesus.

Saint Philip Neri

Saint of the Joyous Heart

Philip grew up in the city of Florence, Italy. He was strong, brave, and cheerful.

One time, when his family was trapped in a burning building, he calmly led them all to safety, one by one. Did he boast about this afterward? Not at all; instead, he thanked God for His mercy and protection.

This was the first of many experiences, for Philip Neri's life was to be dedicated to helping people in trouble.

Philip often went to visit the Monastery of St. Mark where the holy Dominicans taught. The monks liked Philip, for they could tell that he had rare and beautiful qualities of soul. They asked him to study under them, and Philip was eager to do so.

The boy's father, however, had other ideas. "You have known little except poverty till now, son," he said. "I would like to send you to live with my brother on his farm where you will have plenty to eat and a warm bed at night. You will be like a son to him and will be able to enjoy some of the comforts of life."

Philip obeyed, and went to live with his uncle. He was so cheerful and generous that his uncle and aunt liked him right away and treated him as if he were their own. They put him in charge of the men who worked in the fields. Philip enjoyed the long hours spent beneath the wide blue sky, planting and harvesting. The countryside was beautiful; he lived in a fine house; what could be missing?

Something was missing, but he did not have to seek far for it. Against the skyline loomed the great, stone monastery of Montecassino. It called him gently, but irresistibly. Thus, Philip began to visit the monks in the evening, after the day's work was done.

"Why don't you join us, Philip?" the monks began to ask after they had known him a little while. "Remain here, and your soul will know true peace!"

Philip wished he could say, yes, but he knew deep down inside that his call was to another type of life. God wanted him, yes, but not as a monk meditating in his cell or laboring under the lonely sky. God wanted him to go about among the poor, the sick, the criminals, the unguided teenagers—in short, all the suffering—and bring them food, clothing, tenderness, mercy. . . . Philip bade an affectionate farewell to his uncle and aunt, and set out for Rome!

In Rome, the youth found a job teaching a friend's children. He lived in a simple little room with only a sack for a bed. During the night, he would rise and kneel in prayer before his sole treasure, a crucifix. He would continue praying until just before dawn. Penance, mortification, study— these were Philip's life now. Why did he study? Not to make money, but to know things which would help the people whom he met and cared for daily.

Philip visited the sick in private homes and hospitals and cared for them patiently and tenderly. He begged alms for the poor. He gave good advice.

One group who were especially fond of Philip were the teenagers. Often they would come to visit him to listen to him talk. He had a knack of enkindling in their young hearts the same ardor for God which burned in his own. His words conquered souls who had begun to go astray, and spurred them to lead Christlike lives. "Well, my brothers," he would often say, "when shall we begin to do good?"

Philip started a home for the sick, then an inn for travelers, then the Oratory, that famous school which grew like a snowball rolling downhill and soon had four thousand pupils!

Then. . . .

"The Oratory needs a priest," Philip's friends told him. "These boys must have a spiritual father. Philip, you should study for the priesthood!"

"Yet I am not worthy," sighed Philip, who saw the need as clearly as they.

"You can do so much more as a priest!" the friends insisted, and Philip at last agreed. He resumed his studies, and at the age of thirty-six he was ordained.

Now the Oratory had a Father!

As a priest, Philip Neri showed himself to be a marvelous confessor, who drew penitents to himself like a magnet. From dawn's first rays until the noon bells rang, he heard one confession after another: rich and poor, young and old, hardened sinners and those of tender conscience came to him with faith and heard comforting words, urging them to battle the strong currents which strove to sweep them away from God.

※　※　※

One day Philip was approached by a boy who had sinned so much that he did not have the courage to open up his heart.

"Come," the saint urged. "You'll feel better soon."

"Father, I've made mistakes so often. . . ."

"They will all be forgiven you."

"Maybe, but at the cost of so much penance!"

"Nothing exceptional!" Philip assured him. "Only this: every time you fall again, come back right away and put yourself in the state of grace."

The young man promised. He confessed himself, received absolution, and went on his way happy.

But he returned almost at once, head down, humiliated.

Philip Neri comforted him and encouraged him one, two, three, many, many times; every time he returned with bowed head, weary and dejected.

But then he began to return less frequently; the falls were becoming smaller and more widely separated from one another.

Philip's smile, which had never faded, now grew brighter as he saw that the boy, aided by grace and abetted by virtue, was becoming a good Christian.

✿ ✿ ✿

There was another lad, also weak and dissolute, who said, "Father, I am tangled up in such vice. . . ."

"Never fear!" replied Philip. "I will help you to withdraw yourself."

"But what must I do?"

"Simply this: say the 'Hail, Holy Queen' seven times every day, and kiss the earth, saying 'Tomorrow I might be dead!' "

The penitent put the priest's advice into practice and promptly began to lead a holy life, thanking God and His servant Philip.

To another lad one day, Philip said, "Oh, how soiled you are! Go cleanse yourself." The lad understood at once. He made a good confession.

"Now you smell clean and fresh," said the saint happily.

❊ ❊ ❊

Philip also had the gift of prophecy. One day one of his young friends told him that he planned to take a trip to Naples.

"It would be best for you not to go," the priest advised at once.

"But, why not, Father? It's a wholesome outing. Naples is a beautiful city. I don't see anything wrong in visiting it."

"Listen to me; don't be stubborn."

"Father, I really want to go."

"All right, do so if you wish. But you will be ambushed by the Turks and almost drowned."

The youth did not listen, and set sail for Naples.

At sea, the Turkish pirates attacked the ship. The boy, not knowing what else to do, flung himself over the side and struggled to keep himself afloat in the water. He went down once. . . again. . . .

"Father," he screamed, "Father, save me!"

Lo! Philip Neri, who was miles away in Rome, appeared before his eyes, seized him by the hair, and carried him to safety. What a miracle!

❊ ❊ ❊

From hour to hour Philip acted according to the impulses of tender charity. He was gentle with one soul, stern with another, playful with a third, and so on–in all following the interior movements of the Holy Spirit Who enlightened him as to what that particular soul needed most.

Always Philip prayed for guidance. He distrusted his own powers and relied always on God's grace. "Lord, watch over me today," he would pray, "or I shall betray You!"

* * *

One time Philip's friend and follower the Baron, came into the sacristy as Philip was taking off his vestments after Mass. "Father, will you hear my confession?"

"You must go to the hospital at once," the priest replied.

"But, Father, I have just returned from there! The sick are resting quietly. They don't need anything."

"Baron," repeated the saint, "go to the hospital at once."

"Well, if you want me to, but why don't you hear my confession before I go."

"No, go at once; it is necessary."

The Baron stopped protesting and went back to the hospital.

Nothing seemed to have changed; the sick were resting peacefully. Nevertheless, the young man made the rounds carefully. Suddenly he came upon a man who had just been admitted. He was already in his death agony. In fact, it seemed to be too late, but the Baron succeeded in getting the man to open his eyes, and he read therein that dying soul's ardent desire for confession. He called a priest at once; the poor man made a good confession and passed away peacefully.

"You see?" Philip Neri said to the Baron. "Maybe now you have learned to obey without wasting time."

✿ ✿ ✿

One day, Charles Borromeo, the nephew of Pope Pius IV, presented himself to Philip. He was almost trembling.

"Oh, Father!"

"My good, young friend, I'm happy to see you."

"I need your advice because I'm weighed down by a great worry."

"Tell me about it." Philip listened intently while Charles told him that the Pope wished to make him a cardinal and consecrate him archbishop of Milan.

"Wonderful!" exclaimed Philip. "I'm happy to hear it!"

"But, Father, I am only twenty-three years old!"

"That doesn't matter. Don't put obstacles in the way of God's plans. Resign yourself to His will and obey."

"But then? What of problems which must be waiting?"

"Your burdens will be lightened by the hand of God."

"I tremble at the thought of what awaits me."

"Have courage! The Lord never abandons those whom He chooses."

Charles Borromeo, consoled by the words of a great saint, became Cardinal, Archbishop of Milan, and another great saint.

* * *

One day, Philip saw two Jesuits entering his little cell. To his astonishment he saw a halo of light encircling the head of one of them. Deeply moved, he threw himself to the floor and kissed the man's feet.

"Get up! What's the matter?" exclaimed the religious.

"Tell me," replied Philip, still astonished, "what is your name?"

"I am Ignatius of Loyola—and my companion is Francis Xavier, whom God has given me to preach His word in distant lands."

It was the meeting of three great saints!

* * *

No matter how distinguished Philip's visitors were, however, they found him working at ordinary tasks. Often he would greet them with an apron on and his shirt sleeves rolled up. He had been scrubbing pots in the kitchen!

He went to great lengths to be humble. Often when he was to meet the most important people he would dress in a fantastic costume, or with his clothes inside out and long white shoes on his feet. Sometimes he would strut through the streets carrying a huge bunch of brooms in his hand like a bouquet of flowers, pausing every now and then to sniff them. He would do anything to make people think he was foolish. This not only hid his holiness but it also made people laugh–and that was very important to him.

Why was laughter so important? Because he felt that one cannot advance in the spiritual life unless he is cheerful. "Never commit sin, and be always cheerful," was his favorite advice. "A cheerful soul attains perfection quickly." He was convinced that a happy heart is a sign of innocence.

When boys and young men played games in the house, often bouncing a ball against the wall of Philip's room, the other priests protested against the noise. "Don't listen to them," Philip told the boys. "Go on playing."

"How can you put up with that racket?" a visitor asked.

"They may chop wood on my back," Philip replied, "as long as they keep out of sin."

Mischief might have been Philip's middle name. He took delight in the ridiculous. One day at a wedding he intoned the penitential psalm, *Miserere*.

* * *

The celebration of Holy Mass became an almost continuous ecstasy for Philip. Often he was seen suspended in the air, as if he wished to ascend to Heaven. Often he would burst into tears or start to tremble from head to foot; at other times he would become as still as a statue, his gaze directed upward.

At last, he began to celebrate Mass in a separate cell where no one would see him. After the

Agnus Dei, he would ask the altar boy to leave and not return until he was called. It was not unusual for the altar boy to wait two hours before Philip called him. He would find the saint pale and trembling.

When he was nearly eighty, Philip fell sick. Cardinal Frederick Borromeo, brother of Charles Borromeo, brought him Viaticum. Philip received the Eucharist with great joy, saying, "Anyone who wants anything but Jesus, does not know what he wants. All is vanity."

One of his young friends looked worried. "Are you afraid?" asked Philip. "Well, I'm not!"

One day he got up. He confessed himself, and celebrated a high Mass. He spent the day praying, reading the lives of saints, and hearing confessions. But by six o'clock that evening he was in his death agony.

"If you don't have any more medicines," he joked with his friends, "don't worry about it. I can't use them any more."

With tears in his eyes, the Baron asked, "Father, will you leave us without saying anything? At least give us your blessing."

Philip Neri reopened his eyes, raised his gaze to Heaven, and then looked around at his attendants. He lifted a hand and blessed them weakly.

This was his last gesture. When his hand fell, his great heart stopped beating. That heart had known heavenly joys even on earth–so much so that at times Philip had cried out: "No more, Lord, no more; I cannot bear so much joy!" Now that same Lord drew near and opened new floodgates of joy.

True joy comes from avoiding sin and doing good deeds. Joy is the mark of a Christian. We, too, will find joy when we do things which please our parents and brothers and sisters, because God wants us to love them.

Saint Benedict

The Holy Moor

Benedict the Moor was a Negro, the son of Christopher and Diana Manasseri, two Christian slaves who worked on a farm on the beautiful island of Sicily in the blue Mediterranean Sea.

Since Christopher and Diana's master was quite a good man, he promised them that their first child would be set free when he reached the age of eighteen. That first child was Benedict. The name means "Blessed".

Good parents that they were, Christopher and Diana instructed Benedict and his younger brother and sisters in the Christian Faith. They instilled in the children, while they were as yet very small, a great devotion to Our Lady. Benedict especially would carry this devotion with him all through his life.

When the boy had grown into a strong young man of eighteen, he was given his freedom, as the master had promised. From that time on, he would be able to choose his own occupation. As a slave, he had tended sheep; now, as a free man, he decided to buy a team of oxen and hire himself out as a plowman.

Sturdy and able, Benedict spent the next three years walking the furrow behind the plow. Most of his pay was given to his parents, whom he loved so much. Some went to the poor and needy. Benedict kept almost nothing for himself.

Everyone liked the cheerful, generous young man. They could see that he was very good. In fact, they began to call him, "The Holy Moor."

But there was prejudice in those days just as there is in these. Some of the neighboring youths did not like Negroes. One day they met Benedict on the road. Making a ring around him, they started to make fun of him, of his parents, and of *all* Negroes!

Taller and muscular, Benedict could have probably whipped the lot of them single handed. And who would blame him if he did? But he was a follower of Christ, and Him crucified. No matter how much anger was bubbling and boiling around inside of him, he couldn't let it out. He stood there and took it.

Someone had been watching this episode. Now he strode forward, and spoke sharply to the youths: "In a few years, this man's name will be famous!"

The boys looked surprised, then ashamed—for the man who was speaking to them was a holy her-

mit named Jerome, of whom they were very fond.
Murmuring apologies, they walked away, leaving
the two men of God in peace.

Benedict thanked Jerome warmly, and the two
parted company, but only for a few days. Soon Jerome was back, with the invitation: "Sell your team
and come to our hermitage with me!"

Maybe Benedict had been thinking of something like that already, for he was quick to carry
out the idea. He sold the team, said goodbye to his
parents, and joined the Franciscan hermits in their
woodland retreat.

What a severe life the hermits led! Only the
strong could practice all the penances and mortifications of those Franciscans. Strength of body was
something Benedict had. He soon showed that he
had strength of spirit, too. The secret of his success—
was the same as the secret of any saint's success—
the grace of God, given through the hands of His
loving Mother Mary.

The people of the countryside had not forgotten
Benedict. They came to visit him in his forest hide-
away. For them, he was "the Holy Moor," and as
time went on that reputation spread and spread. At
last the Franciscans became worried. How could
they pray in peace, with so many people coming
and going? They must move.

They moved. Not once, but three times. Everywhere they went, people got wind of it, and came
flocking to speak with Benedict, to tell him their
troubles and ask for his prayers. Would so much
attention make the Moor proud? So far, it hadn't,

but there was always that danger. "But we can't keep moving forever," moaned one of the hermits. And so, they agreed to just stay where they were and make the best of the situation.

It was not long after that that the Pope issued a new decree. All the hermits were to enter the regular religious orders. So the little band of hermits to which Benedict belonged, broke up, and each went to the monastery of his choice. Benedict himself asked permission to enter a Franciscan monastery near Palermo, and he was accepted.

One of the first assignments he was given was that of cook. And, of course, since he did everything well, he was a very good cook indeed. But when it came time to elect a new Superior, Benedict found out to his surprise that *he* had been chosen!

The brothers had made a wise choice. They had known that he was the kind of man who will spend himself tirelessly for others. He would never give up in time of difficulty, but would go on and on, asking God and His Mother for guidance and doing his very best to carry out their wishes.

Benedict was a perfect example to the brothers. He did all the hard work, all the dull work—everything that was usually given to the lowliest brothers to do. What an example he set! The other brothers began to watch him with admiration and to imitate him.

Benedict was Superior for three years and then assistant to the new Superior for another three. After that—what do you think? He became cook again! And what a relief it was for him. Benedict was a good leader, but he had always preferred to be a follower, as Jesus had been at Nazareth.

As they had in the old days in the forest, people came flocking to see the humble cook, to pour out their troubles to him, to ask his wise advice, to beg for his prayers which were known to work many miracles.

Benedict was one of those saints who had the grace of seeing the Blessed Mother and of holding the Infant Jesus in his arms. In fact, once the Infant Jesus embraced him!

When Benedict was on his deathbed, as humble as ever, he begged the brothers to forgive him all the faults he had committed against them. His last words were those of Our Lord Himself: "Father, into Thy hands I commend my spirit."

People loved Benedict because of his humility. We can practice humility, too, by giving in to the good opinions and desires of our companions.

Saint Stanislaus Kostka

Angelic Novice

"Why, what has happened to Stanislaus?" the guest asked, horrified. The little boy had crumpled in a heap to the floor.

Embarrassed, the child's father stooped over and picked him up. "It's my fault," he murmured sheepishly as he carried the lad out of the room.

"You see," explained another member of the family as the guest still looked confused, "the boy cannot bear the sound of any obscene language. We generally warn our guests, but this time we forgot!"

Yes, even from his childhood, Stanislaus was remarkable for his purity. He loved God so much that he could not stand the thought of anything that would mar that delicate virtue.

As he grew older, his attitude was unchanged. When at the age of fourteen he went with his brother Paul and a tutor to attend a Jesuit school in Austria, Stanislaus refused to join his comrades in their worldly living. While they went out to parties, he practiced prayer and penance. He joined the Congregation of St. Barbara, and led such a model life that brother Paul became thoroughly annoyed.

"He's trying to shame me," thought Paul. He started making fun of his brother, and when this did not seem to bother Stanislaus, Paul began to strike and beat him. But Stanislaus took it all cheerfully. "Jesus," he prayed, "I offer this little suffering to You so that You will make Paul change his ways."

But Stanislaus' health was very delicate. It always had been. The blows he received from Paul so often upset him. He became ill.

"Paul," begged Stanislaus one day as he lay very sick in his bed, "please call for a priest. I may be dying."

"No," retorted Paul. "You know that the landlord doesn't want any priests on his property!" He walked out, and left the sick boy alone.

Stanislaus remembered that his patron, St. Barbara, never let anyone who was devoted to her die without receiving Holy Communion. "St. Barbara, please come to help me, " he prayed fervently.

And lo! St. Barbara herself appeared before him! Two Angels were with her, and one of them was holding the Holy Host. He gave Stanislaus Holy Communion.

But what was that radiant glow? A Lady was advancing toward him, with a Child in her arms. Stanislaus was dazzled by the splendor. He knew that it was the Blessed Virgin herself. She placed the Infant Jesus right in Stanislaus' arms and when the Infant had vanished, the boy found he was completely well.

Stanislaus went to the nearest Jesuit house and begged to be admitted. But the priests were afraid to do so. They knew that the boy's father was a rich, powerful noble in Poland. They knew that he wouldn't want his son to enter religion. In short, they were afraid of getting into trouble. "But go to Rome," they urged. "Seek admission at the Novitiate in Rome!"

Eagerly the boy set out on his journey. He was dressed in rags, like a beggar, and carried a traveler's staff. He walked from town to town. On the way he stopped at a Jesuit house in Bavaria, where St. Peter Canisius was Superior. He spent a little while there, helping in the kitchen. Everyone was impressed by the humility and obedience of the nobleman's son.

When he arrived in Rome, Stanislaus was admitted into the Jesuit Novitiate by St. Francis Borgia, the Superior General. The boy became a very good religious—so cheerful in his obedience, so prayerful and devoted to the Society, that he pleased everyone.

And yet . . . Stanislaus kept remembering how radiant the Blessed Mother had looked when she appeared to him. He recalled how it felt to hold the Child Jesus. "Mother," he prayed, "on the next celebration of the Feast of your Assumption, take me to Heaven to be with you!"

His prayer was granted. It was less than a year after his arrival in Rome that Stanislaus became very ill. On the Feast of the Assumption, 1568, his pure soul sped to Heaven.

St. Stanislaus always longed for his homeland, Heaven. When something pleasant happens, let us think that Heaven will be much more wonderful, and let us say a prayer to Our Lady to help us reach it.

Saint Camillus de Lellis

Patron of the Sick

It was a beautiful spring day, the twenty-fifth of May, 1550. All nature seemed joyful.

Camilla, the wife of Captain John de Lellis, was about to give birth to a child, in spite of the fact that she was past middle age. Knowing that her baby would soon be born, she had herself taken, in humility, to a stable; there baby Camillus first saw the light of day.

Neighbors asked each other, "What will this child become, born of such an elderly mother?" They thought, and so did Camilla, that he would be the honor of the family and the consolation of his parents.

Instead, they soon saw that Camillus was of a rebellious nature, reckless and quarrelsome, given to throwing off discipline and restraint.

"We must correct him!" said his father.

His mother, of course, was gentler, but she suffered from his conduct too.

They would tell him he was doing wrong, and when he was small Camillus would tremble in fear and obey, but the older he grew, the less attention he paid to the corrections. He did more and more as he pleased.

How sad his mother Camilla felt! She wept and wept, and prayed that God would touch the heart of her irresponsible son.

"So!" exclaimed his father after an especially rebellious act. "If you're going to be like this, you'll have to leave my house!" And he sent Camillus out on his own.

Camillus became absorbed in gambling, attracted to bad company, and lost among the vanities of the world. He had his moments of remorse and deep discontent–probably caused by memories of his holy mother–but these passed quickly, and he continued to gamble as before.

Then a sore formed on the top of his right foot. It was not large, but it was a great nuisance, especially for a young man with his nose in the air like Camillus!

He went to the St. James Hospital in Rome and had the sore tended. When he was well enough to be up and about, someone suggested that he help the other sick people while finishing his own recovery. True to form–independent and lazy–Camillus said, "No."

At last he was discharged from the hospital. And where was he going now, this impulsive young man of nineteen? Well, it was a time of war, and Camillus was a captain's son. So then, he became a soldier of fortune! He led a very unstable life, and was always in some fight or adventure. Was he happy? Not at all, but he continued to lead his wild and reckless life until discharged from the army.

Now Camillus had no more money. How should he make a living? Well, construction work was as good a way as any, so he became a workman on a new Capuchin monastery that was being built. And that was when God's grace touched him.

He could have rejected the grace and forgotten about it. But Camillus was now fed up with the world. He could see that it had nothing to offer him. So when the invitation came: "Repent, my son;" it seemed to whisper, "Serve Me!" Camillus listened to it. He mulled it over and decided to speak to Father Angelo, a holy Capuchin monk. By the end of the conversation, Camillus was a changed man.

So Camillus became a Capuchin. Ah, but how far a saint must go to become a saint! How many difficulties he must overcome; how many disappointments he must bear! The sore on his foot broke out again.

That sore made him unfit for the strict life of a Capuchin, so Camillus had to leave the order and get it healed. He left not once, but three times! What a blow it must have been to him each time he was sent away! Yet more trials lay ahead.

Camillus went back to St. James Hospital, and began to care for the sick–especially those who had no hope of ever getting well. He did everything he could to make them happy.

"How careless some of the attendants are!" he thought. They didn't seem to realize that the poor sick they cared for were human beings just like themselves. They were so rough and unkind! "One should be dedicated to God's service if one is going to serve the sick well," decided Camillus, "and since our Lord does not wish me to be a Capuchin monk, why don't I dedicate myself entirely to the sick?"

Of course, there would be a lot of sacrifice involved. He didn't mind the thought of it for himself, for by now he was eager to give himself to God in every way he could–but it might be hard to find followers generous enough to embrace a life so contrary to natural liking. Who would want to tend such horrible and disgusting diseases? Who would run the risk of death daily, and sacrifice precious hours of sleep nightly–and all for the love of the Suffering Christ?

Camillus soon found other problems, too–so many, in fact, that one night in a dream he poured out a long stream of woes to his bedside crucifix and begged for help in a tone of desperation.

"You're a weak one, Camillus!" The crucifix replied. "What are you afraid of? Go ahead, go ahead! I am with you!"

It was only a dream, but what more inspiration does a spiritual man need?

He went ahead!

Another trial, another plea before the crucifix. And this time it was not a dream. Camillus had just asked, "O Lord, will it *always* be this way?" when the arms of the image of Jesus detached themselves from the cross and stretched out toward him. "Camillus, go ahead without fear. This is My work, not yours. I'll always help you. Go ahead!"

And so the Company of the Servants of the Sick came into being. They wore a black habit with a bright red cross on it. And their leader was now called *Father* Camillus, for he had studied and had become a priest!

What a surprise the people of his village had when he returned there to sell his property! Was this giant of a man the same little baby who was born in a stable? Was this serious priest the reckless boy they had known? It was hard to believe.

Meanwhile, as they marveled, Father Camillus calmly went about the business of selling his property and distributing the money among the poor!

In the years 1590 and 1591, a terrible epidemic swept through Rome, taking many lives. Hunger added to the misery, so that the people who survived looked like walking skeletons. Often someone would fall over right in the street and lie there dead, and no one would come and carry away the body because everybody had too much else to worry about. Misery and tears—they were everywhere.

Through the midst of all this suffering moved big, broad-shouldered Father Camillus, the red cross blazing on his chest. Wherever he went, he brought comfort and consolation. Once, when he was tending some plague-stricken people in the street, he saw a fine carriage approaching, full of important citizens.

"Coachman, coachman!" called the priest. As the carriage pulled to a stop, he hurried over and asked the men inside, "Gentlemen, there's a man here who is very ill and must be taken to Holy Spirit Hospital. Would you be willing. . . ?"

The gentlemen dismounted from the coach, and Father Camillus placed the sick man inside— and then as many other sick as he could fit. He smiled happily as he watched the full carriage roll away toward the hospital.

There are very many stories which could be told about St. Camillus, for he was so humble and good! For example, one day a sick man whom he was tending said to him, "Father, could you remake my bed? It's very hard!"

"You said something wrong, my brother," replied the priest.

"Why, Father?"

"Because you asked as one making a plea and not as one giving an order. Do you not yet see that I'm your servant and your slave?"

To another poor sick man who was crying, he said, "I want to spend myself for you. Don't cry; I am your slave; command me!"

Then there was another unfortunate whom no one would go near, for his entire face was disfigured by the most horrible cancer, giving off the most unbearable smell.

But Camillus dared to care for him. Not only that, he would hold the man in his arms, place his face close to his, and rock him like a baby. After tending this man, the priest would drop to his knees beside the bed. "Praised be the Lord! I have served His Divine Majesty!"

Almost four hundred years have passed since the death of St. Camillus. But his work lives on. Science has brought many technical improvements to medicine, but a continuing source of spiritual consolation for the sick is the same as it was in Camillus' own time—it is found in the dedicated lives of religious who serve the sick, the spiritual children of St. Camillus.

St. Camillus was so good to the sick because in them he served Jesus suffering. If we feel dislike for a person, let us remember that Jesus suffered and died for that person.

Saint Aloysius

Patron of Youth

The tiny baby, slumbering so peacefully, was the son of a prince—and his father was already dreaming of a royal future for his child.

"We'll make a great soldier of him!" This boy, his first son, would carry on the great family name of Gonzaga; he would be the bravest of fighters, the most honored of men.

And, indeed, that baby *would be* both brave and honored, but not in the way his father intended. There is a bravery much greater than that found on the battlefield, and a glory much more lasting than that of a few years' reign.

Little Aloysius' mother was of a very different character than his father. She loved to pray and to think about God; the passing joys of this world meant little to her. Perhaps it was she who taught the little boy to love the things of the spirit. At any rate, as he grew, the child resembled his mother more than his father.

That didn't mean that he was a coward. He was as daring as any other boy. When he was seven, his father took him with him to visit an army camp. Aloysius, attracted by a small cannon nearby, decided that he could fire it himself. He had seen it done often. It would be fun to try. . . . Quick as a wink, the boy ran over to the cannon and set off the charge of powder like a real cannoneer.

The big gun jerked backward. This was the recoil from the big, booming shot Aloysius had fired. The force of the jolt sent the boy spinning away, and his father and a soldier who had seen all this were afraid that he had been seriously hurt or even killed. They ran over to Aloysius, only to be met by a boyish grin. Aloysius was as calm as if he had been playing with a toy.

Of course, his father was delighted. "What a soldier we will make of him!"

So Aloysius grew, and his father's hopes rose. When the boy was twelve, a fire broke out in his room one night. A candle, which served as a night light, had toppled over and set fire to the bed curtains. The brightness of the flames awakened the boy, who jumped up quickly and found something to throw on top of the blaze to smother it. Indeed, here was a brave and cool-headed lad!

"Ah, yes!" exclaimed the Marquis Gonzaga. "My son will make a splendid soldier indeed!"

But, as we have said, there was another side to Aloysius' character. He had picked up many expressions from his father's soldiers. One day, when he found out that these words were vulgar, he fainted from shock. Why? Because such language offended God, Who is all-pure.

The Archbishop of Milan, Charles Borromeo (also destined to become a great saint), gave Jesus to Aloysius in First Holy Communion with his own hands. As Aloysius knelt in adoration, treasuring that union which is the closest of all unions, he told Jesus in the depths of his heart, "I am Yours—completely— and I always will be!" It was about the same time in his life that the boy consecrated his purity to God and asked the Blessed Virgin to protect his innocence for life.

Jesus had suffered on the cross for love of men— for love of *each* man. Aloysius wanted to suffer too, to show his love for Jesus. He made mortifications. He tried not to take the most delicious food; he avoided wearing the most handsome clothing. He put bits of wood in his bed at night, so as to have some pain to suffer. Any pleasures which his nature might want to enjoy, his spirit told him to ignore.

*   *   *

The boy was now in his early teens. He was at the age when young nobles entered into the gay, glittering, worldly life of the royal court. Of course, Aloysius' father wanted the best for his son, so he sent him and his younger brother to become pages in the court of King Philip II of Spain. We can imagine what Aloysius must have felt, since court life was exactly what he wanted to avoid at all costs!

But obedient as ever, Aloysius determined to make the best of it. He entered the life of the royal court, and mixed in well with everybody. He was well-liked, for he was intelligent, handsome, polite, and always had something interesting to say. Yet he still tried not to dress richly, nor to take the best food.

He felt that he had to imitate the poverty of Jesus in a small way at least.

Aloysius lived at the time of the great Spanish saints. Only a few years before, a wounded Spanish soldier had decided to found a new army of Christ. His name was Ignatius of Loyola, and the spiritual army he began was called the Jesuit Order—a dedicated band of priests and brothers. Aloysius had heard much about them, and he longed to become one of them!

What would his father say? Aloysius knew very well what he would say: "The son of the Marquis Gonzaga a priest? Never!" And yet, Aloysius *had* to tell him. . . .

Surprise, anger, blind rage—that was the reaction of the marquis to his son's request. "I forbid you to become a priest!" When Marquis Gonzaga's temper cooled somewhat, he began to make systematic plans for detaching Aloysius' heart from God, and making him love the things of this world. Exposure to plenty of temptations would take care of everything, the marquis decided.

So Aloysius was recalled from the Spanish court and sent on missions to various cities to act as his father's representative. He was very young for such an assignment, but he had great ability and carried out his duties well. Of course, he had to meet often with princes and officials and had to attend balls and dinners and parties without end. It was a gay, glittering life, and as the boy's father had foreseen, there were temptations on all sides. But Aloysius remained pure.

Not only that–his purity made others think twice about the things they were doing and saying. For instance, there was the time when he and an elderly gentleman were waiting to be received by Aloysius' uncle, the Archbishop of Turin. The elderly gentleman looked distinguished, but his speech was vulgar. Sixteen-year-old Aloysius turned to him and asked softly, "Sir, aren't you ashamed of yourself to be speaking like that at your age?"

The gentleman looked at Aloysius in stunned silence. Shame filled his eyes. The remark had hit home.

One day there was a tournament in Milan, and all the young noblemen were asked to join in. Aloysius put on the beautiful garments that young men of his rank always wore on such occasions, but instead of choosing a sleek, fiery warhorse, he picked an old, broken-down nag to ride through the streets. The crowds laughed at him. Insult after insult followed him. How humiliating it must have been for him to do that! Yet that was exactly Aloysius' reason for doing it; he wanted to mortify his pride for the good of his soul.

A ball was given one evening for Aloysius' brother, and of course, Aloysius was expected to attend it.

He did not want to dance, and when asked to do so, he left the room. In fact, he did not return. Finally, someone went to look for him. Where did they find him, but in a quiet room in another part of the castle, praying intently.

The Marquis Gonzaga's plans did not seem to be working out so well. His boy was as other-worldly as ever. Even the urgings of Aloysius' closest friends could not cause him to abandon his ideal: the Jesuits were still his heart's desire. At last the exasperated father asked him point blank: would he obey him and forget all this foolishness or not?

"I will not, Father." There are times when God must be obeyed rather than men.

"Then take yourself out of my sight, and come back only when you have changed your mind!"

Aloysius left the room, tears in his eyes, and sought the Lord in prayer. "Tell me, Lord, what should I do?" He knelt on his bedroom floor and scourged himself with a whip. "Tell me, Lord! Tell me, Lord!" He wanted to sacrifice himself for God, and there seemed to be no way to do it.

Aloysius had scourged himself many times before, but this time he was watched, without his knowing it. The person who saw him, hurried away to find the Marquis Gonzaga. He told him what his son had done. This, at last, was too much for the proud father. "The Lord wants him? Then He shall have him!" Aloysius would be free to enter the Jesuits.

How happy was the young prince as he put aside forever the fine clothes of his rank, and donned the plain habit of a Jesuit! Now he was poor like Jesus. For the rest of his life, he would be poor like Jesus.

Now the noise and distractions of the world were behind. At last Aloysius could settle down to a life of prayer and penance. His heart burned with love for God, so much so that at times he begged, "My Lord, withdraw from me a little!" The love he felt was more than he could bear.

He learned to do each one of his new duties well. Every day he worked upon himself to become more humble, more obedient, more pure. He still had a great desire to sacrifice himself–the same desire which had led him into the religious life.

In the year 1591 a terrible plague broke out in Rome. The hospitals were soon filled to overflowing, and people began to die in their homes and even in the streets with no one to help or comfort them.

The Jesuit Fathers hurriedly opened a hospital of their own, and Aloysius went about the city in patched clothing begging money to buy food for the sick patients. He who had been a nobleman himself now begged from the most wealthy princes.

Aloysius helped in the hospitals as well. He tended the sick tenderly, dressing their wounds, washing their feet, making their beds, carrying them in his arms, and comforting them in every way he could. He tried to prepare the dying for a good confession and a holy death.

One day he saw a poor man who was so diseased that no one could go near him. "Here is Jesus," Aloysius thought. He went over to the man and picked him up in his arms. He carried him to the hospital and found him a bed. It was the same day that Aloysius felt himself very warm and dizzy. By evening he was very ill. He, too, had the plague!

His fellow religious did everything they could to help him, but it was clear right from the start that Aloysius would not live long. In those times, people did not have the medical knowledge and equipment that would have been needed to save him.

For three months the youth lay in a little white bed, while the fever burned inside him. "God's will be done," he thought. He would have liked to serve Him longer, but first and foremost he wanted to do what the Lord Himself wished of him. In this time of pain, prayer as usual was his consolation.

And so, peacefully, on June 21, 1591, Aloysius passed away. He was carried up into a glory far surpassing the earthly fame which his father had desired so stubbornly for him.

Now, from Heaven he watches over all Christian youth, for he has been named their special patron.

Christians have to be brave, and St. Aloysius is a fine example of courage. Let us be brave especially in admitting our guilt with humility, when we have done something wrong.

Saint Jane Frances de Chantal

Model of Fortitude

Jane was the daughter of a nobleman who lived in Burgundy. She loved her religion even when she was very small.

One day a visiting nobleman told Jane's father, "I do not believe that Jesus is present in the tabernacle."

Five-year-old Jane was horrified. "But, Sir," she protested, "you *must* believe that Jesus Christ is in the Blessed Sacrament! He Himself said so! If you do not believe it, you are making Him a liar!"

The nobleman looked surprised. He started to argue with Jane, but she knew her catechism—and her Gospel—too well for him! She had the right answer to everything he said!

At last, the guest tried to change the subject. "How would you like a piece of candy?" he asked.

Little Jane took the candy, but instead of eating it, she went over to the fireplace with it and threw it into the flames. "There!" she exclaimed. "That is how people will burn in the fire of hell, if they do not believe the words of Jesus Christ!"

It was the best way Jane could think of to convince the nobleman to change his ways before it was too late!

As she grew older, Jane loved her Faith more and more. Her mother had died when she was young, and the governess who took care of her was very worldly. So Jane prayed to the Blessed Virgin to keep her safe and pure. This Our Lady did.

From the time of her First Communion, Jane had desired to serve God in some way. During her teen years, she served Him by helping the sick and the poor. Now she desired to serve Him as a wife and mother.

Baron Christopher de Chantal was the man Jane married. He was a very good Christian. The couple dedicated each of their children to the Blessed Mother, and raised them in a real Christian atmosphere. Their family life was very happy.

But then sorrow struck. Christopher was killed accidentally by a hunting companion! It was a terrible shock to Jane, for she and Christopher had been deeply in love. But when she recovered from her first grief, Jane pardoned the man who had killed her husband, and later became the godmother of his son!

It wasn't long before friends and relatives were urging her to remarry. After all, that was the usual thing. But Jane surprised them. "I have made a vow of chastity," she said.

She took care of the children for the next few years, wanting to make sure that they grew up well educated and virtuous and able to take care of themselves. At last she decided that they would be able to do without her. She told the family that she was planning to enter religion!

This was a hard step to take. It is painful to part from people we love, and Jane had been a very loving mother. A lot of courage was needed, especially since her relatives were begging her not to leave. Jane said goodbye to each one, with tears in her eyes. She turned to leave the house–and there was her teenage son lying stretched across the doorway!

"If you go, Mother, you'll have to step over me."

Jane summoned up all the courage she had. She stepped over the boy. Kneeling at the feet of her father, a grief-stricken old man, she asked his blessing. He blessed her, and she left.

St. Francis de Sales, the Bishop of Geneva and one of the firmest defenders of Catholicism, had asked Jane to collaborate in the foundation of a new religious order, the Order of the Visitation. Humility and meekness were to be the foundation of the community's rule, and for the sisters St. Francis de Sales wrote his famous treatise, "On the Love of God."

Mother de Chantal founded many convents in cities throughout France. In the face of all kinds of obstacles, she was always meek and patient, as St. Francis had encouraged her and her followers to be. She won the admiration of everyone.

Many trials awaited her. First, St. Francis died, then many of her close relatives, including the son who had tried to keep her from leaving home a few years before. Then, too, she had interior sufferings and spiritual dryness which no one but she knew about. She always appeared calm and cheerful, in spite of all that she was suffering.

St. Jane Frances de Chantal died in 1641, after a long life of trying always to do the will of God.

One of her favorite expressions through the years had been: "May God's will be done—today, tomorrow and forever—without an *if* or a *but!*"

When our parents and teachers give us something difficult to do, let us realize that this is what God wishes of us, and try to do it well, no matter how hard it may be.

Saint Germaine

Shepherdess of Pibrac

She was very pale and worn—this fragile little girl—but a light seemed to glow from her face as if the features were transparent. At first, a person would not notice the swollen glands in her neck, and her partly paralyzed right arm and hand.

Germaine had been sickly from birth, and most people would have felt sorry for a little girl so delicate. But Germaine's stepmother, for some strange reason, disliked the child bitterly, even though Germaine tried so hard to please her.

"Let me do this for you!" she would say. Or, "How would you like that thing done?"

But it was useless; no matter how hard Germaine tried to do everything well, she was given a beating and kicking almost once every day by the harsh stepmother. And she didn't flinch an inch. She just stood and took it without a word—as weak as she was. Always, Germaine's body was scarred and bruised. Often her face was bloody and puffed out of shape.

The little girl's daily food was a crust or two of black bread. Her clothes were rags. Her sleeping place was a pile of leaves under a stairway of the barn.

Each day Germaine went out to the pasture with the sheep, taking a distaff with her in order to spin wool during the day so that she might bring it home to her stepmother. There in the fields, the village children—the only souls who loved her—would gather around the young shepherdess eagerly.

"Tell us a story from the catechism," they would beg. And Germaine would think back to one of the lessons she had learned on Sundays, when she went to classes after Mass (the only schooling she had ever had), and would explain the catechism in such a beautiful, clear, different way that the children listened spellbound.

"How good God is!" Germaine would tell the children. "How much He loves us. We must show our love for Him by being very kind and patient."

Like St. Patrick, Germaine learned about God from the beautiful loneliness of the fields and hills, beneath His wide, blue sky. She made a little cross of twigs and a rosary of knotted string. She spoke to Him in prayer and then waited and listened to His quiet voice in her heart.

So Germaine worked and prayed, smiled and suffered until one summer night when she was twenty-two years old. On that night, two monks not far from the barn where she slept, saw a band of virgins, clothed in light, coming down from Heaven and then going up again with another maiden even more radiant with light than they. The next day the villagers discovered that Germaine was dead.

What sorrow there was then! Now that they saw Germaine's face peaceful in death, now that she no longer walked smiling among them, they realized that she had been a saint.

They buried her in a new dress, with a wreath of flowers on her head and a candle in her hand.

But Germaine's story did not end there. In a way, it was just beginning, for in the centuries that followed, great miracles, and many of them, were worked through her intercession. She who had seemed so unimportant in life turned out to be a joy unending to the gaze of God.

It is not so important to be popular as it is to be good. When our friends wish us to do something that offends God, let us put God's approval before theirs.

Saint Rose of Lima

Flower of the Andes

The first saint of the Americas was born in Lima, Peru, on April 20, 1586. Her father was Spanish; her mother, part Indian. Christened Isabel, the baby was renamed Rose because her mother found a rose in the little one's cradle. We know her today as St. Rose of Lima.

She was both beautiful and religious as a child. Once, when about four or five, she was playing with her brother. To be mean, he plastered some thick, gooey mud on her gleaming curls.

"Stop that!" cried Rose.

"You're making an awful fuss," retorted the mischievous boy. "Don't you know that the fires of hell will burn a girl's hair if she's proud of it?"

Rose's attitude changed immediately, and she burst into tears. Determined not to let pride come between her and Heaven, she hastily cut off her bright, coppery curls. Her furious parents punished her, but she took the punishment calmly.

When she was five, Rose made a private vow of virginity, so as to always love Jesus and no one else. She asked the Blessed Virgin to help her keep this vow forever.

From her mother, Rose had inherited a very timid nature. They were so afraid of the dark that they would never enter an unlighted room. When Rose was at prayer, however, the dark did not bother her, because her mind and heart were entirely centered on God.

One night, when she was praying in a shack in the garden, Rose lingered longer than usual. Her mother became afraid that something had happened to the girl. Perhaps she had become ill. Too timid to run down to the shack alone, she called Rose's father, and they went out into the dark together.

When the girl saw her parents coming, she stopped her prayers and apologized for having taken so long. Then, while returning to the house with her parents, she asked herself, "If Mother, as timid as I, feels safe when Daddy is with her, how can my heart be fearful when Jesus, my Spouse, is always with me?" This reflection impressed her so much that she lost all her fear of the dark.

Young as she was, Rose understood that suffering can become an avenue of God's graces. Willingly accepted, does it not make one resemble God's Son? Did He not once have a crown of thorns upon His head and spikes in His hands and feet?

Thus to be like Jesus, Rose found many opportunities to suffer. For instance, often she ate only bread and water, or nothing at all! As she grew older, she found other mortifications: rubbing painful chemicals on her hands, placing stinging plants in her gloves, scourging herself until blood flowed. When granted permission, she moved out of the house into the shack in the garden, where she made a bed of bricks and roots, piling them in such a way that the pain they produced kept her awake most of the night. When her mother suggested that she wear a crown of roses, Rose did so, but she made sure that the crown was lined with thorns to prick her head.

Not all saints have the joy of seeing Jesus or Mary before they reach Heaven, but Rose was one of those who received that great grace. Jesus came to visit her several times, appearing as a Child her own age.

Rose's devotion to Mary was intense. She confided in her and relied upon her. At times—dozing off after a night of pain—she would beg Jesus' Mother to wake her in time for Mass. When she awoke, she would see the Blessed Mother's face for an instant in the rays of the morning sun.

The girl was also visited by one of those wonderful beings who give us so many good thoughts, and often save us from dangers without our even knowing about it. It was her Guardian Angel, who came to pray with her, comfort her, and teach her holy things.

As the years passed, Rose grew more and more severe in her mortifications. She would drag a heavy wooden cross about the garden and scourge herself with an iron chain, because she wished to suffer as much of Our Lord's Passion as she could.

She joined the Third Order of St. Dominic, as St. Catherine of Siena had done, and donned the Dominican habit. Over its veil she wore a crown of roses, but hidden underneath the veil was an *iron* crown, from which ninety-nine spikes pierced the flesh of her head!

Once Jesus had asked two of His Apostles if they could drink from the chalice of His Passion; Rose was a soul who could, and did.

Hardly anyone knew of her sufferings, for she endured them in the way Our Lord had taught, secretly and silently. Everything painful which she wore was hidden, and her other bodily mortifications were practiced in the shack or the secluded garden. Thus, when Rose went among the people they saw no sign of sufferings; all that they saw was her joy.

She was *full* of joy, as is anyone who endures pain for love of God. The more she suffered for Him, the more He filled her soul with His peace. And Rose went among the people, taking Him to them with her good words and kind deeds. She helped and prayed for the sick and the poor; she counseled those of weak faith.

Rose's apostolate had a hidden side, too. Her prayers and mortifications were offered to God for the salvation of the souls with whom she came in daily contact, for other souls whom she had never met, and for souls being purified in the flames of purgatory.

When Rose was thirty-one, she was overtaken by a terrible illness. Knowing that her life was almost over, she asked God for still more suffering and an even greater degree of love for Him. He granted her both graces: she endured more and more pain, and felt a stronger and stronger love for Jesus. Then, on August 24, 1617, she died. Many, many miracles were wrought after Rose's death. They were an extra witness to the holiness of her life, spent so unselfishly for the salvation of souls.

Although boys and girls should not perform big penances without the permission of a priest, they can make many small ones each day, for instance, by studying an extra few minutes when they would rather be playing, or by helping around the house when they have not even been asked to do so.

Saint Martin de Porres

Everyone's Brother

"Martin! Martin! Where are you? Come quickly!"

"Yes Mother," called ten-year-old Martin. He came running around the corner of the house, with his little sister Jane right behind him. "Here I am."

"You must go to the market to buy a few vegetables. This is the only money we have left, so be careful. . . ."

"Mother," Martin cut in, "you look worried. Smile. You are so beautiful when you smile!"

And who could resist the boy's wide grin? The worried woman's dark face broke into a bright smile, which was as beautiful as Martin had said. "Flatterer. Run along now, you and Jane, but be careful of the money. And hurry home!"

"Yes, Mother! Bye, Mother!" The two children set off for the market, looking neither to right nor left, for Martin had a soft heart for beggars, and he was afraid that if he saw one, he would give him the money which they needed so much themselves.

"Martin," asked Jane, her little face all screwed up into a frown, "why are we poor now if we weren't before?"

"Because Daddy has been away so long now and has not sent any money. It is hard for Mother to earn enough money by herself."

"Oh, Martin, don't look over there!"

"What is it?" asked Martin, and of course he looked at once. There was a ragged beggar asking for alms. "Come on," he said to Jane, and hurried by the poor man.

"Just a little charity," he heard the beggar pleading.

Mother had told him that these were the last coins they had. Martin started to walk faster, then he stopped. Mother wouldn't have let the beggar starve either. Turning back, he held out the money and said, "In the name of God, take this!"

How happy the beggar was. "Thank you, thank you!" he said. "May God bless you!"

Martin and Jane started back toward the house. They walked slowly and dragged their feet. When they came to the big cathedral of Lima, Martin said, "Come, Jane, let's go inside and say a prayer that God will send us some food."

The two children tiptoed down the great dim cathedral to the altar rail. They genuflected and knelt silently. Martin began to pray, "Dear Jesus, please send us some food. I just gave our last money to a poor beggar. Now we will have to go without supper. And please, dear Lord, don't let Mother be angry. Thank you."

"Amen," said Jane.

Martin and Jane genuflected and left the cathedral. The boy's heart felt light. He knew God would not fail him.

As soon as Martin's mother saw his face, she knew what had happened. But she knew, too, that it was no use spanking or scolding the boy. She herself had taught him to be kind to the poor. In her heart she prayed, "Dear God, please send their father home. Then we will have money for ourselves and for the poor, too!"

A few days later a horse came galloping up the street with a richly-dressed Spanish officer on its back. Martin and Jane broke out into cries of joy, "Father! Father!"

Yes, Don Juan de Porres had come to take his two children to Ecuador, where they would live with his uncle and receive some schooling.

"And what of Mother?" asked Martin anxiously.

"She will be a housekeeper for a nice lady here in Lima," the father replied. "She will be waiting for you when you come back a few years from now."

So Martin and little Jane went to live with their great uncle. He was very kind to them and hired very good tutors so that they learned many interesting things. Martin was a good pupil, who learned his lessons quickly. Soon he had learned everything that was necessary, so his father said, "Jane should stay here with Uncle James until she is old enough to marry, but I shall take you back to Lima, Martin, where you will be near your mother. You shall study as a barber's apprentice. I hope you will study hard and will always be a good Christian."

"I will do my best, Daddy," the serious twelve-year-old replied. "I will learn to be a good barber, and I will be a good Christian always."

Barbers in those days were doctors as well! They knew how to bind up wounds, to treat fevers, to set broken bones and mix drugs. They had all the medical knowledge of the times. "What a great thing it is to be a barber's apprentice!" Martin told his mother. "Now I can help the poor!"

"You're a good boy, Martin," his mother smiled. "May God bless you and always keep you this way."

"That is what I pray for every morning at Holy Mass, dear Mother, and God is helping me. He makes it easier for me to learn my lessons."

Every morning Martin assisted at and served as many Masses as he could at the Church of St. Lazarus. Then he would spend the day going about the city, visiting all the sick and poor, tending and healing them without any charge. Sometimes he would spend the whole night with someone who was ill, urging them to trust in God and offer Him their sufferings.

When he was fifteen, Martin presented himself to the Prior of a Dominican Monastery. "Reverend Father, please accept me as a lay helper. Put me to do any work which the others don't wish to do, but please let me serve God here!"

The Prior had heard of Martin and his goodness. "We will be happy to have you with us, Martin," he said, "but since you are so young, we must obtain your mother's consent."

At first Martin's mother did not like the idea of his being only a lay helper. "Why not a priest or a brother at least?" she asked.

"Because I want to be unimportant," answered Martin. "I want to do little things well for love of God. Please, Mother, say I may go. Please!"

Who could resist those earnest, brown eyes? "All right, my son. May God be with you. Be whatever you like in the monastery, only pray for me."

And Martin rushed off to the monastery, where he received the white habit of the Dominican lay helpers. Now he felt that he belonged entirely to God and to His Blessed Mother.

Martin's duties were varied. He took turns being barber and keeper of the linen closet. Then he was called to help in the infirmary. He was overjoyed.

The first patient Martin visited was Father Peter. Father Peter had a badly infected leg, and the doctors had said that it would have to be cut off if his life were to be saved. Because Father Peter was in great pain, he was very impatient. Martin prepared a nice salad of fresh vegetables and olives and brought it to the door of the sick priest's room. He knocked gently.

"Go away and leave me in peace!"

Martin ignored the cold reception and walked in. "Wouldn't you like some nice, fresh salad, Father Peter?" he asked gently.

Father Peter opened his eyes right in the middle of a groan, and said in surprise, "Why I was just wishing for some salad. How did you guess it?" He sat up in bed and ate with a hearty appetite. "Thank you, Martin."

"Now let us dress your leg," Martin smiled. "If you have faith, Father Peter, I am sure God will heal it." He deftly changed the bandage as he spoke.

"Pray that He will, Martin," Father Peter exclaimed. He knew that if he were operated on, he would probably die.

As soon as he had left Father Peter, Martin hurried off to the chapel where he knelt before the tabernacle and began to pray fervently: "Please, dear Lord, heal Father Peter's leg. You have healed so many others, please heal him, too. Nothing is impossible to You."

That night, Martin went to visit Father Peter again. He found him walking about the room.

"Martin, Martin!" exclaimed Father Peter. "You have cured me! How can I thank you? Half an hour after you left me, the swelling went down and the pain disappeared. You have worked a miracle!"

"Please do not say that," Martin said. "I only changed the bandage on your leg. It is God who healed it!"

"Very well, Martin, but remember that if it had not been for your prayers, I would not have been cured."

✼ ✼ ✼

Not only was Martin the friend of all people, he was also the friend of every living creature. The birds came to him for food, as did the stray cats and dogs. He always had something for them.

One day, the Brother Sacristan found that the rats and mice had eaten some of the vestments. He went to the Prior and asked him to send Martin to get rid of them.

Martin knew that to get rid of the rats and mice he would have to kill them. But he did not feel that he could harm them. He prayed to God, then he went to the sacristy. There he saw a large rat running across the floor. "Come here," Martin called.

The rat came at once.

"Now listen carefully," Martin told him. "You and all the other rats and mice must leave this sacristy. You have been eating the vestments. God is not pleased with this. Go to live in the barn. I will bring you food there. Do you understand?"

The rat nodded his head and ran off. Soon he came back followed by a multitude of rats and mice. Martin led all of them to the barn.

The brother sacristan happened to be passing that way, when the strange procession went by. He looked on with open mouth. Then he turned and ran to tell the Prior!

From that day on, there were no more rats or mice in the sacristy.

One day the Prior announced, "Martin, you will be a lay helper no longer. You are to become a brother."

"But Reverend Father," protested Martin, "I'm not worthy."

"Let me be the judge of that. Invite your mother to the profession ceremony!"

Need we say how happy Martin's good mother was?

New duties came to Martin after his religious profession. One of them was that of feeding the poor who came begging at the monastery gate. Before he distributed the food, Martin always gave it a special blessing: "May the Lord bless and increase this food, and may He sanctify all who eat it."

This prayer was always effective. No matter how little food was on hand, no beggar was ever sent away empty-handed or hungry. Each one received enough to satisfy him.

One day when Martin took the last piece of bread from the pantry, the cook went to the Prior to complain. But the Prior answered calmly, "Do not fear. Martin will not finish it. There will still be enough for all of us too."

And the Prior was right. No matter how much Martin gave away, the brothers never lacked anything necessary. God always provided for everybody.

Martin served God as a Dominican for forty-five years. During that time he worked so many miracles that the people of Lima would have been surprised if he had failed to work one. He served God lovingly in the sick, the poor and the orphans.

Then, not long after his sixtieth birthday, Martin became very ill. He went through three days of suffering, while the poor whom he had helped gathered outside the monastery to weep and pray. Then on the fourth day Martin became calm and peaceful. The Blessed Mother and St. Dominic appeared to him to encourage him.

Martin called all the brothers together and they said the prayers for the dying. "Is there any special hymn you would like us to sing, Brother Martin?" asked the Prior.

"The Creed," was the reply.

The brothers lifted their voices in that beautiful act of faith. As the words rolled on, "God the

Father Almighty, Maker of heaven and earth, and of all things visible and invisible," Martin closed his eyes. Peacefully his soul went forth to meet Him of Whom the brothers sang. It was the third of November, 1639.

St. Martin was a friend to everyone, without making distinctions between them. We, too, should be pleasant to everyone we meet, no matter how different their family, race or religion may be from our own.

Saint John Berchmans

Patron of Altar Boys

"If I do not become a saint while I am young," John Berchmans once remarked, "I shall never become one." He died at the age of twenty-two, and numerous miracles followed his death. John had reached his goal!

He was born in Diest, Belgium, in March, 1599, the eldest son of a shoemaker. He was a lively lad, always kind and cheerful. In spite of high spirits, he liked to pray, and could often be found off in a corner, saying his rosary. By the time he was seven, he was rising early each morning and hurrying off to serve two or three Masses in the parish church.

Whenever his playmates quarreled with one another, cheerful John was right on hand to help them settle their differences and to keep peace. He never argued himself, and so had many friends

When he was nine, his mother became ill. As the oldest of the five children, John took care of her, and left her bedside only to attend school and to run errands. He was always very patient and considerate.

The following year he went to study Latin and other subjects under a priest named Father Emmerich. By this time John had decided that he would become a priest himself. Father Emmerich grew very fond of the boy, and the two of them often went on walks to various shrines in the neighborhood. At night John would pray in some secluded corner of the house.

When he was thirteen, his father said to him, "Son, I know this will disappoint you, but it will be necessary for you to stop your studies and learn a trade. I am finding it harder and harder to support the family, especially since your mother's illness."

What a blow it was to poor John! "But, Father," he protested, "if I don't continue my studies, I shall never become a priest. Is there no other way?"

John's good father looked for another way, and at last he found it. "Canon Froymont at Mechlin needs a servant," he said. "While living with him, you may continue your studies at the archdiocesan junior seminary."

"Thank you very much, Father!" exclaimed the boy. "I know Our Lord will bless our family very much because of your sacrifice!"

So John went to Mechlin to be a servant to Canon Froymont. He performed all his duties with a quiet efficiency and cheerfulness which made him liked by all. When the canon went duck hunting John went with him. Patient as usual, the boy set about training the canon's dog to retrieve the ducks as they were shot down.

In 1615, the Jesuit Fathers opened a college in Mechlin, and John enrolled himself there at once. Soon he was pleading with his father to let him enter the Society of Jesus. Finally the father gave his consent. Soon the parents received an invitation from John to come to Mechlin to say goodbye and give him back to God, Who had given him to them seventeen years before.

John made a wonderful novice. He saw God represented by each of his superiors, and so he obeyed their slightest wish, often before it was even spoken. He was kind to all his companions and never had an argument with any of them. They in turn respected him for his gentleness and thoughtfulness; whenever he spoke they listened attentively.

After two years of novitiate, John pronounced his first vows. What a joyous day it was for him! Soon afterwards he and a companion were sent to Rome to study philosophy. They went on foot, stopping over at monasteries by night, and walked the whole distance from Antwerp to Rome in ten weeks!

In Rome John began his study of philosophy, but of course he had other duties as well. He was always looking for a chance to make merits—by doing even the smallest of duties perfectly, for the love of God; by smiling when someone said an unkind word; by correcting every fault of his as soon as he was told about it. He did not perform great penances. "My greatest penance is to do common life," he said. By that he meant that he did penance by obeying his rule and his superiors exactly and by getting along well with his companions.

Before beginning any task, John would ask God to enlighten him so that he would do it in the very best way. He was always conscious of the fact that God was with him and he was careful never to offend Him in any way.

Sometimes he found it hard to pray—as everyone does at one time or another. Realizing that at such times God wants us to be patient and to keep on trying, John would pray just the same. He knew that God does not want us to give up just because we do not feel like praying.

John always looked happy, but he never talked during the times when he was supposed to keep silence. When he had to speak he asked God to help him say the right thing, and then he spoke in as few words as possible. At recreation time, even though he liked to joke, he was careful never to hurt anyone's feelings.

His companions all noticed what a good sport John was. He never minded being paired with a poor player, and would put his whole heart into the game no matter what. If his side lost, he would flash his usual bright smile; if it won, he was quiet, in order not to hurt the feelings of the losers.

After two and a half years of hard study, John began to feel tired and weak. Perhaps it was just the summer heat, he thought, but perhaps it was something else. . . . Nevertheless, he was scheduled to take part in a debate, so he prepared himself and participated. The next day, he was in bed with a fever.

But he was as cheerful as ever.

* * *

"Here, son, drink this."

John drank the medicine obediently. It was horribly bitter. "Thank you, Father. Perhaps you should say the grace after meals?"

* * *

"Father, I hope my death won't cause friction between this province and the Belgian one. I'll be the second Belgian Jesuit to die in Rome within a few weeks!"

* * *

"To subdue your fever," the doctor ordered solemnly, "the attendant will bathe your forehead with aged wine."

"It's a good thing my expensive illness won't last long!"

* * *

John knew he was dying, even though the doctors could not find out the cause. He received Extreme Unction and Viaticum with great devotion and, after two more days, he passed away very peacefully. Clutched in his hands were a crucifix, the rosary he had said so devotedly, and the rules of the Society which he had always obeyed. It was August 13, 1621. Was it a coincidence that he had died just before the feast of Our Lady's Assumption?

One beautiful quality of St. John Berchmans was his cheerfulness. Cheerfulness is charity, for when we are happy, we make other people happy, too.

Saint Isaac Jogues

North American Martyr

In the days when the first white men were exploring America, several Jesuit missionaries from France settled among the Huron Indians in what is now southern Canada. They lived in the same kind of huts as the Indians, ate the same food, and spoke the same language. Their purpose? To save the red men's souls.

One of these missionaries was Father Isaac Jogues; young, active and eagle-eyed, he was well-liked by the Hurons. They accepted a white man only if he knew how to walk long miles, carry heavy burdens and eat vermin-infested food without complaint. And Father Jogues, with his broad smile, knew how to do all that and more. The Hurons gave him the name Ondessonk, or Hawk, and considered him one of their favorite "Blackrobes." Blackrobe was an Indian name for any priest.

One summer, Father Jogues was traveling between Quebec and a Huron village with a band of his Huron converts and three other Frenchmen. They journeyed in twelve canoes manned by about thirty-five Huron braves under the command of their fiercest chief, Ahatsistari. He was a famous warrior who had taken the baptismal name Eustace. Other leaders of the Huron Christians were Charles, Stephen, Joseph, and Eustace's nephew, Paul. Among the Frenchmen were René, a young doctor, and William, a woodsman.

One morning, as they approached a stretch of river where hostile Iroquois war parties might be lurking, the Hurons and Frenchmen held a council.

"If we are attacked, brothers," said Father Jogues, "remember always to be faithful to that God Who has given His life for you!"

The Hurons croaked in approval; one by one each pledged his loyalty to the Faith. Eustace was the last to speak:

"Brothers," he said, "if captured I will tell the Iroquois that no matter how severely they torture me, even if they try to tear the soul from my body, they will not be able to tear from my heart the consolation that after death I shall be supremely happy. I shall tell them that while they are burning me.

"Charles, my brother, if God should decree my capture and your escape, go to my kinsmen in our country. Tell them that if they love me, if they love themselves, they must accept the Faith and adore the Divine Majesty which is invisible to our eyes but makes Itself felt in the very depths of our souls when we do not close our eyes to His truths—when we submit our wills to His commands. Tell them I am convinced of this. Warn them that we shall be separated forever unless they become followers of God, Who alone is my hope, and in Whom, wherever I may be, I wish to live and die."

It was to win to Christ souls like Eustace, that Father Jogues had dedicated his life to the missions!

With strong, sure strokes, the Huron braves shot their canoes out into the choppy water. They paddled steadily, hour after hour. By nightfall they had covered almost thirty miles.

"Brothers," said Eustace, "we must determine the route we shall follow tomorrow. We may travel in the open waters, secure from all ambush, but that way is long, as you know. Or we may pass through the north channel—a shorter route which holds many dangers."

"We have heard of no bands of Iroquois nearby," ventured an older brave. "Let us take the channel."

At the end of the discussion, the northern route was chosen.

In the dawn hush, the Hurons and Frenchmen gathered about Father Jogues as he led them in prayer. Then they boarded their canoes and slipped cautiously through inshore reeds until they reached open water. The entrance to the northern channel lay a short distance beyond.

Suddenly one of the braves clucked a warning. Each Huron seized his bow and arrow and gazed at the shore intently. In a patch of clay by the water's edge were marks which could only have been made by canoes!

Eustace and some of his men paddled over to examine the markings and the fresh footprints next to them. "Iroquois," Eustace decided. "But only three canoes of them. There are enough of us; let us continue without fear."

The twelve canoes stroked on into the channel, where they had to string out single file. Anxious Huron eyes searched the forested island to their left, probed the thicketed mainland to their right. When a stretch of weedy swampland opened up between the channel and the shore, each member of the party sighed in relief.

Then war whoops rent the air. The swamp-weeds came alive with red-painted bodies. While muskets blazed and lead balls whistled overhead, Eustace and his men shrieked defiance and drove their canoes fiercely toward the enemy.

Above the tumult the chief thundered, "Great God, to You alone I look for help!" Father Jogues raised his hand and pronounced words of absolution over his people. Then he turned to a young brave in his own canoe, one who had never become a Christian. The man had been wounded by a musket ball.

"Would you like Baptism, Atieronhonk?"

"Yes."

The priest cupped some water in his hand, and sprinkled it on Atieronhonk's head, baptizing him Bernard. Then the canoe rammed into the weedy shore.

Only half of the Huron canoes had come within range of the Iroquois muskets. The others swirled about swiftly and shot back down river to safety. Eustace was left with about fifteen braves, plus Renè and William, to face thirty Iroquois. The latter had retreated to the forest's edge while the Hurons crept toward them through the swamp grass.

Another blood-curdling shriek—this time from the river! Eustace whirled. There, bearing down upon them were eight canoes of screaming Iroquois! The Hurons had been surrounded completely.

Soon the Indians were fighting hand-to-hand—about five Iroquois to each Huron. One by one the Hurons fell—Charles, Stephen, Paul, Bernard, Joseph. . . . The Iroquois roared in savage triumph at each new victory.

In the tall river grass crouched Father Jogues. As a priest, he was forbidden to join in the battle—for Christ Himself had given His life for those savage Iroquois who danced with glee about their prisoners. All he could do was pray—and wait.

Yet what could he wait for? Now, almost all the Hurons had been captured; Eustace, still fighting valiantly, had vanished amongst the trees; William, too, had disappeared.

"If I crept through the weeds to that thicket on the right," he mused, "I could steal through the forest and escape downriver. The Iroquois are too busy. . ."

But some unbaptised Huron braves had been captured. Were they to suffer torment and death without gaining eternal life? That could not be. Father Jogues rose to his feet, and picked his way through the weeds toward the Iroquois who guarded Renè. The braves stared in amazement, crouching tensely, prepared for some kind of attack.

"Don't be afraid!" the priest shouted. He stretched out his arms as a sign of surrender. Several Iroquois braves approached slowly, cautiously–then leaped upon the priest, knocked him to the ground, beat him, kicked him, and tore off the black robe. They dragged him to the other prisoners.

"Do not bind me," Father Jogues told his captors. "I shall not try to escape so long as even one of these Huron braves remains your prisoner. *They* are my bonds."

The Iroquois listened bewildered; however, they did not bind the priest. Father Jogues approached René and said, "My Brother, God is our Lord and Master. He has permitted only what He knows is good. So be it."

"Yes, my Father," the young doctor replied. "He has permitted it; He has willed it. His holy Will be done. I love it, I cherish it, I embrace it with all the strength of my heart."

Father Jogues next turned to his Huron friends. "Take courage, brothers. The torments we will suffer now are as nothing compared with the glory to come. God will not let us suffer anything beyond our strength."

He turned to the unbaptized.

"We are near death, brothers. Do you not wish to enjoy life everlasting with the good God of Whom we have spoken so often?"

They said they did, and Father Jogues used drops of water squeezed from his own torn, wet garments to baptize them in the name of the Father and of the Son and of the Holy Ghost.

Scarcely had he finished, when shrieks and whoops of glee rang through the forest. A large band of Iroquois erupted from the gloom jubilantly leading a brawny, bloodstained chieftain—Eustace! He whom the Iroquois had sought above all else!

The priest hurried to the great chief's side, only to be torn from him by angry Iroquois, who cast Eustace to the ground and bound him tightly. Without expression, the chief spoke: "My Father, as I have promised, I will remain faithful to you whether I live or die."

Meanwhile, the other Frenchman, William Couture, had managed to outdistance the Iroquois. He struck out down a forest trail, slowing down to a dog-trot which would eat up the miles. A day's journey distant was the French settlement; surely he could make it.

Yes, he could make it. But what of his comrades—Father Jogues, René, their Huron friends? Could William return to security while they must face torture and death? No, he must die with them. William halted, turned, and began to walk back toward the swamp.

* * *

Thus, with twenty Huron captives and three Frenchmen, all ripe for torture, the Iroquois boarded their canoes and threaded their way through a maze of channels until they reached the main river. After they felt safe from pursuit, they beached the canoes, held a council, and celebrated.

One of the newly-baptized Hurons annoyed the Iroquois. He was an old man with a sharp tongue. Eager for blood, the captors smashed in his skull, scalped him, and left his body on the beach as a monument of their raid.

That night, on a hilltop south of the St. Lawrence, Father Jogues wept over his loss. He grieved not because he and his comrades would have sufferings to offer to God, but because almost no leaders remained among the Huron Christians. These men who had been captured were the cream of the crop; they were to have been his apostles among their brethren. Now they would suffer and die for their Faith–but they would never preach it.

One comforting thought came to him in the blackness. "The blood of martyrs has ever been the seed of the Church." Yet he could not help but weep.

Rivers, rapids, lakes passed behind the travelers as they made their way southward into the land of the Mohawk Iroquois. Father Jogues felt hot tears spring to his eyes whenever he looked upon Eustace, Joseph, Stephen, Charles and Paul–"the sustaining columns of the Church among the Hurons." He would write later, "It is a hard thing to bear–nay, a cruel thing–when one sees the triumph

of demons over whole peoples who were redeemed
with so much love and paid for with such adorable
Blood."

René Goupil, himself covered with scars from
the battle, tended the injuries of his fellow prisoners
and the wounded Iroquois. Father Jogues marveled
at the young doctor's gentle cheerfulness, his submission to God's will, his eagerness to give up his
life for the Lord Jesus.

René's ill health had prevented him from making the vows of religion years before and after becoming well he had felt unworthy to make them.
Now, however, he asked Father Jogues' permission
to do so, that his sacrifice to God might be complete.

Father Jogues agreed gladly. In an Iroquois war
canoe, René Goupil pronounced the formula of consecration he had memorized years before and had
always longed to say. Now, he, too, was a Jesuit.

On the eighth day after the capture, the travelers met a band of two hundred Iroquois camped
on an island in Lake Champlain. They greeted the
raiding party with shrieks of glee—eager to honor
their pagan war gods by torturing the prisoners.
They sprang upon the Frenchmen and Hurons, beating and pounding them.

"The gauntlet!" urged one brave.

"The gauntlet!" went up the cry.

Each warrior rushed off and returned with a
club or thorny rod. They formed two lines from the
beach up a long hillside. All the prisoners were
stripped naked and lined up, with the old men first,
then William, more Hurons, René, more braves and

lastly Father Jogues. The Iroquois hated the French even more than they hated the Hurons, and they hated Blackrobes most of all. They wanted Father Jogues' punishment to be the worst.

The first Huron was pushed between the two lines of Iroquois, and began to run up the hill, while stinging, numbing blows rained on his head, his back, his legs. The shrieks grew savage, as one man after another ran in between the two lines; the blood lust of the frenzied Iroquois mounted and mounted.

Father Jogues watched it all. God alone knows what he thought in those moments. He knew that the worst was meant for him.

The last Huron—and, now, his turn. He stepped forward, tensed, and began to run up the hill between the lines of savage, swinging clubs. Pain—stabbing pain, dull pain, pain that sent his head reeling and spinning... Someone tripped him; he stumbled to his feet and ran on blindly only to feel his path blocked by another mocking savage, and another, and another... And all the time the blows. And all the time the frenzied screams and wild mocking laughter. He broke away again and again and stumbled on....

And fell. Blows and kicks rained upon him, but he knew no more.

* * *

When the priest came to, he found himself near a platform on the hilltop. He was dragged up onto it, to find William and René there already. The Iroquois tried to make him stand, but he sank to the floor. At this, the savages took blazing sticks and held them against his arms and legs. One seized his hand and crunched the thumb between his teeth. Another held a burning coal against the fingers. Father Jogues lost consciousness again.

He opened his eyes to see frenzied Iroquois braves chopping William's and René's fingers from their hands and sealing the wounds with red-hot stones. A cry went up as the braves saw that the Blackrobe was conscious. They lunged for him, but a wiry young figure stepped before them—Paul, Eustace's nephew. "Torture me!" he urged them. "Torture me as cruelly as you like! I will take this man's place."

The Iroquois were ready to vent rage on the Hurons. They threw the Frenchmen down from the platform but instead of Paul they set upon Eustace, the Huron chief, slashing his flesh from head to foot, holding blazing torches against the wounds to seal them so that he would not lose too much blood and die before time. True to his race and to his Faith, the chief remained expressionless. He threw insults at his enemies and defied them.

They cut both thumbs from his hands; they took a sharp-pointed stake, rammed it into the thumb socket, forced it up the arm till it protruded at the elbow. Eustace was unmoved.

Father Jogues burst into tears at the scene, and the Iroquois began to jeer and taunt him. "The Blackrobe is a woman!" they shouted.

The Huron chief still had strength enough to roar: "The blackrobe is *not* a woman. Your cruelty, my pains, and his love for me are the reason for his tears."

"Keep remembering," the priest called out to the chieftain, "keep remembering that there is a God Who sees everything and Who will reward everything which we endure for His sake."

"I will remain firm even until death!" the chief replied.

Knife in hand, an Iroquois brave approached the priest. He reached out, grasped Father Jogues' nose with one hand, and held the knife poised in the other.

"Lord," prayed the priest silently, "take not only my nose, but also my head."

Slowly the brave put down his knife. He turned and walked away. A half hour later he came back again, prepared to carry out the deed. Again, he hesitated and turned away.

The fury of the Iroquois had spent itself for the night. They stumbled sleepily down the hill to their camp ground, leaving the Frenchmen and Hurons lying bruised and bleeding in the moonlight.

Those were the first tortures. The next day the Iroquois and their prisoners resumed the journey southward. Most of this trip was overland on foot, at a dog-trot, with packs on their backs. Father Jogues and René, worn out as they were from torture and lack of food, could not keep pace with the party no matter how hard they tried. They dragged along behind—and talked of escape.

"I must stay with the Huron Christians," the priest told René. "But you could easily escape now that they've relaxed their guard. Perhaps we can persuade William to go with you."

"I shall never leave you, Father," replied René. "I will die with you!" And so, they remained with their Huron comrades, while the Iroquois taunted them with the promise of roasting them alive and eating their white flesh.

They arrived at Ossernenon, the first Mohawk Iroquois village, located where Auriesville, New York, is today.

The date, Father Jogues calculated, was August 14 — Vigil of the Assumption.

"Lord Jesus Christ," he prayed, "I thank You that on the day that the whole world rejoices in the glory of Your Mother's Assumption, I may share some part of Your sufferings and cross."

Another gauntlet awaited them, bruised and exhausted as they were. In the middle, someone struck René a blow on the face that sent him reeling, and his body was thrown out of the double line. When Father Jogues staggered up to him after his own ordeal, he found the young doctor's face smashed and swollen beyond recognition.

The tortures which followed were more horrible than those inflicted at Lake Champlain. In the process, Father Jogues' hands were mangled severely and his left thumb torn from its socket. And the Mohawk children poured hot coals on the Frenchmen's helpless bodies.

Another journey. Another Mohawk village. More torture. Whatever one of his Huron companions suffered, Father Jogues felt was happening to himself. Most of them were *his* converts; he it was who had poured the saving waters of Baptism on their heads. Through all their anguish, he comforted them and encouraged them to remain firm in their Faith: " 'You weep and lament,' says the Gospel, 'but your sorrow shall be turned into joy.' "

Another Mohawk village. More torture. How long could this go on before they died of their torments? It seemed impossible that they would live through another day.

Then the Mohawks took Father Jogues and hung him by his arms from the cross-piece of a cabin. As the weight of his body pulled on his arms more and more, he lost his composure for the first time and begged his tormenters to loosen the ropes a little. They tightened them. "They acted justly; I thank you, Lord Jesus, for letting me experience how much You deigned to suffer for me on the cross, since the whole weight of Your Most Sacred Body hung, not from ropes, but from Your hands and feet pierced by nails." A young brave cut him down as he was about to lose consciousness.

The next day four new prisoners were brought into the village. His face drawn with anguish, the priest watched them run the gauntlet. He knew these Hurons; they were not Christians. After they had been tortured, he and Eustace approached them and spoke of the consolations and reward of the Christian Faith.

"Father, these two are to be burned tonight," someone whispered.

"Very well," replied the priest. "We shall concentrate on them."

After the two Hurons had consented and had received instructions, Father Jogues sprinkled on their heads some drops of water he had gathered from wet leaves, and baptized them. The next day he baptized their two comrades while wading through a little stream on the way back to the second village.

A council was held by the Mohawks—and at first it seemed that the Frenchmen would die. But many of the braves wished to end the war with the French and urged that the Blackrobe and his companions be left alive. At last that group won out: the Frenchmen would live as slaves among the Mohawks.

And their Huron comrades? Three would die, one in each village; the others would become slaves.

In Ossernenon that night, Father Jogues and René witnessed the bloody death of Eustace's nephew Paul, a generous young brave who had often offered himself to the Iroquois as a victim in place of the priest. Shouting out his hope in a better life to come, Paul died with the courage of a young lion.

Over the next village some miles distant, the sky glared red. There, Stephen was being burned.

And in the farthest village William watched Eustace die, bearing his tortures with calm, telling

Huron friends not to let his death stand in the way of a future peace between them and the Iroquois.

Father Jogues and René were taken as slaves by the chief who had captured them. The two Frenchmen were so weak that they could not work, and could hardly drag themselves from place to place. Pus oozed from their unhealed wounds, and clouds of fleas, lice and bugs swarmed about. With their maimed hands, the prisoners could not ward off the insects. To add to their misery, they were half-starved, and since food was scarce among the Indians, they were given only a little ground corn and some raw squash each day.

At last the Mohawks realized how sick their prisoners were, and gave them a few little fish and some pieces of meat, that they might regain their strength. As soon as they could hobble about again, they were sent into the fields with the squaws to help them harvest corn and vegetables.

Father Jogues knew how to get along well with Indians, for he had lived among the Hurons six years. He understood how suspicious the savages could be, and avoided doing anything which would arouse their anger. He warned René to do likewise. However the young doctor, accustomed to openness and sincerity, did not understand how he could irritate the Iroquois.

But he did irritate them. His face was so scarred and battered from the gauntlet that it created a feeling of disgust, and so did his natural clumsiness. His expression showed how sickening he found the filth and the food. His gestures when at prayer suggested that he was a sorcerer weaving spells against the savages. His Christian virtues of gentleness and kindness seemed cowardly. The Indians desired to kill him.

If the Mohawks were to kill Father Jogues, the French would never agree to peace, for he was a Blackrobe. But the younger paleface was less important. If he were to die, so what? A story could be made up to explain his disappearance. To make their deed easier the Iroquois separated the two Frenchmen, giving Father Jogues to another master.

Still, the younger Jesuit did not know his days were numbered.

In the young Mohawk children, René found kindred souls. They were gentle and simple like himself, not having learned craft and cruelty. He liked to play with them. One day he picked up a boy of three or four and placed his own cap on the child's head. The little fellow chuckled happily. René took the tiny hand in his own mangled one, moved it from the child's forehead to his breast, to one shoulder, to the other—in the sign of the cross.

A wild scream came from the boy's grandfather who had been sitting in the shadows watching. The paleface had invoked an evil spirit upon the child! The old man flew at René in a rage, tore the boy away from him, and began to beat and kick and pound the prisoner.

Later the same day Father Jogues came to the cabin and called René to him. "Come pray with me," he urged. They walked through the village and up a lonely hill toward their favorite prayer spot.

"I heard about what happened this morning," the priest began. "Our lives are in danger, especially yours."

"I do not fear death, Father," the young man replied, "so long as I am in God's grace. May I confess myself again?"

The priest heard René's confession, as he had done every other day, and absolved him of his sins. They knelt together and offered the Lord Jesus their lives and their blood, asking Him to unite their sacrifice to His own for the salvation of the Iroquois.

On their way down the hill, they began the rosary, as was their custom, the priest leading and René answering. Two braves met them on the trail. One of them was the uncle of the child on whom René had made the sign of the cross. "Go back to the village," he growled.

They walked down the slope together, the missionaries saying their Hail Mary's softly, the braves stalking grimly behind them.

"You walk ahead," one of them abruptly commanded Father Jogues. "You stay here," he ordered René. The priest gazed intently at the glaring savage, then walked on a few steps. A rustle made him whirl—just in time to see a tomahawk crashing down on René's head. "Jesus, Jesus, Jesus," called the young Jesuit, as he crumbled to the earth.

The priest murmured absolution. Now it is my turn, he thought. "Just a moment," he told the Mohawks, and kneeling he said an act of contrition.

"Get up," growled the grim-faced brave. "I have no power over you. You belong to another family."

The priest approached his comrade. René still breathed. As Father Jogues made a sign of the cross over the split head, the braves tore him away and finished their job.

A mob from the village swarmed to the spot, babbling excitedly and milling about. The priest was led away to his cabin, for fear that some wild young brave would kill him, too.

"How calm you are," marveled the priest's master. And indeed Father Jogues *was* calm. René had been so cheerful, so kind, so obedient, and he had just recently made the vows of religion; his beautiful soul must have winged its way straight to Heaven. It was September 29, 1642–the feast of St. Michael the Archangel.

The following morning he went in search of René's body, which had been dragged about the village by the children and then thrown into a ravine. The Mohawks watched him, and he knew that death might come any minute, but it didn't matter.

He found the body, but not having a spade with which to dig a grave, he could only conceal it in a stream bed under a mound of stones. At the first opportunity he came back with a spade to give the martyr's bones a fitting burial, but the Mohawks, now knowing how much those remains meant to him, had stolen them away.

✧ ✧ ✧

Death stalked the priest continually, for only
a few of the Mohawks wanted to keep him alive
in case of a truce with the French. Most suspected
him as being in league with evil spirits, and would
have cut him down at the first opportunity. Yet day
after day passed, and Father Jogues did not die.

"If I am to live after all," he thought, "I must
try to find a way to teach them about God." He
busied himself in learning the language well, and
in finding ways to slip in a word here and there
about the Creator of all men. After all, were not
these Mohawks his brothers, bought by the Blood of
Christ?

That fall the priest accompanied a hunting
party into the Adirondack mountains. He helped
the squaws carry the food and equipment. During
the weeks that they camped in the mountains, he
would go off into the forest daily to honor God in
the vast solitude He had created, where no lips had
ever before spoken His Name. Peeling the bark from
a tree in the form of a cross, the priest interceded
for his new people.

But his new people, spying on him continuously, blamed the scarcity of elk and deer on his
prayer and on the cross. They jeered at him and
beat him often. This, coupled with hunger, lack of
clothing, the cold of the November snows, the
memory of his past sins and the fear of torture and
death, plunged the priest into the depths of near-
despair. Then it seemed that a voice spoke to him,
saying, "Serve God from love not from fear; do not

worry about yourself." Renewed in spirit, Father Jogues returned to the village with the hunting party.

One snowy day, when crossing a swift stream on a mossy tree trunk, a Mohawk woman slipped and fell into the icy waters. The bundles and papoose cradle which were strapped to her kept pulling her under. Father Jogues plunged into the current, freed the woman from the bundles and cradle, and dragged her and the baby to safety. As he lifted the baby from the stream he baptized it without letting the Mohawks see what he was doing. The child died a few days later.

Back in the village, the Mohawks put him to work tending a sick brave—one who had tortured him severely a few months before. The man was dying of a horrible disease which covered him with foul-smelling sores. Although he could hardly stand the sight and the smell, Father Jogues nursed the sick man for two weeks.

Little by little, his master's family began to like the priest. They asked him many questions about the sun and moon and tides and accepted his answers eagerly, but as soon as he began to speak of a Creator, they lost interest.

Father Jogues was more successful among the sick. He visited them daily, as he had once done among the Hurons, and as he tended their diseases he told them of Heaven and hell. A few adults consented to be baptized. He also baptized many infants who were near death.

One day, while visiting a neighboring village he chanced upon a cabin where five children were all seriously ill. He baptized them, and a few days later learned of their death. How good God had been to lead him to them in time!

Father Jogues went among the Huron and Algonquin prisoners in the three Mohawk villages, comforting them and hearing confessions. He warned them against praying openly, for fear of arousing their captors. Joseph for one, became accustomed to carrying on an almost continual conversation with God. He was grateful when Father Jogues taught him the rosary, and he recited it often in secret.

In his travels, the priest often saw William, who had been adopted by a family in the third village. He was still fervent, and well except for having frozen one of his feet.

In March, some children told the priest that they had found René's bones in the ravine. He hurried to the spot and searched, but found nothing. The children mocked him gleefully, but after he had searched for a whole day they told him the exact spot. Tenderly, the priest gathered up those precious relics and buried them in the earth beneath a pine tree. He said the *De Profundis* over the remains of North America's first martyr.

On Holy Saturday six Algonquin prisoners were led triumphantly into the village. Having undergone the usual bloody tortures, they lay awaiting death in one of the cabins. Father Jogues tended their wounds and told them of God, the commandments, and Heaven. Like the catechumens in the early Church in Rome these men received Baptism on Easter Sunday.

* * *

The sister of Father Jogues' master had grown very fond of the priest. She was a kind old woman who called Father Jogues her "nephew." In May, she took him with her when she and a band of braves went down to the Dutch settlement to trade skins and furs.

At Rensselaerswyck also called Fort Orange, Father Jogues met and spoke with the Dutch governor, but he did not try to escape. He had his new Christians to look after.

On Pentecost, back in his "own" village, he secretly baptized an Algonquin woman who was about to be burned alive–by pretending to give her a drink of water.

A few days later new prisoners arrived–Huron Christians and a Frenchman. Fortunately they had not been tortured, but the priest's heart sank to see so many of his people captives and in exile. A few days later, the Mohawks butchered and burned a hundred Hurons in the neighboring villages. Father Jogues' grief knew no bounds.

That summer the Iroquois warred continuously on the French, Hurons and Algonquins along the St. Lawrence. One of the war parties took the Hurons, Joseph and Charles, with them to carry baggage, and this gave them the chance they were waiting for. The Huron warriors slipped away from their masters and hurried to tell the French about René, William and Father Jogues.

Meanwhile, Father Jogues was paddling his master's canoe down the rivers south of the Catskill mountains. He acted as the chief's official beast of burden, as his master and other chiefs went about collecting tribute from the Susquehannock Indians. The journey gave Father Jogues a chance to visit the sick. He baptized all the children in danger of death, and every dying adult who was interested in instruction.

One day he met a very sick young man who called him by name. "Do you remember the man who cut your bonds in the third Mohawk village when you were at the end of your strength?"

The priest thought back to that terrible night he had been suspended from the wooden beams. "Yes, I remember very well. I owe a lot to that man. I've never been able to thank him. If you know him, please tell me where he is."

"It was I who did it. I took pity on you and loosed the bonds."

The priest embraced him. "I have often prayed for you," he said. "And now I have a gift for you."

He told the dying man of the reward of eternal life and what he must believe to attain it. After he had spoken, the man begged for Baptism, and he died a few hours after receiving it.

They began the two hundred-mile journey "home" to the Mohawk villages. Father Jogues could hardly wait to get there, for he feared lest some new prisoners be tortured and killed in his absence before receiving the grace of Baptism. In his year among the Mohawks he had baptized seventy children and adults belonging to five different tribes, and he was content to remain among the savages as long as God should be pleased to keep him there.

"Nephew," the old chief's sister said to Father Jogues almost as soon as he had come home, "prepare to go fishing with the braves and me in the great river below the Dutch settlement."

So Father Jogues was off again. He and his companions stopped at Rensselaerswyck for about a week, during which time he wrote a long report of René's martyrdom, his own sufferings and labors among the Iroquois. He addressed it to his superior in France. The Dutch promised to send it with the first ship.

A few weeks later the priest passed through Rensselaerswyck again on his return trip from the fishing area. To his astonishment an angry band of braves met him there.

"Dog! Traitor! Sorcerer!" they roared. "You shall be torn to pieces and roasted alive!"

What had happened? A Mohawk chief had delivered a message from Father Jogues to a French fort on the St. Lawrence. Since the message had contained a warning to beware of the Iroquois, the French had fired upon them immediately after reading it.

"You have betrayed us!" screamed the angry braves. "You shall die!"

The Dutch governor urged Father Jogues to escape on a ship bound for France. The priest hesitated, then said he would pray about it. Lying awake that night he thought the matter through. Now that he knew the Iroquois so well, it seemed he would be more valuable to the missions alive than dead. He could escape to France, return to Canada, and go back to his Iroquois people when the heat of their anger had cooled.

After a hair-raising escape in which he was bitten by a huge dog, the priest spent almost a month lying on hard planks in a hot Rensselaerswyck attic while his bitten leg swelled with infection. At last he was smuggled on board a ship going downriver.

✜   ✜   ✜

It was Christmas morning, 1643, when Father Jogues set foot on French soil. His heart pounding with joy, he headed for the nearest church, and for the first time in seventeen months he made his confession and received the Sacred Host!

A few days later, tattered and worn, he presented himself before his Superior in Rennes. What joy flooded the community, as they gathered around their brother who had suffered so much for Christ. They gasped at the sight of his scarred and twisted hands and the thinness of his once powerful body. They shuddered when he related the tortures, and exulted when he told them of René's martyrdom and the seventy baptisms. They venerated him as if he were one dead and canonized.

But Father Jogues had only three things on his mind. He visited his mother. He wrote to the Holy Father and requested permission to celebrate Mass even though he could not hold his battered hands in the required position. Having received that permission, he set sail again for Canada.

As the ship cleaved its way through the Atlantic swell, Father Jogues recalled what the Holy Father had said when he granted the dispensation: "It would be a shame if a martyr of Christ were not allowed to drink the Blood of Christ." Well, he was not a martyr yet, he reflected, but it would be very surprising if he died a natural death. He was then thirty-seven years old.

A terrible storm overtook the little ship in mid-ocean, tossing her about like a cork. "We're lost! We're lost!" screamed the passengers in terror. Father Jogues rose in their midst. Clinging to a doorpost as the vessel pitched and bucked, he cried out in a calm, penetrating voice, urging the men to have sorrow for their sins and to put their trust in God's mercy. As he spoke the storm gradually abated.

Before they reached the St. Lawrence, every passenger on the ship had made his confession to Father Jogues.

How the priest's heart swelled as he saw the wooded shores of his beloved St. Lawrence! Through the trees, here and there, he glimpsed the log cabins and bark huts of copper-skinned Algonquin braves. He was home, among "his people" again!

At Quebec, his fellow Blackrobes greeted him with open arms. They were overjoyed to find him alive and well. Their own news was not so pleasant as his, for the Iroquois were still raiding the Hurons and Algonquins, destroying them little by little.

Father Jogues' Superior assigned him to the island of Montreal where a fervent little Christian community lived. There he spent the winter.

The following spring, council was held with the Iroquois, and some Iroquois prisoners were released to them. Peace was made–temporarily–and renewed again the following fall. However, the French were uneasy, for they knew how treacherous the Iroquois could be.

"Eat a little meat, Father Isaac," his companion urged Father Jogues often during the long winter months at Montreal.

"No, thank you," was the reply. "When I go back among the Iroquois I do not wish my thoughts to keep turning to the pleasures and comforts of this place."

His one desire was to return to his people–not the Hurons with whom he had lived six years, but the Iroquois who had captured, tortured and enslaved him; *they* were his brothers!

His chance came in midwinter, when Iroquois ambassadors returned to renew the peace. They told Father Jogues that the Mohawks would be happy to have him return among them; his "aunt's" cabin was waiting. Father Jogues asked his Superior to send him among the Mohawks.

He went in May, as ambassador of the French governor, accompanied by a surveyor named John Bourdon. He went joyfully, for this was what he had asked to do, and yet his will had had to bend his nature to accept it. To his Superior he admitted, "My poor nature trembled as it remembered everything that had gone before. But Our Lord, in His goodness, calmed it and will calm it still more. Father, I desire what Our Lord desires—and I desire it at the peril of a thousand lives. How I would regret it if I lost such a wonderful opportunity, one in which I might be responsible if some souls were not saved."

Most of the Mohawks were happy to see Father Jogues again, especially when they saw that he was as kind and friendly as ever. The Turtle Clan and the Wolf Clan (to which Father Jogues' "aunt" belonged) welcomed him eagerly. However, among the warlike Bears—who had murdered René Goupil—there were grumbles and mutterings. They listened grim-faced to the peace pledges between the Frenchmen and their tribesmen.

After the peace councils, Father Jogues found time to instruct several sick, old people and to baptize them and a few dying infants. He also reassured the Mohawks about a little black strongbox he had left in his "aunt's" cabin three years before. The wily Mohawks suspected he had a demon inside the mysterious box. Father Jogues smiled at them, and showed them how to open the box by means of a key. He took out all the little odds and ends the box contained and let the braves examine everything. At last they seemed convinced that the box was harmless, and they agreed to keep it for the priest's return.

The two Frenchmen travelled the long route back to Montreal, where they made their report.

The following fall, Father Jogues and a youth named John de la Lande set out for the Mohawk country to spend the winter instructing the savages in the Faith. With one Huron as their companion, they paddled the long lonely river route through the still forests. About twenty days after leaving the St. Lawrence they left lakes and rivers behind, and set out through the mountains on foot. It was a route which Father Jogues knew well. He hurried faster and faster; he was going "home"!

There–coming up the trail to meet them–was a band of Indians. The priest called out to them, only to see them disappear into the brush beside the trail. A moment later, furious shrieks pierced the air, and red-painted savages leaped out of the forest, seized the missionaries, and beat them cruelly. They dragged them down the trail to the village.

A huge mob bore down on them, and Father Jogues could see that the Bear and Wolf Clans were fighting among themselves. Some of the Wolfs grabbed the Frenchmen and rushed them to the safety of the "aunt's" cabin.

Why had the Mohawks had this sudden change of heart?

Two tragedies had befallen them that summer. An epidemic had swept through their villages, killing many, and the corn crop had been destroyed by worms. They had blamed both on the "magical" black box of Father Jogues! The Bear Clan had aroused the people to take the warpath against the Algonquins, Hurons and French. It was one of the war parties which had met Father Jogues and John on the trail!

All night long the Wolves and Bears argued over the fate of the Blackrobe and his young companion. The next day the warriors left, to hold council in another village, leaving the Frenchmen free until an agreement should be reached. At sundown Father Jogues went with a young Wolf brave to have supper in a Bear cabin, for he had received an invitation and dared not give the insult of refusing.

As Father Jogues stooped to put his head through the low doorway, his young Wolf friend sensed the danger and leaped to protect him—but it was too late. A tomahawk came crashing down on the skull of the missionary, and Father Jogues crumpled to the ground, dead. With shouts of glee, the Bears hacked off his head and defiantly placed it on a tall spike overlooking the forests, facing the distant St. Lawrence. The Mohawks screamed defiance against the French.

Wolf braves guarded young John de la Lande closely, warning him not to leave the cabin. However, as the hours passed by and all was silent outside, and his guards fell asleep around the fire, the youth felt an urge to see his friend's body and save some relic of the martyr. He crept silently out of the cabin—and felt a stabbing pain, and then, nothing.

John's head was placed on a spike next to that of Father Jogues. The two heads were on the spikes the next day when the warriors came home to announce the council's decision—to free their prisoners!

* * *

Within a year after Father Jogues' death, the brave who had tried to save him had been baptized, and the murderer had repented and had received baptism before being burned by Algonquin captors.

However, the Iroquois had taken the warpath in earnest. They massacred the Hurons and Algon- quins and, in 1649, killed five more Jesuit Fathers- John de Brebeuf, Anthony Daniel, Charles Gar- nier, Noel Chabanel, and Gabriel Lalement. The blood of the eight Jesuit martyrs cried to God, Who poured an abundance of graces upon the Iroquois. Many of them were soon converted by other Black- robes. A few years later, the Mohawks had a saint of their own—Katherine Tekakwitha.

Father Jogues grew to love the Iroquois at once, and he worked to save their souls as earnestly as he had worked among the Hurons. A very good way to love God is to be happy wherever we are and to thank Him for placing us there.

Katherine Tekakwitha

Lily of the Mohawks

The billowy clouds appeared to be almost still, as if waiting to be admired by the young Indian maiden who stood leaning against a birch tree. Bright Star, for that was her name, had heard her people speak of war. She shuddered. Everything about her was so peaceful, yet . . .

Suddenly she heard the distant sound of drums. War drums!

She must hide and pray for her dear Algonquin Tribe. Only the White Manitou–God–could save them from the fierce Iroquois. Swift as a deer, Bright Star ran into the deep forest to pray.

Soon everything was wrapped in silence and darkness. Bright Star was alone. She prayed and prayed, all night long. "O God, do not let my people be destroyed," she begged. And then, "I *know* You won't; I *know* You will take pity on them." She sighed, and gazed up at the sky.

The last star was about to go to sleep when Bright Star heard a wild, triumphant cry behind her. An Iroquois! The blood froze in her veins.

With a silent prayer she began to run–but it was too late. Another Iroquois rose from the bushes in her path and grabbed her by the wrists. "Now we will burn the squaw at the stake!" he cried in savage glee.

"Wait!" ordered the first Indian. "I, chief of the Turtle Clan, will speak!"

The brave relaxed his grip a little and listened.

The chief looked at the young maiden. Never had he seen a more beautiful squaw. "The squaw has found favor in Great Turtle's eyes. She will be *my* squaw. I have spoken."

"That is good," answered the brave.

Erect and unafraid, Bright Star followed Great Turtle. "All for You, Jesus," she whispered.

❊   ❊   ❊

Great Turtle took Bright Star to live with him in the valley of the Mohawks.

Although she was an Algonquin, the Iroquois did not treat her harshly. She was kind and everyone soon loved her.

God loved her too, and one day He sent her a beautiful baby girl.

Great Turtle forgot all about his many worries, his war councils and his tribal meetings. He proudly held the infant in his arms and asked: "Bright Star, what shall we name our little one?"

Bright Star sighed. She wanted to give her child a Christian name, but she did not dare to ask Great Turtle.

"Let us call her Tekakwitha," she said.

"That is well," agreed Great Turtle. "Tekakwitha will do just what her name means: she will *move-all-that-is-before-her.*"

He then gently placed the sleeping child in her mother's arms and left.

Bright Star's eyes filled with tears. "Some day," she said softly, "some day I will have the Blackrobes pour the water of life on you, my little one. Then you, too, will be a child of God."

"Hush! You must be careful of what you say," warned Anastasia, an old Christian squaw who loved Bright Star. "If you are not careful, our Great Chief will have all of us Christians punished."

"You are right, Anastasia," said Bright Star. "I will try to make Great Turtle love the White Manitou. He must become a Christian too!"

The young squaw kissed her child and placed her on a mat. "The Blackrobes are far away," she said to Anastasia, "but I will do my best to tell her about Jesus and His Blessed Mother Mary."

"You do well, but be careful, for her aunts are not Christians either. In fact, they hate the Christians."

"I know. Will you promise me to take care of my Tekakwitha if something should happen to me?"

"Yes, I promise."

* * *

Almost every night, when the stars were twinkling brightly in the sky, Bright Star would creep out of her cabin and kneel in prayer. She had never given up hope that Great Turtle and Tekakwitha would be baptized. Soon she was praying also for the baptism of a new little son!

One morning Anastasia smilingly said to Tekakwitha's mother, "Your prayers have been heard by the Great White Manitou. The Blackrobes have come to stay nearby."

"I shall go at once and ask them to baptize my children!" cried Bright Star joyfully.

"Wait, you must remember that if you make Great Turtle angry, he will have all of us Christians killed!"

"You are right, Anastasia; I must be patient," sighed Bright Star.

Just then Tekakwitha came out to play.

"Where are you going, my little one?" asked Bright Star.

"Into the woods, to watch Fuzzy Tail!" answered Tekakwitha, and off she went.

Once in the woods, Tekakwitha took off her little red moccasins and ran barefooted on all the soft ground.

Whenever she caught sight of some birds–or her favorite pet, a gray squirrel–she would stop.

Fuzzy Tail, as she called the squirrel, would come and play near her. None of the birds or animals feared her, for they knew that she loved them and would not hurt them. Tekakwitha loved the forest, the flowers, the birds. They made her think of Heaven.

*　*　*

Wherever Bright Star went, her little daughter followed her. She was a lively child of four, full of curiosity and always asking questions. She loved to hear stories, especially those about Jesus, His Mother and the Saints.

"'Mamma, where do the birds come from?" asked Tekakwitha. She had heard the answer many times, but she liked to hear her mother repeat it again and again.

"God made them, my little one. God made all the beautiful things of this world: He made the trees, the flowers, the birds and the lakes; He made everything. Then He made Adam and Eve. They were our first parents.

"Because God loved Adam and Eve, He gave them each a soul which would live forever. That soul was made to God's image and likeness."

"I wish I could see the soul. It must be beautiful," said Tekakwitha.

"Yes, dear, and we must keep it beautiful by never committing any sins."

"Adam and Eve did."

"Yes, they disobeyed God and He punished them just as I punish you and your little brother when you are naughty. God sent them out of their beautiful garden, because by sinning they had lost sanctifying grace, God's special gift to man. But to show His love for our first parents and for us, He promised them a Redeemer, a Savior, Who would come on earth and take away the sin from man and regain for him sanctifying grace. He would reopen the gates of Heaven."

"Jesus opened Heaven for us. And the beautiful Mary is His Mother and ours too!" cried Tekakwitha.

"Yes, my little one, and she loves us very much. Love her, and never offend her by sinning," said Bright Star.

One morning, while Tekakwitha was playing in the forest, she heard a heavy rolling of drums.

"What does that mean?" she asked out loud, but her little forest friends just went on playing.

After a while she heard the drums again. It was a strange new way of beating the drums. Little Tekakwitha was frightened.

"Mother, Mother," she cried as she ran towards the lodge.

Bright Star came out and the child threw herself into her mother's protecting arms.

"Why are they beating the drums?" asked Tekakwitha.

Bright Star shook her head sadly. "My little one, the *Purple Devil* has visited our tribe. Many of our dear friends have died already."

"What is the Purple Devil, Mother?"

"It is a sickness. The white man calls it smallpox. When he strikes, he usually kills," answered Bright Star.

"But father is a great chief. He will kill the Purple Devil," said Tekakwitha.

"My little one, it is not in his power. Only the White Manitou can help us."

While she was talking, Bright Star's arms let go her child. Her eyes began to stare and she fell to the ground.

"Mother! Mother!" cried Tekakwitha. "Don't let the Purple Devil get you!"

But Bright Star did not hear. She was hot and feverish.

Anastasia came running as soon as she heard Tekakwitha scream. She tried to help Bright Star, but she could do nothing for her. The good squaw ran to see Tekakwitha's little brother. He lay so still on his mat. . . .

* * *

"My little one, don't cry. You are the daughter of a great chief. You must be strong."

"Yes, Anastasia, I will try to be brave. But I miss my mother, my father and my little brother."

"God thought it wise to take them now. He spared us. We must thank Him for His goodness."

"Anastasia," begged Tekakwitha, "why can't I live with you?"

"My little one, your uncle has the right to take you as his daughter. He loves you. You will be treated well," answered Anastasia. "He is now the chief of the Turtle Clan and you must obey him."

"But his squaw doesn't smile. She does not like me," said Tekakwitha sadly.

"You are a good child. You will obey old Anastasia, won't you?"

"Yes, Anastasia, I will try. But I wish I didn't have to go," insisted the little Indian maiden. "I will never become a Christian now."

Anastasia wrapped her big arms around the little girl. "Don't worry," she said. "You will become a Christian and you will help many others become Christians too!"

Tekakwitha's eyes opened wide. "Will I really? Then I will go to my uncle. I am not afraid."

Her uncle treated her well, but her aunt, Light Feet, disliked her, for she feared she would get too much attention. Yet Light Feet did not dare hurt the child, for fear of the great chief, Thunder Cloud.

* * *

"Tekakwitha, my little one, what are you doing here?"

"O, Anastasia, I miss you so much! My aunt never talks about God. She always scolds me when she sees me thinking. She said that I think too much."

"What do you mean, my child?" asked Anastasia.

"Well, sometimes when I think I'm alone, I think of the things you tell me."

"What, for example?"

"Well, I think of how good God is. He is our Father and watches over us. You said that He takes care of us and sends us rain when we need it. But when my aunt sees me thinking, she scolds me and makes me work."

"But you are only a child of nine."

"Yes, but she said that I must work and not be a lazy child."

"Tekakwitha, I think I hear your aunt calling you. Go quickly. I will speak to you again some other time."

Off Tekakwitha flew to her aunt.

"Where have you been?" asked Light Feet.

"I went to visit Anastasia."

"Haven't I told you not to waste time? Come quickly. I will teach you how to clean the lodge. From now on you must do it yourself, do you understand?"

"Yes, aunt," said little Tekakwitha, swallowing her tears. She was the great chief's daughter. She would not let anyone see her cry.

* * *

The little Indian maiden was now eleven years old. It did not seem possible that her small and slender body could stand the strain of so much work. But Tekakwitha had a strong will.

Her eyesight was poor because of the illness she had had as a child. For this reason she always tried to stay indoors. The sunlight hurt her eyes very much.

One day, while she was busily making a new mat, Anastasia came to visit her. She appeared rather excited. What news could she have, to make her so happy?

"Tekakwitha, my own," she cried excitedly, "the Blackrobes are coming! I heard them speaking with your uncle. They are to stay at *your uncle's lodge* for three days!"

"Anastasia!" exclaimed Tekakwitha happily.

"Your good mother's prayers will be answered now. Perhaps you will receive Baptism now."

"I hope so, Anastasia. I do want to become a child of God."

"Tekakwitha, Tekakwitha, where are you?" called Light Feet. "Oh, there you are! Quickly: prepare the meal. We have guests. But don't you let me see you speak to them!"

Tekakwitha prepared for the guests. Then she went out to fetch some water. On her return she saw three Blackrobes–Jesuit missionaries who had come to speak to the Mohawk chiefs about a peace treaty with the French.

After the meal, Tekakwitha was busy cleaning the lodge as usual. One of the missionaries came up to her and asked: "Are you Tekakwitha?"

"Yes, I am," she answered.

"I am Father Pirron. Tell me, do you love the White Manitou as much as Anastasia said you do?"

"O, yes. I love Him and His Mother. I would be so happy if I could hear more about them."

"Well, pray to them and try to always be good and patient with all. You will be happy soon."

But Tekakwitha had to wait many years to be baptized.

* * *

"Tekakwitha," screamed Light Feet one day, "come here at once! We must gather all our belongings. We are moving!"

Heavy packs on their backs, the Turtle Clan walked many miles through the forest. They halted on the north bank of the Mohawk River. This was to be their new home.

"Tekakwitha," called Light Feet, "hurry! Don't be lazy! We must build our bark cabin quickly, because it might rain tonight."

The little Indian maiden never complained. She was very tired, but it was the women's duty to build their houses. The men only carried the heavy logs. The women did the rest.

"Anastasia," confided Tekakwitha that night, "I wish I could do something to show my love for God."

"You can, my pet."

"How?"

"Instead of suffering everything in silence because you are the daughter of a chief, suffer it for the love of God. Make some mortifications for the conversion of our people."

"Oh, yes, that I will do willingly. What else can I do?"

"Make acts of charity. For example, be as kind as you can to those who hurt you."

"Thank you, dear Anastasia, I will try my best to do so."

"Try to imitate the Blessed Virgin in her humility, modesty and charity, and you will live as a Christian."

* * *

"Tekakwitha," called Light Feet, "come quickly. We must dress well. We are having guests tonight."

Soon all was ready and the guests arrived. The men sat in a group and talked and smoked. The women were sitting nearby. They, too, were busy talking.

When the men stopped smoking, Thunder Cloud gave Light Feet a signal.

Light Feet understood. She gave a bowl of porridge to Tekakwitha. The brave next to her put out his hands to accept the bowl from her. By this action they would be married. Tekakwitha understood that she was being tricked into marriage.

Poor Tekakwitha! She wanted to belong only to the White Manitou, so she threw down the bowl of porridge and ran out of the lodge! Her uncle and the brave ran after her, but could not find her.

"I will punish her for this," said Light Feet. "She has brought dishonor upon our family."

From then on, Tekakwitha was given the very hardest work. She was sent to gather firewood in the winter cold. Tekakwitha's fingers would freeze. The sunlight made the snow sparkle and its brightness hurt her eyes.

But the girl never complained; she was happy to have something to offer to God.

Whenever someone hurt her, she repaid them by being very kind to them.

One day, while she was home alone, she was surprised by a visitor. It was a Blackrobe!

"Father De Lamberville is my name," he said smiling. "Anastasia told me you would like to see a Blackrobe."

"Oh, yes! Please, O Blackrobe, may I be baptized? I want to belong wholly to the White Manitou."

"But first you must know something of the Catholic Faith."

"O Blackrobe, my mother was a Christian. She taught me many things and so did Anastasia."

Father De Lamberville asked Tekakwitha many questions. He was very surprised when she answered all of them quickly and correctly.

"You know a great deal about the Catholic Faith, but before I can baptize you, you must have your uncle's consent. Then I will prepare you for Baptism."

Tekakwitha asked her uncle that very night. "Dear uncle, you know how much I desire to be baptized. May I?"

Thunder Cloud looked at her for a long time. He loved his niece. Finally he gave his consent.

Tekakwitha flew to Anastasia. "Anastasia!" she called. "Tell the Blackrobe I have permission to become a Christian!"

Of course Light Feet was angry. She did not want Tekakwitha to be baptized. But Thunder Cloud had spoken. . . .

On Easter Sunday, April 18, 1676—Tekakwitha's twentieth birthday—she heard the beautiful words: "Katherine, I baptize you in the Name of the Father, and of the Son, and of the Holy Ghost." Katherine was the happiest girl in the whole Turtle Clan.

But her joy was soon turned to sorrow.

"I have come to say good-bye," said Anastasia. "I am going to the Christian village. There I will worship God in peace."

"Take me with you," pleaded Katherine. "I will ask my uncle to let me come with you."

But Thunder Cloud would not let Katherine go. "Never will I let you leave our clan," he said.

So Katherine remained with her uncle and aunt. After the girl's Baptism, Light Feet tried to find new ways of hurting her to make her suffer as much as possible.

Not only did Katherine's aunt make her suffer, but also many of the neighbors hurt her, scolding when she refused to work in the fields on Sunday, laughing when she prayed.

But Katherine did not listen to them. She always did her duty. She recited the rosary while working and did double work before the holydays.

One day there was great excitement in the village. An Oneida Chief, who had become a Christian, had come to the village. His Christian name was Louis. He and a companion were now preaching among the tribes of the Mohawk Valley.

Katherine was filled with joy. How she drank in all the words of those Indian missionaries!

In the evening Katherine ran to the missionaries' cabin. "Please," she pleaded, "please take me to Canada where you and all the other Indian converts live. I want to be free to live as a true Christian."

"We will gladly take you, but do you have permission to come?" asked Louis.

"No, I don't. I know my uncle will never grant it, but my aunt would be happy to see me go. Please take me!"

So early one morning Katherine slipped out of the cabin while her uncle was not at home and sped into the forest where the missionaries were waiting to take the trail north.

* * *

"Anastasia, will you take care of this young girl?" asked Father Cholonec.

"Katherine! How happy I am to see you!" exclaimed Anastasia. "Did your uncle give his consent?"

"No, he didn't. I know that my uncle misses me. In fact, he followed us for quite a distance. But God is good to me and did not let him find me," answered Katherine.

"You will live with me," said Anastasia. "Come, I will show you our cabin. Then we will go to visit our good neighbors."

How happy Katherine was! She immediately began living as she had always desired. Even when it was bitter cold, she went to church every morning at four o'clock. Then she would wait for the later Mass, which was celebrated for all the Indians.

Anastasia enjoyed Katherine's company. She told her many things about God and His saints. She explained how the saints used to do penance for their faults.

Katherine listened attentively. She tried to remember God's presence all the time. As often as possible, she recited the rosary, because she loved the Blessed Mother tenderly.

Always she was found helping someone in need. Her greatest pleasure was taking care of children.

Because of her goodness, one of the priests granted her permission to receive Holy Communion, although Indian converts usually had to wait several years for this privilege. Katherine received Jesus on a Christmas morning. Who can describe her joy? From that day on, she went to receive Our Lord frequently.

"What are you doing?" asked Anastasia one day.

"Nothing," answered Katherine, blushing. She had been putting ashes in her porridge! It was one of the many mortifications that she made, but she did not want anyone to know about her penances.

One night Katherine sprinkled her sleeping mat with long, sharp thorns. Then she lay down to sleep. Every movement she made caused her pain. She did this for three nights. Then her friend Anastasia, who had noticed the new kind of penance, told her to stop.

Katherine was very obedient. She thought that she had sinned, so she went to confession and said what she had done. Father Cholonec smiled. "You must not do that," he said, "you are ill, and that penance won't make you better. You must also try to get rid of your bad cold."

One day Katherine could not get up. She was too ill to go to Mass!

"What is the trouble?" asked Anastasia.

"I—I can't move. I feel pains all over," said Katherine.

Anastasia went to speak to the priest.

"I will come at once," said Father Cholonec.

Katherine smiled when she saw him. "Don't worry," she said, "I won't die until tomorrow. You may rest tonight."

The following day she received Holy Communion and Extreme Unction. Then she died peacefully. She was twenty-four years old.

A few minutes after Katherine's death something strange and wonderful happened.

Her face had been scarred from the small pox which she had suffered when a child. Yet, fifteen minutes after her death everyone noticed a great change. Her skin was smooth and lovely! She was beautiful!

Sometimes we have to wait many years for something we want very much, just as Katherine Tekakwitha waited years for her baptism. The important thing is never to stop praying and trusting that God will give us what we wish, if it is for our good.

Saint Margaret Mary

Apostle of the Sacred Heart

From early childhood, Margaret loved God. She always had a great hatred and horror of sin.

When she was seven, she felt something urging her to pray with these words: "My God, I consecrate my purity to You and I make the vow of chastity." She repeated her promise over and over. She did not know the exact meaning of all the words, but she understood that she was giving herself completely to God for all her life. Margaret was inspired to make this vow, but ordinarily such a vow should not be made without asking the opinion of a priest.

A few years later, Margaret became very sick. Her family feared that she would not recover, so they offered her to Mary, hoping that the Madonna would cure her. Soon Margaret became well again, and that was when the trouble began.

"It is your duty to marry," her mother told her. Margaret did not know what to say, for she knew that she could not marry. Time after time, her mother would urge, "Choose one young man, or another, but choose *someone*."

What should Margaret do? She had no spiritual director to help her. She began to weaken. After all, the world and its pleasures were very inviting. . . .

She was thanking Our Lord after Holy Communion one day, when He Himself appeared before her. He was so powerful and handsome! But He looked sad, too. "I have chosen you for My spouse," said Jesus. "We were happily promised to each other when you made Me your vow of chastity. It was I Who urged you to do this before the world had any part in your heart, for I desired you to be completely innocent."

And now Margaret was thinking of forsaking God for an earthly spouse!

"Oh, if you do Me this injury," Jesus told her, "know that I shall abandon you forever; but if you are faithful to Me, I shall never forsake you."

Margaret was crying. She saw how foolish she had been. "My Lord," she promised, "even if it should cost me a million lives, I will never be anything but a religious."

Her mind was made up now, and she was firm when she told her family that she wished to become a sister. "Please send away all the young men who wish to marry me," she said. She entered the Order of the Visitation and took the name, Sister Margaret Mary.

Sister Margaret Mary's love for God grew deeper all the time. She spent hours adoring Him in the Blessed Sacrament. "Oh, my God," she would say, "I love You so much that I want to be consumed by love, just as a candle is consumed by the flame!"

One day, the Feast of St. John the Evangelist, Jesus appeared to Margaret and invited her to rest her head on His Heart, just as St. John had done at the Last Supper.

It was the first of many visions. Jesus told Margaret that she had been chosen to spread devotion to His Sacred Heart, which loves men so much that It has given Itself to them completely. He told her how much it hurts Him to know that most people do not care that He has given His *all* for them.

He told her about the pain He suffers because people hardly seem to know that He is waiting for them in every tabernacle all over the world, longing to be their closest Friend. They hardly talk to Him at all; they hardly ever tell Him they love Him; they hardly ever give their whole hearts to Him Who has given His whole Heart to them!

Jesus told Sister Margaret Mary, "My divine Heart is so on fire with love for mankind that It cannot hold the flames of love inside any longer. It must spread them by means of you!"

Jesus told her, too, that a great many people were in danger of going to hell because of their sins. He asked her to have a special feast day established to honor His Sacred Heart so that those who loved Him could pray for those who did not love Him. Even though the sinners had hurt Him so much, His Heart still burned with love for them and longed for them to be saved.

Sister Margaret Mary found it very hard to tell other people about the Sacred Heart's love for them. They laughed. For a while it seemed as if Our Lord would be forgotten as much as ever, but Margaret was determined that this would not be so. She continued to pray and to plead. In the end, Our Lord rewarded her self-sacrifice and determination by giving the proud and blind people the graces needed to convert themselves and come to Him with hearts full of love.

And so, Sister Margaret Mary accomplished the very special mission she had been given, and went to Heaven with her heart full of peace.

"My only need is God, and to lose myself in the Heart of Jesus."

Even if we displease God, we must never despair, but always trust in His mercy. If we are really sorry, He will forgive us and help us to be better.

Saint John Baptist de La Salle

Patron of Teachers

People always like the saints who dedicate their lives to children, and of these St. John Baptist de La Salle is especially lovable. He was born in Rheims, France, in the seventeenth century. It was a cruel age in which to live if one was poor, but the wealthy fared well, as one would expect. John himself was a member of a rich and respected family and could have had a successful and comfortable future ahead of him. However God's plans are often different from those of men, so John chose to become a priest. Shortly after his ordination he became a canon of the Cathedral of Rheims.

This priest would soon devote himself to serving God in the swarms of youngsters who were growing up without instruction or training of any sort, amid conditions of the most squalid spiritual misery. In those days there were no state-supervised public schools, and only the fortunate children of the wealthy went to private schools; the others were influenced only by the conditions in which they lived, and as these were generally bad, their lives were tending toward desolation and misery.

It was upon these children that the pitying gaze of John Baptist de La Salle rested, and as he looked upon them, he began to plan out the program of his life: instruction and training of the young, above all the most abandoned and miserable.

It was in a strange and marvelous way that Our Lord made it possible for Father John de La Salle to begin his wonderful mission.

❖ ❖ ❖

In the city of Rheims there lived a beautiful, rich, much-admired lady, who was very proud. She had no charity toward the poor and always closed her doors to them. One evening the lady's cook came up to her and asked, "Madame, a beggar is asking for shelter. May I let him into the coach house for tonight?"

"A beggar? Here?" The lady was plainly horrified. "No! No! Definitely not!" The cook went away sadly.

But the cook had a kind heart, and could not bear to send the beggar away. "Come," she said to the poor man, "I'll do the best I can for you!" She let him into the coach-house and brought him a little food, and a blanket also because it was very cold. . . .

The next morning, the beggar was found dead in the coach-house.

When the wealthy lady found out, she was furious. She fired the disobedient cook, and ordered that the corpse be removed immediately.

Quickly the servants wrapped the body in a large sheet, took it away, and buried it. Only then did the haughty lady calm down, but her relief did not last long, for that evening she saw the burial sheet draped over an armchair in her room!

"Still here? But then," she gasped, "is that body still in my house?"

"No Madame," the servants tried to reassure her. "We took it and buried it, wrapped securely in this sheet!"

In *that* sheet! The proud lady felt her blood freeze, for the mysterious event showed her in an instant how harsh, and even wicked, she had been. Grace touched her heart; she decided to make reparation for her life of mistakes by using her wealth to do good.

The Providence of God soon brought Father John Baptist de La Salle to her. She gave him the money to realize his great dream—schools open to the poorest children—Christian schools which would not only teach reading and writing but would also hold up the pattern of Christ's life to be copied.

In the face of objections from all sorts of people—some of whom did not understand, and some of whom were downright evil, Father John opened his first school. The children of the poor came flocking to it joyously. A bright, new future was opening up before them.

What envy Father de La Salle was stirring up! Highly-paid teachers, fearful that they would now be jobless, met and murmured among themselves. Then they drew up a long list of charges and filed a lawsuit against Father de La Salle. But the lawsuit came to nothing, for the poor, whom the saint had so helped, sprang to his defense. His enemies were forced to try another method.

They called together a band of ruffians, armed them to the teeth, and ordered, "Break into his school, and destroy everything there without pity."

In the middle of the night they did their dark deed. Morning revealed the destruction: only ruins remained of the school that two hundred children had attended.

"The Lord has allowed this for a reason," said the saint. "We shall move to another section of the city to build our next school."

Now, attracted by his example, the first "recruits" were coming to him; they were men who wished to dedicate their lives to the noble mission of Christian education. Of them Father de La Salle formed the first "Brothers of the Christian Schools."

Father John wanted to live in community with his brothers, so he decided to resign his canonry at the Cathedral. It was a sacrifice which would have been unbearable for most, but not for a saint.

"He's crazy," said some.

"He doesn't realize what he's doing."

"He'll regret it later; you'll see!"

Father John's parents, in particular, tried to change his mind, and so did his fellow canons, for they did not want to lose such a good friend and co-worker as he. But Father de La Salle remained firm in his decision, and went to the archbishop's home to resign the office.

The archbishop did not want to lose Father de La Salle either; he pretended not to be at home.

Father John went into the church and prayed, "Lord, let me renounce my canonry at once so that I may be as poor as You were!"

His prayers were answered. Soon Father John was free to dedicate himself entirely to his schools. The brothers joined him in singing a great hymn of praise to God.

The Institute prospered in spite of all sorts of difficulties. Divine assistance was obvious; at times, in fact, it appeared to be miraculous. There was the time, for example, when the community was moving from Paris to another city. The furniture movers had to be paid, and the brother in charge of the money had almost nothing. He came to Father John, told him of the trouble, and asked him what he should do. "Oh," replied the priest, "the beauty of it is that I haven't a cent either!"

"What, then?"

"Then, never fear. Isn't there Divine Providence? Pray and leave everything up to God!"

Since the brother knew that Father de La Salle was very holy, he went away feeling relieved. However, the day passed, and Divine Providence had not yet appeared, while the movers *had* appeared and were asking their wages! The brother became worried again. He hurried up to Father John, who smiled and told him to have faith.

As the brother went back across the courtyard, his eye lit upon an old bureau. Oh, he thought, if that were only a safe! But the brother knew well that he had gone through every piece of furniture thoroughly before the movers arrived.

Yet he gave in to the temptation to look just one more time. And there, in plain sight, was the sum of money they needed! There was neither a cent more nor a cent less!

"It's a miracle," the brother told Father de La Salle. His eyes were shining with joy. The saint smiled. "Let us thank God," he replied. "He never abandons those who trust in Him."

*   *   *

Father de La Salle prayed so much and drew so close to God that he actually seemed to *enjoy* insults and humiliations. In fact, he *did* enjoy them because they gave him a chance to suffer as Jesus had suffered.

One fine day Father John was relaxing in the garden, at the same time keeping an eye on the horse which the brothers used for long journeys. It was cropping the grass nearby. As the saint became absorbed in prayer, the animal strayed into a neighboring meadow. The meadow's owner appeared on the scene at once.

"Do you think all the fields are made for your beast?" he roared. In a fit of anger he struck the saint on the face.

Father de La Salle stayed perfectly calm. He knelt down and humbly asked his neighbor's pardon!

We can imagine how the shame-stricken neighbor felt then!

And how Father de La Salle used to mortify himself! One day, when there was nothing to eat, the brother cook went out and gathered some strange-looking greens, which had been growing unnoticed in a corner of the garden. No one knew what they were. With them the cook prepared a soup for lunch.

But what a soup it was! It was so horribly bitter that the brothers took only one spoonful and laid down their spoons in disgust. They would rather go hungry than eat that awful *thing!*

But how about Father John? He was eating away, thinking about God, not even seeming to know that he was eating something that tasted so bad.

That night, confused and deeply moved by the example they had been given, all the brothers ate the bitter soup without a word—in tribute to their spiritual father—who knew so well the virtue of mortification.

Although Father de La Salle is long since dead, the great work he began lives after him. From France, his brothers spread into other nations, where their mission continues to thrive, as they bring to youth Christ's truths that will aid them to reflect His image.

Teaching is one of the most important vocations there is. We can help our teachers by praying for them and by paying careful attention in class.

Saint Elizabeth Seton

American-Born Saint

The little four year old sat on the porch steps, watching big, puffy clouds go floating by. She seemed not to care that inside the house, only a few feet away from her, rested a tiny coffin containing the body of a small child.

"Elizabeth," a voice asked, "what are you doing? Your dear sister Kitty is dead, and you are not even crying?"

"No," replied the little girl. "I am not crying because Kitty has gone to Heaven. And I wish I could go to Heaven to be with my mother, too!"

Little Elizabeth Bayley had been taught by her mother that God is a loving Father, and that He has prepared a beautiful reward in Heaven for all who love Him. Now that her mother and little sister had gone to their heavenly home, the little girl wished only to follow them. However, she would have to work and suffer very much before that blessed reunion.

In a few years, Elizabeth was helping a new stepmother around the house and caring for new baby sisters. She enjoyed teaching the little ones their prayers. She was studying hard at school, and also learning self-control and generosity.

Elizabeth's father, Dr. Richard Bayley, gave her many examples of generosity. He helped the poor a great deal; in fact, he was kinder to them than he was to anyone else.

One day another doctor called on him to ask, "Could you come help me perform a difficult and dangerous operation?"

"I have a very full schedule," Dr. Bayley replied, "and I'm tired besides. Surely another doctor can come."

"I doubt if another would be willing," the friend replied. "I'll be sorry to tell that family of your refusal. They are poor people—penniless."

Dr. Bayley jumped to his feet. "Poor?" he asked. "Why didn't you say so before? Let's go at once!"

* * *

Elizabeth grew into a calm and prayerful young woman of eighteen. She had delicate features and beautiful dark eyes. William Seton, a young businessman, fell in love with her and asked her to marry him. Since they were Episcopalians, they were married in an Episcopal church in New York City in 1794.

William and Elizabeth were very happy, but a heavy burden soon fell upon them. Upon his father's death, William, as the oldest son, had to take over the business and support his twelve brothers and sisters. Elizabeth, sad to see him becoming worried and tense, helped with the bookkeeping, and tried to find little ways to keep William's courage up. Now and then, she would speak of the great reward God prepares for those who are resigned to His will. She knew the Bible from cover to cover, and often consoled her husband with a line or two from Scripture.

The young couple were blessed with five children—Anna Mary, William, Richard, Catherine and Rebecca. Elizabeth regarded each child as a gift from God, and was careful to see that each grew up obedient and kind. When they needed punishment, she would punish them, gently but firmly knowing that this was for the good of their souls.

In 1803, William became quite ill, and the doctors suggested that a sea voyage would do him good.

"Leave the younger children with us, Elizabeth," urged kind relatives. "You will be able to take better care of William that way."

Sad as she was to part from her little ones, Elizabeth agreed. She and William and Anna Mary set sail for Italy, where William had spent some time in his youth. There they would stay with old friends of his, the Filicchi family.

But when the ship reached port, William was placed under quarantine, for the officials were afraid he might be carrying yellow fever. They did not know that he was dying of tuberculosis.

The quarantine shack was dirty and cold. William's condition grew worse and worse in spite of the good food and other necessities which his friends the Filicchis sent to him. Helplessly, Elizabeth looked on, as her husband was seized by coughing spell after coughing spell. Soon he was coughing up blood, although he tried not to let her see it.

"What shall we say?" Elizabeth wrote to her sister-in-law, Rebecca. "This is the hour of trial. In permitting it Our Lord gives us support and strength. . . . Let us press forward toward the goal and the reward."

Soon she had overcome herself enough to be able to write, "I have not only resolved to carry my cross, but I have kissed it. When I thank God for having created and preserved me, I do so with more love than ever. To wait on him, my William, soul and body, to console and soothe those long hours of pain, to hear him pronounce the name of Jesus— even in the darkest dungeon I would thank God for letting me perform such a holy task!"

At last William's quarantine was ended, and he was carried away tenderly to the Filicchi home but all hope was gone. Elizabeth watched by his bedside for three days and nights while he suffered intensely—and then it was over. Elizabeth was exhausted, but she knew she had done everything she could.

William was buried the next morning.

The Filicchi family was very kind, and asked Elizabeth and Anna Mary to stay with them for a few weeks. One day Elizabeth went to church with them.

The services amazed her, for she had never before witnessed the drama of the liturgy. She went to church with her new friends again and again.

One morning, at the elevation of the Sacred Host, Elizabeth thought of the words of St. Paul— "discerning the Body of the Lord"—and tears began to flow down her cheeks. Was Jesus truly present here, as St. Paul had said He was? Oh, if He only were! She could speak to Him of all her sorrows; she could tell Him of her sins and receive His forgiveness!

Often the Blessed Sacrament was carried through the streets in procession. Whenever she saw a procession pass her window, Elizabeth had a deep sense of loneliness. If only she could believe that God was present in the Host. One day she fell to her knees, and prayed silently, "My God, bless me if You are truly present. My soul desires only You!"

One of Mrs. Filicchi's prayerbooks was on a table nearby. Elizabeth opened it, and there was a prayer to the Blessed Mother. Elizabeth said the prayer slowly. She was sure that God would not refuse His Mother anything, and that Mary would have only love and mercy for the souls for whom her Son had suffered. Elizabeth prayed, and she felt that the Blessed Mother was her mother, a tender, compassionate mother. She began to cry in relief, and crying she fell asleep.

* * *

The ocean voyage had been long, but Elizabeth forgot the length of it and all her worries when she saw that her younger children were all well. Even though William was gone, God would take care of them.

"I have good reason to place my trust in You, my God," Elizabeth wrote. "Whom do I have in Heaven except You? And whom on earth besides You?"

She had been thinking long and carefully, and had decided to become a Catholic. She knew, now, that Jesus truly was present in the Blessed Sacrament, and she longed to assist at Mass and to receive Him.

Her husband's family objected; and threatened to have nothing to do with her if she should take the step. Elizabeth then went to Father Cheverus, who would one day become Cardinal of Boston, and poured out her story. He told her that she, indeed, was making the right choice—the only one which would bring her happiness. And so, in the only Catholic church in New York City, on March 14, 1805, Elizabeth became a Catholic. She was thirty years old.

After a general confession, Elizabeth prepared for her first Holy Communion, which she received on Annunciation Day. "At last," she wrote, "God is mine, and I am His!"

The relatives abandoned Elizabeth, leaving her and the children without income, but she did not care. She had peace of soul, and no price was too great to pay for that. She opened a school and began to teach. At night she would play the piano while her five youngsters sang and danced, and then when they had gone to bed she would mend and make over their clothes. At midnight she would go to bed, only to rise early and walk several blocks to Mass. It was a hard schedule, but she did not mind. When William had been alive, he had scolded her for working too hard, and she had replied, "Love makes all effort easy." Now that Jesus was her Friend and

her Spouse, should she not say the same—and
more—to Him?

* * *

One day Elizabeth was introduced to a young
priest from Baltimore, who told her of the great
need of that city for a religious community to teach
young girls. Could not Elizabeth found such a community?

Elizabeth felt quite unworthy, but she prayed
about it and consulted her spiritual director. Then
she agreed to try.

In His all-wise Providence, God soon sent
Elizabeth several young women who wished to become teaching sisters. He also sent a generous benefactor who provided the finances necessary to build
a school, academy and hospital in Emmitsburg,
Maryland. The community received its Constitu-
tions in 1812, when already it numbered twenty
sisters.

Of course, trials accompanied the founding of
the new community. One of these was the death of
several of its members because of hardships suffered during the War of 1812. Then Anna Mary,
who had become a novice, became ill and died.
About the same time Rebecca, Elizabeth's youngest,
injured her leg, and a tumor developed. The girl,
who was only ten, suffered patiently for months,
while Elizabeth stayed at her bedside day and
night, telling her of the beauties of Heaven which
would soon be hers. She marveled at Rebecca's
patience, for the girl was in great pain. When
Rebecca died Elizabeth wrote to young William,

"If you had been given the opportunity of seeing our Rebecca fly to Heaven as a little angel, you could not be more certain that she is with God."

Elizabeth made a wonderful Superior, for she gave her sisters a perfect example of prayerfulness, of calm, of mortification and self-sacrifice. She looked after each sister and each young pupil as diligently as she had looked after her own children.

Her thoughts were fixed on Heaven, as they had been when she was a child. Now she knew that her own death was coming, for she was growing weaker day by day. "Eternity seems so near," she would exclaim. "Think of it when you feel oppressed or annoyed. It will be a beautiful endless day!"

After receiving Extreme Unction, Elizabeth said, "Thank you! Oh, how grateful I am!" She was thinking of the great consolation the Church gives to the dying.

"Have pity on me!" she said to her sisters. "Pray for me!" The next day, with the name of "Jesus" on her lips, she passed away peacefully, to rejoin her loved ones forever in the land of eternal joy.

Let us think of Heaven sometimes—especially when we are having a good time. If we remember that we will die some day, we will be careful to have only clean fun; we will avoid everything that could lead us to sin.

Saint Joseph Cottolengo

Model of Faith

"The charity of Christ urges us on!"

Those words were first written by the Apostle St. Paul in one of his epistles. Now they are found in another place also, over a plain little door that faces a side street in the city of Turin, Italy. If you saw the door, you would be very much surprised to learn that a *city*—a "city-within-a-city"—is on the other side.

"The charity of Christ urges us on!"

"On to do what?" we might ask, slightly puzzled. What is the meaning of St. Paul's words above that plain little door?

The answer we would receive is this: To do something which is hardly ever done, something beautiful in its holiness—that is, to search the cities for the sick people who are the most abandoned, who suffer the greatest pain, who are the most unpleasant to look at and care for, and to take these poor souls and treat them, tend them, teach them to see their sufferings as a sign of God's special love, for He rewards every sorrow that is offered up to Him.

A very holy priest, a few years ago, first thought of building this great city for the sick. He started with just one small building, and as that was filled he added a second, a third, a fourth and many others. The number of sick grew from one hundred to several thousand; today there are ten thousand people in that city, which is called, of all things: "The Little House of Divine Providence".

Suppose we were to open the plain little door and enter the city of the sick. The first thing we would see would be a courtyard, and there in the middle a beautiful statue of the Blessed Mother all decorated with roses and other flowers. Near the statue is a place to leave donations—for all the money that comes to support the ten thousand sick people is given by God and men. Truly the "Little House" runs on Divine Providence!

The statue has a beautiful smile. "She's the Gatekeeper of the House," said the holy priest who put her there. It is through her intercession that everything goes smoothly in the city.

Suppose we were to pass through the courtyard and enter the network of streets beyond. We would see one huge building after another, one for the blind, one for the deaf, one for the crippled, one for the terribly deformed, and so on. Some of those poor people would make even the worst criminal cry. They are in such a miserable condition. Some of them cannot understand anything that is happening around them. They cannot even move.

But in spite of the pain and misery, the sick are happy. The cheerful sisters who take care of them are happy, too. There is an atmosphere of peace in the city of suffering. And the reason? The Providence of God.

There are huge dormitories of white beds, and at one end of each is a marble altar. There the priests celebrate Mass every morning. The Mass always has an infinite value, because it is the renewal of Our Lord's own sacrifice. But here, among so many who live in pain, the Mass has an even greater value for us because all those other sufferings are united to His.

You should see the people working in the "Little House"! Even those that have no hands, work with their feet or with special tools. They all have something to do. Think of the feeling of satisfaction that gives them! They really feel that they are doing something useful. If they are too ill to do anything else at all, they have still more time to pray, and prayer is the most important work of all.

As we said before, the "Little House" depends completely on the Providence of God. Often bread is needed, or medicine, or clothes, and there is no money to spend on them. Yet nobody worries. The priests and sisters know that God sees, and that He will provide. And the needed help always comes, usually at the very last moment!

In the heart of the little city is a magnificent church. There are always many people there praying, asking God to bless the "Little House". Among them are the busy sisters who take care of the sick so lovingly.

❀   ❀   ❀

Perhaps you would like to learn more about the priest who founded this marvelous city. His name was Joseph Benedict Cottolengo, and he had wanted to help the sick even when he was very small. One day, he paid a visit to a nearby hospital.

When he came home, he started to measure the rooms in the house.

"Joey, what are you doing?" his mother asked.

"I'm going to bring lots of sick people in here," the little boy answered. "I want to see how many will fit!"

When Joseph grew up, he studied to become a priest. After he was ordained, he went to a large church in Turin to help its pastor. He tried to use every minute of his time well, but still he felt that something was missing from his life.

One day a family from a faraway village came to Turin. There were three small children, their good father, and their mother who had become very ill during the trip. The father hurried to take her to a big hospital, but the hospital would not take her in because she was poor.

The mother was getting more and more ill, moment by moment. "I'm afraid," the father thought to himself. "She's very ill. She may die. I must find a priest."

Father Cottolengo was the priest the poor man called. He hurried to the side of the sick woman, and gave her the Last Sacraments. Then, as he stood by, helpless to do any more, the poor woman died. Her husband and the three little children sobbed desperately.

What a terrible shock it was for that little family which had needed its mother so much! Father Cottolengo thought of how she might have been saved if that hospital had only taken her in and cared for her. As he thought about it, he made a resolution: that sort of thing would never happen again in Turin!

It didn't take the determined priest very long to put his plans into action. He soon found a small building near the center of the city which could be turned into a hospital. He opened it up and brought in the most desperately sick people he could find. But then troubles came, and he had to close the little hospital again.

But Father Cottolengo was not discouraged. He did not give up his great idea. He waited and looked around and pretty soon he found a large meadow with a little house in the center of it. This would be his next hospital!

On April 27, 1832, a little cart pulled by a donkey came bumping along the road to the little house. In the cart was a patient with a diseased leg. Two sisters and a kind lady came with him. And that was when the Little House of Divine Providence really started. It was a poor beginning, but full of joy and faith.

More and more patients came. Soon another house had to be built, then another and another. Streets were built between the houses, and before long there was no meadow left at all—just buildings filled with all kinds of sick people.

Father Cottolengo was working very hard all the time, to make sure that all the needs of the sick, of the sisters and other nurses were provided for. He worked very hard, but he prayed even harder, because only the spiritual and material help from God could keep his great project going. More food,

more medicine, more doctors, sisters, priests. . . .
Truly this was God's work.

Yes, it was God's work. But people began to
wonder what would happen when Father Cottolengo would die. Would God still provide, without
the faith and prayers of that holy priest?

That question bothered the king, too. One day
he sent for Father Cottolengo and asked him if he
had made any plans for the future. For a minute the
priest didn't say anything. He walked over to the
window and looked down into the big square below.
"If you please, Your Majesty, come look at this,"
he said. There below them the palace guard was
changing. One group of soldiers was dismounting
from their horses; other soldiers took their place.
It all happened very calmly and without excitement.

"That's just the way that someone will take my
place when God calls me. Don't you think so, Your
Majesty?"

The king was very much impressed. From that
time on, he had great respect and admiration for
Father Cottolengo. He always spoke of him with
great affection, as: "my friend Cottolengo".

To the holy priest, those poor, suffering patients
in his Little House were the most important people
in all the world. When he was with them, nothing
could take him away. One day an archbishop came
to visit. He found Father Cottolengo playing ball
with a poor crazy man named Doro.

"I would like to speak with you, Father," said
the archbishop.

"I'm delighted to see you, Your Excellency," replied the priest. "I'm playing with this gentleman right now, and he might feel offended if I stop. I hope you don't mind waiting."

So the archbishop waited, and even kept score for the players! He didn't mind, because he realized that Father Cottolengo was very holy.

Saints can be described in many ways, depending on what virtues they show the most, or what virtues we need the most to imitate. Love and Hope both describe St. Joseph Cottolengo very well, but another virtue stood out even more clearly in him, and that was his Faith in Divine Providence. "Everytime someone new enters the Little House," he said, "more bread comes down from heaven—and the best thing about it is that *I'm* not the one who makes it come; it is Divine Providence which takes joy in raining down the loaves one by one."

Never worried, never discouraged—that was Father Cottolengo. When things seemed at their worst, he was the happiest. Then he felt that the Providence of God was really close. Sometimes he could predict the arrival of something they needed almost to the exact minute. One day, for instance, they ran out of flour, rice and noodles; it was almost mealtime, and there were all those thousands of sick people to feed!

The sister-cook was really worried. She hurried up to Father Cottolengo. "Oh, Father, there's nothing to prepare!"

"Really? Well, put the kettles on and start the water boiling. Let's not waste any time."

Waste time? With nothing to cook? But the sister obeyed.

As soon as the water was boiling merrily in the big kettles, the doorbell rang. And who was outside? There was a big wagon full of bread and rice which someone had donated!

"The Little House will grow as long as it does not have a steady source of income," Father Cottolengo often said. "It will grow only as long as it has nothing."

One day Father Cottolengo had to leave on a trip. His brother, Father Louis Cottolengo, came to take his place. "Here is the money bag, Louis," said the saint. "Spend whatever you need to spend, but never look inside the bag to see what is left. If you do as I say, the money will last."

Many, many expenses came up in the days that followed. Father Louis had to pay a great deal of money. He was amazed that the little bag always provided whatever he needed and more! It didn't seem possible that it could have held so much!

Another time, a great sum of money was needed. Father Cottolengo went though the whole house trying to find some. He reached into his pocket several times, and each time there was nothing. But the last time. . .

"Thanks be to God!" Father Cottolengo drew from his pocket the exact sum he needed!

And then there was the time that the Superior of the Sisters came up to him looking quite upset. "What's the trouble, sister?" the saint asked kindly.

"I have so many things to buy, Father, and this is all the money I have!"

"This is all? Let me see it."

She handed it to him. It was a very small sum indeed. "Quite right," said Father Cottolengo. He walked over to the window and tossed the money outside!

Now what do you think of that? Can you imagine how that sister felt? At least she had a little money before; now her hands were completely empty!

"That's all right," said Father Cottolengo. "It's been planted now. Wait a few hours, and it will bear fruit."

Sure enough—that evening a woman came to see Father Cottolengo. She gave him a large sum of money.

＊   ＊   ＊

"Oh, Father," said the sister-cook one day. "We have not even a crumb of bread to eat."

"No?" smiled the priest. "Well, that's fine. I can't do anything about it myself, but this is just the right kind of job for Divine Providence. Come with me, sister."

They went down to the courtyard where the statue of the Blessed Mother stood. Father Cottolengo opened the little box that held the donations. Inside it was a great roll of money. "Thanks be to God!" said the priest. "Isn't this bread?"

"What shall we do for salt, Father?" asked one of the sisters on another day.

"Don't ask me. Just go buy some!"

"That's fine, Father, but what shall we do for money?"

"Don't worry. Go with God."

The sister did as she was told, but she was quite upset about it. Halfway to the store she met a lady. "This is for the priest," said the woman, and she handed the sister a large roll of money. Then she hurried away.

Of course, the sister rushed back home and told the story to Father Cottolengo. When she started to describe the lady, the priest said, "You didn't recognize her; she was the Blessed Mother!"

One day another sister came up to the saint and said, "Father, what are we going to do? There's no bread, no flour, no potatoes—there's nothing! And it's almost dinnertime!" She held up a nickel. "This is all we have!"

"Give it to me," replied the priest. He flung the nickel out the window. "There! Now we have nothing, and Providence *has* to provide!"

"Go to the church and pray," he told the upset sister. "I'll go and pray, too. When noon comes, *send everyone to the dining hall, as usual.*"

Noon came. The obedient sister sent everyone into the dining hall, and they sat down in their empty places. There was a knock at the gate. Someone hurried to open it. And what came rolling in through the gate but wagon after wagon, loaded with ready-prepared meals! Those meals had been intended for a regiment of soldiers who were in the field on battle maneuvers. The soldiers had been delayed, and their officers had decided to send the food to the Little House so as not to waste it.

One day the sister who did all the buying told Father Cottolengo that she didn't want to do it any longer.

"And why not?" asked the priest.

"The storekeepers want us to pay our bills before they sell us anything else!"

"You have no faith," replied the saint. "As a penance, say the psalm 'Miserere'—and then go out as usual."

The sister didn't say a word. She just prayed, and left.

In the first place on her list, the storekeeper came up and handed her a receipt for what had been owed: "A lady came and paid me for you, sister!"

It happened again and again, all along the street. One woman even handed the sister some extra money. "The lady left it for you," she said.

Father Cottolengo listened to the story without surprise. *He* knew who the mysterious Lady was!

Then there was the time that a very angry man came to the Little House and demanded that his bill be paid. "I won't leave until you pay every single cent!" he roared.

"I haven't even one cent," replied Father Cottolengo.

The big man said something nasty.

"Please don't swear," said Father Cottolengo. "Come back tomorrow, and we'll pay it all."

"Nothing doing! It'll be right now. I'm not moving from here until you pay up!"

"All right," agreed the saint. "Wait just a moment, please."

It was very quiet for a minute. Father Cottolengo reached into his pocket very slowly. When he pulled his hand out, it held two large rolls of money.

The big man's eyes were almost popping out of his head. He went away amazed.

There are many more stories like these that we could tell about St. Joseph Cottolengo. His life was full of miracles, because he had such great Faith, and because the Little House needed them so much. In fact, the miracles have continued since his death, almost as if he were guiding the Little House from Heaven. Even to this day, the Little House runs smoothly, operating only on the gifts of God!

The body of the saint lies now in a large glass case. Every day a long line of people who are devoted to him pass by, and as they do, it almost seems to them that he is saying, "Let's not fool ourselves. We are nothing unless we put ourselves in the hands of God's Providence. If we do that, we will surely be able to do great things!"

There is nothing that happens to us which God does not permit. Even when everything seems to go wrong, let us trust that God will bring good from it in the end.

Saint Bartholomea

Lily of Lovere

"Let's see which of us will become a saint first!"

Sister Frances, who had spoken, smiled as the young pupils crowded about her shouting, "I will!"

"No, I!"

"No, me!"

One of the newer girls stared at the sister wide-eyed. A saint? Become a saint?

"Well, let's draw straws."

Sister Frances began to search for straws of various lengths. Meanwhile the wide-eyed girl, who was about eleven years old, ran across the courtyard to the chapel, rushed inside, and fell to her knees before the Blessed Virgin's altar.

"Oh, Heavenly Mother," she begged, "grant that I may draw the long straw! I promise you I *will* become a saint, no matter what the cost!"

Hastily she said three Hail Marys, and hurried back to the courtyard, already confident that her desire would be granted.

The drawing began. With trembling hand, the eleven-year-old approached. Rosy color flooded her face and a strange light glowed in her black eyes. She pulled, and looked.

"Bartholomea has drawn the long straw!"

While her companions watched in wonder mixed with envy, the dark-eyed girl gazed down at the straw—and cried for joy!

In a second she was running back to the chapel, kneeling before the Blessed Virgin's Statue, and offering thanks. Bartholomea knew that picking the straw was not the *reason* she would become a saint, for holiness means the favor of God's grace. But she looked upon the event as encouragement to her great desire.

* * *

Some seven or eight years before, Bartholomea had been a lively little girl, hopping and skipping about, asking a million and one questions. Her bright eyes took in everything around her. As she grew older, she became a leader in games, usually playing the part of the mother or the teacher. Her vivid imagination led her to make up stories to delight her companions. Often she would take smaller neighborhood children to church and teach them their prayers in front of the Blessed Virgin's altar.

After hearing a sermon about how much Jesus suffered because of our sins, Bartholomea promised, "Oh, Jesus, I shall never offend You again!"

The joys she felt when she received First Communion remain a mystery, for Bartholomea never described the experience to anyone. Those who saw her, noticed tears in her eyes and joy in her smile.

But Bartholomea's childhood was far from being all sweetness!

Her father was a drunkard, and had a violent temper. Often he came home reeling, surly and suspicious, ready to quarrel at the slightest excuse. Sometimes he beat Bartholomea's mother; he often drove her out of the house. But he was fond of Bartholomea and listened at least a little when she tried to calm him down. After calming her father the girl would find her mother and console her.

The mother knew that in Bartholomea she had a treasure of innocence, but she feared for her daughter amid such home surroundings. And so she sent her to live at the school of the Sisters of St. Clare—where Bartholomea made her resolution to become a saint.

No sooner had the girl made her decision than she set about finding a way to accomplish it. She wrote:

"I resolve to make myself a saint. That is the goal to which You, my God, invite me.

"It is an ambitious saying, which would be proud if I did not place all my confidence in You, my God.

"I propose to make myself a saint by the practice of three virtues—humility, self-denial and prayer.

"During my visits to You in the Blessed Sacrament You have told me that I must always strive for and long for perfection, and that although I ought to distrust myself and realize that I am capable of nothing except offending You, I should nonetheless trust You completely, hope in You entirely, abandon myself to You totally.

"Mary, my dear Mother, please, help me to become a saint."

Well did Bartholomea know that she would become a saint only by praying much—for prayer would obtain God's help. Her program was prayer and mortification.

For her model Bartholomea took St. Aloysius, whose life she had recently read. At the same time she sent a copy of the book home to her parents, so that they, too, would profit from the saint's example.

❋ ❋ ❋

Bartholomea set about overcoming her natural likes and dislikes.

When her mother brought her baskets of fruit and candy, she divided everything among her companions, who never realized that she took none for herself.

When she had to eat something she disliked, she never mentioned the fact, but ate it without expression. Once a sister asked, "You don't care for this do you?"

Flushing slightly, the girl replied, "It's true that it is hard for me to mortify my palate by eating what I don't like, but let me make these little mortifications. Once I read that one who pleases his own taste will never acquire the spirit of prayer."

Every Saturday, she ate less than usual, in honor of the Blessed Virgin. On Fridays she drank only water with her meals. Often she placed pebbles in her shoes.

They seem small, these acts of virtue—yet such little victories over nature strengthen the will, so that it can later overcome the temptations and difficulties of life. Besides, nothing is small in the eyes of God and He rewards everything done out of love for Him.

Bartholomea was bright and sensitive. She was also proud. Luckily her teachers knew this and were determined not to let pride harm that soul which longed to become a saint. Mother Frances scolded her often for even the smallest faults, until one day someone remarked, "It seems that the teacher hates her." Instead, Mother Frances loved Bartholomea very much, and the girl knew it, and was always grateful to her. She asked Mother Frances' advice in every need—physical or spiritual—and she always tried to take the corrections cheerfully.

One day she was blamed for something someone else had done.

"Kneel on the floor—there—in the middle of the room!" came the order.

Bartholomea knelt, calmly. She knew who the real culprit was, but felt it would be unkind to tell. Her companions began to cry for her.

"If only we knew who really did it!" they whispered among themselves. They were fond of Bartholomea, who was so kind and full of fun.

Another time she received a very good mark.

"You will go back to a lower grade for one month!" the teacher said.

Her companions gasped, and Bartholomea herself was startled, but she obeyed.

For a whole month she joined the beginners' reading class!

When she was fourteen, a new problem entered her life. Camilla, her nine-year-old sister, came to stay at the school. She was stormy and impetuous like their father, accustomed to having her own way. The sisters had to scold her often, and this made Bartholomea suffer greatly, even though she wanted the sisters to correct Camilla for her own good. Often the older sister was blamed for the faults of the younger, but she did not mind.

Bartholomea never tried to hide her own faults. In fact, she said them openly, in front of everyone, and asked pardon for them.

Happy years, they were—those fleeting teen years which provided many boys and girls with nothing but memories, but which gave Bartholomea thousands of merits. In her last two years of school she helped the sisters teach the younger children, and she showed herself a perfect teacher—patient and cheerful, lively and kind, quick to solve any situation that faced her. The children loved and trusted her, for they knew she was their friend. She knew how to encourage the timid, arouse the lazy, and correct those who needed it.

At recess she was always thinking up interesting games to play, and stories of saints to tell.

And then, her parents called her home. They wanted her with them, and much as she would have liked to become a sister, Bartholomea went home to her family. She knew that this was God's will for her—to live in the world although her heart was with God, and to sanctify herself by enduring the anger and blasphemies of her father, by comforting her beaten and sobbing mother, by overlooking the complaints and spitefulness of Camilla.

Indeed Camilla was a real cross for her older sister. She was impatient, and, although five years younger than Bartholomea, she bossed her around continually. Bartholomea always hurried to obey— as if Camilla were the elder. Some days the older girl's patience was really tested, but always she came through the crisis calm and smiling. As time passed, Camilla became gentler. She often joined Bartholomea in her prayers and became a sympathetic listener to her older sister's projects and difficulties. Meekness had won out.

Bartholomea was kind and respectful toward her father, in spite of his violent outbursts. He was fond of her because of this, preferring her over the stubborn and stormy Camilla, who resembled him so much. Bartholomea, however, did not wish to be preferred, and she often prayed that God would give her father more affection for Camilla.

❉ ❉ ❉

Often she would look for him when he was out drinking, in order to lead him home before trouble started.

On one occasion she stopped at a friend's house.

"Yes, your father was here but he has gone to the tavern, now. If you like, I'll go call him."

"No, I'll go," Bartholomea replied.

"Into a tavern? Aren't you afraid of being insulted?"

"Oh, no. I'm not afraid of humiliations." And off she went.

She found her father playing cards. Seating herself nearby, she said, "Daddy, as soon as you finish this hand, I need to speak with you."

She led him out—and home! No one in the smelly, smoky tavern, had said an unkind word to her, because of her courage, modesty and devotedness.

On another occasion, a neighbor insulted Bartholomea's father. He tried to control his anger at first, but as insult followed insult, rage welled up in his heart and he lunged at the other man.

Bartholomea ran up to him and urged, "It's not worth bothering about, Daddy. It's not worth it. Come on, let's go home!" And without even giving the tormentor a scornful glance, father and daughter turned and left.

How did Bartholomea acquire such strength and courage? We would not wonder, if we were to examine the daily program she made out for herself shortly after she returned home. It was a long program, very detailed, including daily Mass, an hour of meditation each morning, and another half hour at night, a daily visit to the Blessed Sacrament, and many ejaculations and spiritual communions.

These are some of the resolutions from that program:

I shall teach classes only for the purpose of glorifying God and helping my neighbor. Besides teaching pupils the regular subjects, I shall teach them piety and virtue.

I shall be pleasant and kind to everyone, especially to my sister. However if anyone does something which should be corrected, I shall reprove her kindly.

I shall never complain about anything nor tell others about the little sufferings which God may send me.

I shall try to hide my likes and dislikes, following instead the preferences of the others. I shall choose the simplest food and clothes unless my companions wish otherwise.

I shall hold my tongue, never saying unkind or useless words.

I shall never pry into the affairs of others, but shall concentrate on my own.

I shall never praise myself nor give excuses, but shall try to remain hidden from the eyes of people in order to be more pleasing to God.

I shall bear insults, sharp words, and other harshness patiently and joyously.

I shall love the poor and enjoy being with them. I shall help them with kind words and with as much material aid as possible. Three times a week I shall put aside some of my own food to give to them.

I shall visit the sick as often as I can—at least once a week.

On every holy day I shall give some religious instruction to persons who need it, and shall encourage them to practice virtue.

I shall never argue nor raise my voice; on the contrary, I shall try to keep peace in the family.

In obeying my confessor, I intend to obey Jesus Himself; in obeying my father, I intend to obey my Guardian Angel; in obeying my mother, I intend to obey the Blessed Virgin; in obeying everyone else, I intend to obey all the saints in Heaven.

I shall never refuse to do someone a favor, no matter how inconvenient it may be.

I shall speak very little before going to Holy Communion. I shall never talk about clothes, physical beauty, etc.

I shall be resigned to God's will, accepting everything as coming from Him and always thanking Him.

I shall never touch anyone, even the young children I am teaching.

I shall respect and love all my elders, but shall not show more affection for one than for another. I shall love them because of God.

I shall have great trust in my sweet Mother Mary and shall turn to her in every need. When tempted I shall call upon her. Through her help I am confident of reaching Heaven.

* * *

Once each day Bartholomea examined herself on these points and on many more. She never forgot that her whole life belonged to Jesus. During the course of every day she would often reflect that Jesus was with her—that it was He calling her to her household duties, urging her to be a kind companion, assuring her that He would never abandon her and commanding her to perform every action only for Him.

When we love someone we want to do something for that person. Bartholomea so loved God that she wanted to bring as many people as she could to love Him, too. Soon after she went home to her parents, she opened a private school right in the house, where the young village children could come to be taught. Soon there was not enough space, and they moved the school to a larger house.

Bartholomea was a born teacher, and her pupils learned quickly. They learned other things besides reading, writing and arithmetic! They learned humility, kindness and patience! At the end of each year, the parents were amazed to see what lambs even their most rebellious children had become. They thanked Bartholomea wholeheartedly.

Bartholomea's teaching method was this—to love her pupils and to sacrifice herself for them. Seeing how truly she loved them, the children responded with all their best efforts. Every day she would propose a virtue for them to practice and told them *how* they could practice it. Often she rewarded those who did the best.

She understood well that some students learn faster than others, and gave her help to each one without showing any partiality. She never hesitated to point out their faults, but did it so kindly that they tried at once to correct themselves.

Pastors of parishes in the nearby towns began to send teenage girls to Bartholomea so that they, too, would learn to teach as she did and would imitate her virtues. In that way, Bartholomea's influence spread throughout the whole region, which comprised about eighty-four villages!

We might think that Bartholomea found teaching a full-time apostolate. But, no. When two older women, Catherine and Rose Gerosa, opened a hospital for the sick poor, they begged their young friend Bartholomea to take charge of the hospital's finances, and she accepted the duty. From then on she often visited the sick in the wards, stopping at every little white bed to say a comforting word and encourage each poor sufferer to prepare well for confession and Communion. Upon her arrival word would pass joyously from bed to bed: "Bartholomea is here!"

She prepared the dying to pass into eternity at peace with God, resigned to His holy will. Such a hope in the joys of the next life she gave them, that it became a saying, "To be admitted to that hospital is a sign of salvation!"

Once two soldiers were admitted to the hospital, more sick in soul than they were in body. They cared little or nothing for God and religion. Yet Bartholomea's holiness, together with her prayers for their conversion, won the grace of a transformation. When the cured soldiers left the hospital, they were God-fearing men.

Another man, who had led a bad life, refused at first to listen to Bartholomea's gentle urgings. After a time, however, her prayers won out. He made a good confession and firm resolutions and, upon leaving the hospital, became a brother. Whenever he heard anyone speak of Lovere, he would say, "There is a saint in that town!"

* * *

Bartholomea had never given up her concern for her father. One summer he fell gravely ill. She

herself had become ill at the same time, but she refused to rest and spent all her time caring for him.
As he grew worse and worse, she prayed with him,
urging him to say with her the acts of love and contrition and acts of resignation to God's will. Like a
lamb, that fiery man did everything she told him
to do.

When the father made his general confession
he confided to the priest that it was his daughter
who had helped him prepare it. He knew well that
Bartholomea was the means of his conversion, and
he kept her near him till the end. When he died,
toward the end of October, 1831, Bartholomea
wept, but she had the consolation of knowing that
he had died a changed man. She assisted at many
Masses for the repose of his soul.

✿ ✿ ✿

There was so much good to be done in the
world—and so few people to do it! Persons were
needed who had a deep spirituality, from whose
union with God would flow acts of kindness and
self-sacrifice for children, the poor and the sick.
Bartholomea saw the need for a new religious congregation.

Her friend Catherine Gerosa joined her in the
project. And, as it always seems to happen in a
worthwhile endeavor, obstacles showed up to block
their path. One by one these were overcome, thanks
to the firm faith and unfailing prayers of the two
holy women.

The Institute of the Sisters of Charity of Lovere was founded on the Feast of the Presentation of Mary, 1832. As it began, Bartholomea's work on earth was ending. Apparently God wished her to offer up her life for the growth of her Congregation.

In April, 1833, she came down with a fever which rose higher and higher. Her mother and sister (and indeed the whole village) were beside themselves with grief, for she was so young—only twenty-six years old.

"Mother, listen," Bartholmea soothed. "You know that everyone has to die. If I were to live forty years more, I would have to die anyway. Suppose God were to let me live those forty years and that I were to give in to my passions and to the pleasures of the world—for, as long as we live we are in danger of foresaking God—and die in sin, then, my Mother you would say, 'Oh, if only my daughter had died when she was ill in 1833, I could hope for her eternal happiness!'

"This is the moment when God in His mercy wills to receive me into Paradise. Do not be saddened by my death, but instead thank God!"

Bartholomea endured many days of suffering with little consolation from God. But, "The sufferings Jesus sends us are never thorns!"

To those who were taking care of her, she said, "Have patience for the troubles you are bearing with now, and be assured that if I have the good fortune of going to Heaven, I will repay you all."

To die meant to abandon the Institute at its very birth and to leave it in other hands. It was a great sacrifice, but to Catherine Gerosa, Bartholomea said, "In Heaven I will be more useful to the Institute than I would have been on earth."

Full of love, she said ejaculation after ejaculation. "Oh, how sweet death is!"

And yet she did not die. It was God's will that she remain suspended between life and death for many hours more.

On July 20, Bartholomea received the Last Sacraments with great fervor. "Do you wish to go to Heaven?" her confessor asked.

"If it were God's will for me to remain in pain till the day of judgment, I would do so willingly to please Him."

On July 26, she went into her death agony, clasping to her a crucifix and a small statue of the Blessed Virgin. From time to time she kissed them. Then murmuring prayers, smiling as if dropping into a deep sleep, she died.

✳ ✳ ✳

"What shall I do now?" Catherine Gerosa kept repeating to herself. "I am good for nothing; it is better for me to return to my home. Without Bartholomea I can do nothing; she was an eagle; I am an ox."

But Bartholomea's confessor scolded Catherine for her discouragement. The Institute was necessary, he declared. She must pray and have faith.

"Let us go ahead then," Catherine agreed. "God wants to do this all by Himself."

Soon young teenage girls, former pupils of Bartholomea, came to join Catherine. Camilla came, too. On the Feast of Our Lady's Presentation, 1835, they received the religious habit.

The Institute grew and grew. It spread throughout northern Italy and sent missionaries to India and Brazil. A hundred years after its founding the Congregation numbered 8,150 sisters working in 1,723 institutions, in more than 600 localities, helping 240,000 people daily—abandoned children, old people, lepers, the mentally ill, the plague-stricken, teenagers who had gone astray. . . . The Congregation labored in asylums, orphanages, public and private schools. All this because an eleven-year-old girl once made a decision to become a saint—and did something about it!

St. Bartholomea's considerateness of others was outstanding. Let us try to see other people's points of view and understand them a little better.

Saint John Bosco

Friend of Youth

The great war caused by Napoleon left much suffering and misery in its wake. Many schools had been destroyed, and young children went out to look for work instead. When they found work, they were forced to spend long hours at their jobs, even on Sundays, for many people had forgotten about God in those days. The wars and the foolish ideas of a few proud men had taken Him out of their hearts.

Some boys could not find work at all. They turned into tramps and thieves, who were picked up by the police and thrown into prisons. There they learned from hardened criminals about worse crimes and blasphemies.

Could anything be done about this sad situation? Yes. Even at that time a little boy was growing up who would change much of it. His name was John Bosco.

John's mother was a good, hard-working widow who taught her son to be cheerful and good. One day she began to scold him when she saw him come home with a big gash in his forehead. She was proud of him when he explained, "My companions don't use bad language when I'm around!"

John used every chance he could find to study the Bible and to read and write. Very often he could be seen out in the fields with a book in his hands. "Come play with us!" his friends would call, for they enjoyed playing with him. But John would reply, "I want to become a priest!" That was why he was studying so hard!

He was a generous boy who often traded his own white lunch bread for the hard, black bread of one of his friends. "I really like the black bread better," he would say. He liked it better only because it was a sacrifice!

Mother would need it . . .

When John was eight, he broke a big jar of oil one day. He knew that his mother would punish him, so he went out to the woods, cut off a tree branch, and handed it to his mother when she came home so that she could give him the whipping he deserved!

One night John had a marvelous dream. He seemed to be in the midst of a group of children who were fighting and swearing. He tried to tell them to stop, but they wouldn't listen. Then he tried to *make* them stop, with his fists, as he had made others stop before. But that didn't work either.

Suddenly he saw a man in white coming toward him. He was smiling. "You will make them your friends with love, not with blows," the man said. "You will show them how to become good."

"Me? But I'm not able. I am poor and ignorant!"

"By being obedient and studying hard you will be able to do it."

"Who are you?" asked the boy.

"I am the Son of the Lady your mother has taught you to pray to so often. Ask My Mother for help!"

And there she was! The Blessed Mother, whom he honored daily in the beautiful prayer, the Angelus. She said sweetly, "Look!" Suddenly the raging children around John were changed into wild beasts. "As I do with these wild beasts, so will you do with the children." And the beasts became meek and snowy little lambs, ready to be led away to pasture!

From then on, John knew that his special purpose in life was to help children.

"My Mother will help you."

One day, his mother took him to a country fair where he watched the stunts of the acrobats. An idea came into his mind. Back home again, he stretched a rope between two trees and tried to walk it.

Of course, he tumbled many times. His brother Anthony laughed heartily. But John was not discouraged; he just said a Hail Mary and tried again and again. . . Soon he was walking the rope quite easily.

Then he learned other acrobatic stunts. At last, one Sunday night, he called some men and boys to see his "show". They enjoyed it and clapped enthusiastically. Then John, who had another motive besides giving healthy entertainment, began to sing a hymn to Mary. Everyone joined in, and the beautiful notes soared toward heaven. Then the boy said, "Now unless you say the rosary while I perform, I'll fall and break my head!" The people began to pray. At the close of his performance, John sat down and repeated the sermon the priest had given that morning at Mass, so that everyone would remember it better.

One night there was a public dance scheduled— not a nice one, but the kind that could lead to sin. John, who was twelve at the time, tried to think of a way to keep the people away from the dance. At last he hit upon an idea. God had given him a very good voice, so he stood near the square and sang— so sweetly that a crowd gathered. He led the way to the church, and the people followed him, to assist at vespers and listen to the sermon!

It wasn't easy . . .

John had never stopped wanting to be a priest. But he knew that his mother would have to really scrimp and save if he were going to study. He didn't like to ask her to make such a sacrifice. . . . But the boy had a very good mother. She told him not to worry about her, but to do what God wanted him to do. "I was born poor," she said, "I *am* poor, and I wish to die poor." So at the age of sixteen, John Bosco entered the seminary.

Whenever he could spare a moment from his studies, the youth would gather together all the ragged and lonely boys he could find. He would take them on outings and instruct them in the catechism.

When John was ordained to the priesthood, the whole village turned out to assist at his first Mass. Tears of joy streamed down his mother's cheeks. Now her boy was no longer Johnny, but Father, or Don Bosco.

A few months later, Don Bosco was in the sacristy, preparing to say Mass, when he heard a commotion. Turning around, he saw the sacristan mistreating a boy because he did not know how to serve Mass.

The young priest hurried over. He sent the sacristan away. "Would you like me to teach you how to serve?" he asked the boy. Gratefully the youngster nodded his head. After Don Bosco had finished the lesson, he asked the boy to bring his friends with him the next day.

Soon Don Bosco had many pupils. Every feast-day morning they came to assist at Mass and go to

Working his way

The sacristan screamed at the boy

The
thug fled

confession; in the evening they would come to study catechism and sing sacred hymns. So many of the boys were homeless that the priest soon found himself looking for places for them to live, and his own mother came to join him to help him care for his little flock.

One evening as Don Bosco was out walking alone a strange thing happened. Four grim-looking thugs appeared before him. They looked as if they meant to beat him, even kill him. But a huge dog came flashing out of the shadows and leaped at one of the robbers. The rest turned and fled, and Don Bosco called the dog away from the one he seemed about to kill. The dog walked home with the priest, and then disappeared into the night shadows again. Many other times in Don Bosco's life, that big dog came to help him when he was in danger.

Often the devil appeared in person to Don Bosco to discourage him. He would shake the walls of his room; he would shake the bed; he would appear in the form of strange and horrible monsters. . . . But Don Bosco always prayed hard to the Blessed Mother and put his trust in her. Because of this, the devil did not scare him away from his great work.

After a few years, Don Bosco saw that a religious order was needed to take care of the boys— not only boys in his own city, but all over the world. So he founded the Salesians, whom he named after St. Francis de Sales, who today do that work all over the world.

A scare that didn't work

Whenever one of "his boys" looked troubled, Don Bosco would take him aside and quietly ask him about it. Often it was a matter for confession. How peaceful and happy each boy looked when he had made a good confession!

One day, when a boy said, "And that's all I have to confess, Father," Don Bosco had the feeling that the boy had more to tell. How could he help him to say it? In a very grave voice the saint said, "Look who you have at your shoulder." The boy turned and let out a horrible scream. He had just stared into the ugly, twisted face of the devil himself! He hurriedly told the saint the sin he had been keeping back.

Happily, Don Bosco watched his Salesian Order grow and spread to South America, France and Spain. It was a consolation to him in his old age to see how much was being done for boys all over the world.

Don Bosco's health was now failing him, and he passed away in the winter of 1888. He was canonized by one of his greatest admirers, Pope Pius XI, in 1934.

From his early childhood, St. John Bosco wanted to help others to draw closer to God. One way we can do this is by being good ourselves. Our example will help our friends.

"Look behind you!"

Saint Dominic Savio

The Teenager Saint

Although Dominic Savio was only fifteen when he died, he had already reached a high degree of holiness. This is the story of how he did it. Would you like to do it, too?

Dominic, born in Italy about a hundred years ago, was the son of a blacksmith. Even when he was very small he liked to pray. In fact, once when his father forgot the blessing before the meal, Dominic reminded him right away!

When he was five years old he became an altar boy. Each morning he would rise at five o'clock with his father. He would hurry to dress and then would scurry off to the church–which was usually still closed. While he was waiting for the priest to come, the little boy would kneel there on the steps, even in the cold and slush of wintertime, and pray to the Blessed Mother the same prayer that you say each day, "Hail Mary, full of grace. . . ."

Now, at that time children did not have your privilege of receiving First Holy Communion at the age of seven or eight. Usually they had to be at least ten. That would have been a long, painful wait for Dominic, who was so eager to take the living Jesus into his heart, and because his pastor realized this and knew that the boy understood his catechism thoroughly, he made an exception. So Dominic prepared to receive First Communion at the age of seven.

On that wonderful day, the boy poured out to Jesus all the secret desires of his young, loving heart. He made a promise to Him and took for himself this motto which he afterwards told the pastor: "Death, but not sin!" Truly, that was the sort of motto which a hero would take, and Dominic would prove to be a hero in living up to it.

What strength of character he had! One day two classmates asked him to go swimming. Dominic thought about how much he enjoyed the water. Then he thought about what a friend had told him of the danger of swimming in deep water. "No thanks," he said.

"Oh, come on," urged his comrades. "It's great fun. If you're not good at swimming yet, we'll teach you. Come on!"

Dominic reflected that it is a sin to go into danger without a good reason. What would his mother say? he wondered.

"I'll ask Mother if it's all right," decided Dominic.

"Don't you dare!" exclaimed one of the would-be buddies. "She won't let you come! Why, she might even tell *our* mothers, and then we'd catch it for sure!"

Now Dominic saw clearly how matters stood. "God always punishes boys who are foolhardly enough to disobey their parents!" he retorted grimly, and turned away.

Then there was the time when Dominic had just changed schools. The new teacher, a priest, didn't know him well yet, although he thought that

Dominic was a good boy. One day some of the pupils thought of a clever scheme.

"Let's put some snow in the wood stove," said one.

"Then it'll be so cold in class that Father will let us out early," agreed another. "Whoopie!"

But Father looked into the wood stove to see what had made the fire go out, and when he saw the melting snow he became very stern. "Who did this?"

The frightened boys pointed to Dominic.

Although surprised, the priest believed them. He ordered Dominic to kneel down on the floor and stay there for half a day. Dominic obeyed without a protest.

He could have talked; he could have told Father that the others had done it. But if he did, they would be punished much worse than he was being punished, because they were always in trouble. Dominic thought of how Jesus had suffered when He was accused of things that weren't true. He was happy to imitate Jesus.

Somehow, Father learned that Dominic was innocent. Then the good priest was full of admiration for the boy who had taken another's punishment so willingly. It was an example of virtue which he never forgot.

When you walk to school, or take the bus, or ride your bicycle, maybe you can picture Dominic and the long walk he took each day. He was poor, so he used to take off his shoes, tie the laces together and sling them over his shoulder. That way he saved leather until he reached the village. On the way, he prayed and talked to the Guardian Angel who he knew was with him. Of course, when he was with the other boys, Dominic was just as lively as they were, and just as full of fun. But it was always *clean* fun.

God willing, the boy decided, I will become a priest. Dominic was now twelve, and eager to begin the studies which would prepare him for that great goal. Holy Don Bosco, who was a living saint himself, encouraged the boy and admitted him to the Salesian Oratory he had founded. There Dominic set to work at his studies joyfully. He wanted to learn all he could, so that he could save souls—his own soul and many others.

When not studying, Dominic often visited the Blessed Sacrament by himself or with other boys whom he invited along. Many times you could find him, with an eager little group gathered around him, telling stories about the great saints and the wonderful things they did. On Fridays, Dominic gave up the usual games and went to chapel to honor the sorrows of the Blessed Virgin in a special way; often he asked his companions to join in these prayers. On Sundays he taught catechism to younger children.

Once, Dominic came upon some boys who were looking at indecent magazines. Quick as a flash, he tore them up! "You ought to be really ashamed!" he told them.

Dominic never looked at anything that would harm his soul. If he did see something by accident, he ignored it and said a prayer to the Blessed Virgin. In fact, sometimes he would not permit himself to look at things which were harmless—just so he could offer the sacrifice to Our Lord and at the same time strengthen his own will so that he would not give in to temptations which would come later on. Practicing mortifications like that sometimes gave Dominic a bad headache. But he offered that up to God, too, because he knew that mortifications and headaches are a very small price to pay for all the brightness and beauty of eternity in Heaven.

The boy wanted his soul to be always in complete control of his body. He tried to avoid comforts. When it was cold, he would move slowly so he felt the cold more deeply. When he went to bed, he would put bits of wood and nutshells under the sheet so he would not be comfortable.

* * *

Did Dominic ever fight? Well, not exactly. But he was right in the middle of a fight once.

Two of his companions, almost blind with rage, were slugging it out. One of them grabbed a rock big enough to smash in the other's head. The other boy grabbed another rock, and there they stood glaring at one another. That was when Dominic stepped between them!

"Get out of the way!" growled one. Dominic refused to budge.

"Hit me first."

For a minute, it seemed they were going to do it! Dominic held out his little crucifix and added, "You won't hit me? Then hit Him!"

That was too much for the boys. They knew they were in the wrong. Not long afterwards they were shaking hands in embarrassment and preparing to go to confession.

Dominic himself went to confession each week and received Communion every day. He urged his friends to go to confession often and he founded the Sodality of the Immaculate Conception for the frequent reception of Holy Communion. The members of the Sodality strove to be model Catholics in every way and to have a great devotion to Mary.

Dominic once said to Don Bosco, "I have to become a saint, Father!" He never lost sight of that goal. He knew that you can't become a saint by putting things off till "tomorrow" or even till "this afternoon." He knew that it is always "now" that matters and the happiness you have for all eternity depends on how good and cheerful and obedient and generous and hard-working and prayerful you are right at the time you think about the great things you want to do. He was practical. He didn't just dream about becoming a saint; he cooperated every instant with God's graces.

God wishes us to help our neighbors save their souls, too. That was why Dominic was always urging his companions to do good deeds and to avoid everything (like bad magazines) which could lead them to sin. Of course, he did not pretend to be wearing a halo, either! He was a lively, high-spirited teenager like his companions, and they regarded him as their buddy, "a regular guy."

Sometimes God takes us when we are young. That was what happened to Dominic. He was only fourteen when he became very ill and was sent home to his parents in the hope that the change of climate would make him feel better. How hard it was for the boy to leave his dear teacher and friend, Don Bosco! He had a feeling that they would never meet again except in Heaven.

At home, Dominic grew worse instead of better. The priest came and gave him Communion and anointed him. The boy felt all the strength draining out of his body, so he prayed harder and harder to resist any temptations the devil might send him in his last moments. "Jesus, Mary, Joseph, assist me in my last agony!"

"Good-bye, Dad," the boy murmured tenderly. Suddenly a change came over him. He sat up straight and held out his arms eagerly. His eyes shone. "Oh, what a beautiful sight!" he exclaimed.

Then, with a smile on his lips, St. Dominic Savio died.

One doesn't have to be a "goody-goody" to become a saint. We can be in the midst of many good times if we remember never to displease God while we enjoy ourselves.

Saint Bernadette

On February 11, 1858, the city of Lourdes in southern France was enveloped in a blanket of fog. In the poor little room of the Soubirous family there was not even a bit of wood to light a fire.

"We'll go get some, Mamma," volunteered the girls, Bernadette and Mary. Their friend Joan was eager to go, too.

Thinking of her older girl's asthma, Mamma Soubirous protested, "Bernadette, don't go out. Your cough might come back again."

"Mamma, don't worry," replied Bernadette quickly. I'll put on my cloak and I won't be cold." Her mother nodded consent.

"We'll be back very soon," promised Mary and Joan.

All three chorused, "Good-bye."

Cheerful, dark-eyed, Bernadette was the oldest child in her family, but she was not as strong as her sister Mary because of her asthma, and she was very slow in schoolwork. At fourteen, she had not learned her catechism well, and had not yet made her First Communion. But Bernadette loved God very much.

Bernadette, Mary and their friend ran off lightheartedly toward the grotto of Massabielle, where they would find dry branches. The water of the stream was cold. Unafraid, Mary waded in quickly.

Bernadette, who was not able to go into such cold water, watched her sister.

Then, to make a crossing for herself, Bernadette threw stones into the stream, but the water was high and covered them.

Off to the grotto

The Lady moved her rosary beads, too.

The sound of the Angelus bell rolled across the valley. She stopped a moment and, like Gabriel, greeted the Most Holy Virgin, whom she dearly loved. While Mary and Joan moved away to gather

wood, a light breeze touched Bernadette, although
the air all around was still and the branches of the
trees were not moving at all.

Only a wild rosebush, under the arch of rock,
stirred. Then, in the grotto, a beautiful, young Lady
appeared. Bernadette gasped, dropped to her knees
and reached for her dear worn-out rosary. The Vision smiled and taught Bernadette to make the Sign
of the Cross devoutly and well. Then taking the rosary which hung on her arm, she passed the beads
through her fingers, encouraging Bernadette to recite the rosary. At the end of each decade, the Lady
joined with the girl in saying the "Glory be to the
Father."

Bernadette's eyes, her thoughts, her very soul
were fixed on the radiant Vision.

After the Lady had disappeared, Bernadette
rejoined Mary and Joan. She mentioned the Vision–
without really meaning to–and the other girls excitedly made her tell what she had seen. Unable to
keep the secret, they told her parents and some
friends. Her parents thought it nonsense; the friends
were curious.

The next Sunday, Bernadette took a bottle of
holy water and, with several girls, went to the grotto. There, she knelt and began to say the rosary and
the others followed her example, waiting expectantly. She gazed upward, toward the wild rosebush,
her eyes wide and intent. . . . Her companions saw
nothing, but they knew that the Lady had come.

"Quick, quick!" urged one of the girls. "Throw
the holy water!"

Bernadette threw some of the holy water. "If you come from God, come forward!" she said to the Vision.

Obediently the Lady advanced, bowed her head and smiled. Bernadette's face lit up with a divine light. Her eyes were fixed on the spot, on a Vision that filled her soul with a heavenly joy.

After this apparition, the news reached the city officials. They did not believe the story, but were eager to find out more about it, thinking it to be some sort of trick of Bernadette's to make money for her parents.

On Thursday, February 18, the Lady again appeared—smiling and wonderfully sweet. The girl begged her, "My Lady, be so good as to write your name and what you desire of me."

As soon as Bernadette had made the request, she grew worried—had she been too bold with the Lady? She held her breath, but the Vision smiled.

"There is no need to write what I want," she said. "Will you be kind enough to come back here fifteen times?"

"Yes, my Lady!"

The Lady continued, "I promise to make you happy, but not in this world. I desire to have many people come here."

That voice filled Bernadette with happiness and made her certain that the Lady loved her.

Soon after this, Bernadette was taken to the office of Police Commissioner Jacomet, who asked many confusing questions and then accused her of lying.

"Give me back my child!"

"Now listen," stormed Jacomet, "first you say one thing, then you say another. You're trying to fool me! I tell you, girl, if you don't promise not to return to the grotto, I'll call in the police!" He was

shouting in uncontrollable anger when Francis Soubirous entered.

"I am her father, Commissioner," Francis introduced himself. "Give me back my child."

Immediately Jacomet turned his anger upon
him: "When are you going to end this lie you started
in order to get money? If you don't end it, I will!"

"Believe me, sir, my wife and I are weary of
the whole thing," Francis declared. "And I promise
you that Bernadette will not go to Massabielle
again."

"All right," snapped Jacomet. "So be it. But if
not, I have my police . . . and you know them!
Now go!"

But Bernadette's father did let her see the Lady
again.

One morning Bernadette made her way
through an especially large crowd and knelt in
prayer as usual. As the girl began to say her rosary,
the Lady said,

"Go to drink and wash yourself in the spring.
Then eat some of the grass you will find there."

The spring? But there was no spring! Perhaps
it doesn't matter where I take the water from, Bernadette thought, as she rose and began to walk
toward the river.

The Lady was calling her softly. "Not in the
river," she said, and motioned to the earth near the
grotto. Bernadette hastened to the spot, and—not
knowing what else to do—began to dig in the sand.
It became moist. Soon she had a small hole filled
with muddy water. It was a real struggle to make

herself drink it, but as soon as some of the mud had
settled out, she scooped up some of the water and
drank it. Then she washed her face, and began to
eat some of the grass which grew beside her. How
bitter it tasted!

The onlookers gasped. They did not understand that Bernadette was making penance for
sinners.

During the following days, the little trickle of
water swelled into a stream which in our own times
flows into nine great tanks where the sick are
bathed and often cured.

Another day the Lady asked Bernadette,
"Would it tire or disturb you to kiss the ground for
sinners?"

"No, my Lady," the girl replied. She kissed the
ground several times, then stood up with her face
wet with tears. Turning to the crowd, she ordered,
"Kiss the ground."

The people did not understand. Bernadette
motioned to them again, and a murmur went
through the crowd; all bent to kiss the ground.

On the following day Bernadette went to see
the pastor. He had heard of the events at the grotto,
but had shown no interest in them. However, now
he would have to take some sort of position regarding them, for the Lady had given Bernadette a
message.

"Who are you?" asked the pastor.

"I am Bernadette Soubirous," the girl replied.

"Oh, that Bernadette about whom I've heard
certain stories. What do you want?"

"The lady charged me to tell the priests that she wishes to have a chapel at Massabielle."

"The Lady! What's her name?"

"I don't know, Father," Bernadette replied.

He towered above Bernadette

"She is a very beautiful young woman who appears to me at the grotto."

"Neither you nor I know who she is. So . . . tell her that the pastor doesn't deal with people he doesn't know and that therefore, she must tell you her name."

On March 25, Bernadette hurried to Massabielle with the first rays of dawn, but she was late, for the Vision was already smiling at her from the rocks. Oh, that smile! Bernadette gathered courage and pleaded, "My Lady, won't you be kind enough to tell me who you are?"

Three times the young girl dared to question her sweet Friend. Finally, the Lady opened her arms, extended them toward the earth; lifted her gaze to Heaven, then joined her hands over her heart, and said, "I am the Immaculate Conception."

After that, the Lady disappeared in a great cloud of light.

Eagerly the crowd questioned Bernadette:

"Did she tell you her name?"

"Is it really the Blessed Virgin?"

Bernadette hesitated, for the name the Lady had told her was one which she had never heard before. "I don't know," she murmured, and then ran off to tell the pastor—for he should learn the beautiful Lady's name.

"Is she the Blessed Virgin?" he asked.

Her tone slightly puzzled, Bernadette replied, "She said, 'I am the Immaculate Conception.' "

The pastor gasped, "The Immaculate Conception! . . . Maybe you don't remember, Bernadette?"

But the girl was sure. "Oh, I do, Reverend Father, because I repeated the name all the way from Massabielle until now."

When the girl had left, the priest thought long and seriously about what she had said. Only four years before, Pope Pius IX had proclaimed the Immaculate Conception a dogma of the Church. Was Heaven itself now voicing its approval of that declaration?

* * *

On June 3, of that year, Bernadette received her first visit from the King of Heaven—in Holy Communion. She had learned about Him by studying her Catechism, and her little heart was purer than a lily and burning with love. In the silence of her heart she spoke to her God: O Jesus, I love You. Forgive all sinners and save them. For them I offer You my life. Accept it, O Jesus."

The joy of her First Holy Communion prepared her for the parting with her beautiful Lady. It was the evening of July 16, when Bernadette urged her aunt, "Aunt Lucille, come with me! The Blessed Virgin is waiting for me."

Willingly her aunt accompanied her to the grotto. A barricade had been placed about it; they paused on the other side of the river. How Bernadette's heart beat!

Suddenly she exclaimed: "She is there! She is looking at us and smiling at us across the barricade."

Fifteen minutes of wonderful happiness passed by. This was the farewell visit, and Bernadette felt it. She fixed her gaze on the splendor of her Lady, who appeared more beautiful than ever before. As the figure of the Virgin slowly disappeared, Bernadette was left with a sweet peace of heart.

"I shall not see her again on this earth ... But I'll see her again!"

* * *

Bernadette, the little flower of Mary Immaculate, was soon seeking a shelter from the world. First she stayed at the convent of the Sisters of Lourdes. One day the Bishop asked her, "What do you intend to do, Bernadette, in order to make some return to the Blessed Virgin for her favors to you?"

"I would like to live with the sisters as their maid, Your Excellency," Bernadette replied. "Wouldn't that be possible?"

"And have you never thought of entering their Congregation?" the Bishop continued.

"Your Excellency," Bernadette protested. "I am poor and ignorant."

But poverty and ignorance matter little when a person wants to serve God. Thus, Bernadette soon left Lourdes for Nevers, where the Mother General of the Sisters of Charity was happy to receive her.

"My child," said the Mother General, "I hope you will be happy among us. What do you know how to do?"

"Very little, Reverend Mother. I know how to peel potatoes and scrub pots."

"In the house of the Lord," replied the Mother General kindly, "one action is just as noble and meritorious as another. Now, then, you will help the sister in the kitchen."

Bernadette smiled, "I am very grateful to you for this, Reverend Mother."

Bernadette's new home

On July 29, 1866, His Excellency, the Most Reverend Bishop, came personally to give her the holy habit of the Congregation.

"From now on," said the Bishop, "you will be called Sister Mary Bernard." And she was very happy.

One day a sister asked Sister Mary Bernard, "Have you ever felt a temptation to pride because you were so favored by the Blessed Virgin?"

Sister Mary Bernard was amazed. "But don't you know that the Blessed Virgin chose me because I was the most ignorant? If she had found anyone more ignorant, she would have chosen that person."

Another time she said, "I served as a broom for the Blessed Virgin. And when she no longer had any use for me she put me in my place, behind the door. There I am and there I shall remain."

What humility!

✾   ✾   ✾

The short life of the Immaculate Virgin's privileged one was soon to come to an end amid great suffering from tuberculosis.

The Virgin had told her, "I shall not make you happy on this earth," and Sister Mary Bernard knew that suffering was her mission.

"I can suffer more," she would say. "Thus I'll earn Heaven."

As Sister Mary Bernard lay dying, her sweet Friend from Heaven came down to visit her; her smile lightened the pain, made it easier to bear.

Fervently the dying sister begged, "Mary Most Holy, Mother of God, pray for me, a poor sinner."

Then Sister Mary Bernard's large eyes shone with happiness; her lips curved into a smile. Slowly she bowed her head. . . . She had taken flight with her Lady–toward the gates of Heaven.

❊ ❊ ❊

Although Sister Mary Bernard has gone from this earth, the spring which she dug continues to bubble up and calls people to Mary's shrine. The white trains bring the suffering to Lourdes from all over the world–those sick with the most dread and painful illnesses. For although doctors cannot cure their afflictions, the Immaculate Virgin can.

In the shrine at Lourdes, the house of our heavenly Mother, people find Jesus. In the Most Blessed Sacrament, He passes among the row of sufferers waiting in the square in front of the basilica. While He blesses them, they pray:

"Jesus, have pity on us."

"Lord, that I may see!"

"Lord, make me walk!"

And at His passing, the lame walk, the blind see, the dying rise from their stretchers of pain. Then a powerful shout rises up from the crowd. The people thank God with the words of the Blessed Virgin, "My soul magnifies the Lord!"

In the niche where Our Lady stood are the crutches of the sick who have been cured through her intercession. Long processions wend their way along the square in front of the basilica toward the grotto. Just as Bernadette used to do, the faithful recite the rosary before the Immaculate Virgin. Many different languages are all joined in one melody—to greet the Blessed Virgin: "Ave, ave, ave, Maria."

And the beautiful Lady in white is there, listening to us and watching over us. Certainly we would see her, if our eyes were as pure as Bernadette's.

St. Bernadette never became proud of the graces God gave her, because she knew they were His, not hers. Let us never look down on boys and girls who are not as smart, or as strong, or as well-dressed as we are, because everything we have is God's gift to us.

Saint Frances Xavier Cabrini

First United States Citizen Saint

Little Mary Frances liked to listen to the stories of missionaries, which her father read aloud to the family in the evening.

"I'm going to be a missionary, too!" she told her big sister, Rose, one day.

"You? You're too small. Missionaries must be strong!"

"I'll grow," Frances promised. She thought of St. Francis Xavier with his great love for Jesus Crucified and how he had travelled up and down the Orient and was headed for China when he died.

"Do Chinese children know about Jesus?" she asked.

"Some do, but many have never heard of Him," answered Rose patiently.

"Oh, how much I would like to tell them about Him!" the little girl exclaimed.

As Frances grew older, her desire to be a missionary grew with her. Yet her health was poor and every time she tried to enter religious life, she was told, "This is not for you; you are too weak for such a life!"

Each time, Frances said to herself, "God's will be done," but she still wanted to serve Him as completely as possible. She finished high school and became a teacher, but she wanted to do much, much more than that.

When she was twenty-four, Frances received a message from a monsignor she knew. He wanted her to take charge of an orphanage which had been managed poorly. Could she put it in order in two weeks time? Frances said she would try. She went to work with an energetic will, and fervent prayers –and succeeded.

The monsignor asked Frances to remain at the orphanage and keep things running smoothly. This was difficult, since she was not really in charge, and had to work with people who always wanted their own way and argued among themselves. It was hard for Frances to keep the peace and still get things done. But saints are made in such trials.

With seven young women who had become her pupils, Frances made her first religious vows–six years after arriving at the orphanage. Soon afterward the local bishop directed her to form a new missionary community and be its superior. Frances didn't bat an eye. "I'll look for a house," she said.

"The Missionary Sisters of the Sacred Heart!" Frances exclaimed. How beautiful it sounded. She and her sisters would go throughout the world telling everyone of the great love of Jesus for mankind Perhaps they would go to China. . . . The childhood dream had not been forgotten.

Orphanages, schools, catechism classes, and more sisters to staff them! The little community grew rapidly. Soon it had several houses in Italy, and an invitation to go to America.

Why America? That was what Mother Cabrini wondered, too. She had had her heart set on the Orient.

"The Italian immigrants need you there," explained Bishop Scalabrini, who had founded an order of priests to work among the immigrants. "They have no one to teach catechism to the children. There is no one to tend the sick, for they are too poor to be admitted into the regular hospitals. People are taking advantage of them materially and they are starving spiritually as well."

Frances was not sure what she should do. Knowing that one never makes a mistake by obeying, she asked the Holy Father himself whether she should send missionaries to America or to China. After a moment of reflection, the saintly Leo XIII told her, "You must not go to the East but to the West." America, it would be.

Frances and some of her sisters arrived in New York on March 31, 1889. The first institution they opened was a day school. Next came an orphanage. In four months' time there were four hundred orphans!

Then came a wonderful offer of a beautiful piece of property which could be used for another orphanage and a novitiate house. The price was low, but there was one hitch—no water. Mother Cabrini smiled, and bought the property. "God will provide," she said.

And provide He did! The sisters began a novena to Our Lady, and on the 5th day of it they marched out onto the grounds with an array of hoes and shovels.

"Dig here," Mother Cabrini said, pointing to a certain spot.

Soon the shovels were turning up rich, brown soil instead of dry sand. And then—"Water, water! clear, running water!"

In the depths of her heart, Mother Cabrini thanked God. "We shall build a shrine to Our Lady near the spring," she promised.

All of Mother Cabrini's undertakings were full of the same kind of faith that she showed when searching for the spring. She traveled from the United States to Italy to Central and South America, founding orphanages, hospitals and schools in an amazingly short space of time in the face of all kinds of obstacles. She succeeded only through prayer, courage and faith.

Her faith was great when confronted with natural dangers, too. How many times in her frequent sea journeys violent storms arose, forcing her companions to take to their berths but leaving her calm and prayerful–a consolation to all who saw her. When traveling from Chile to Argentina, she undertook a perilous journey over the Andes mountains by muleback without batting an eye. Her motto was a line from St. Paul: *I can do all things in Him Who strengthens me.*

Life was hard for Mother Cabrini's sisters, especially in New Orleans and in the Central American missions. Mother Cabrini realized this full well, and knew, too, that the sisters must strive to become always more fervent. Once she wrote:

"Our great Patron, St. Francis Xavier, said, 'He who goes holy to the missions will find many occasions to sanctify himself more, but he who goes poorly provided with holiness, runs the risk of losing what he has and of falling away.' I become more convinced of this truth every day, and as experience is a great master, let us take advantage of the lessons it teaches and never let a day pass without examining our conscience and making serious resolutions to acquire the virtues we need."

The sisters in New York went often to visit the prisons, encouraging the prisoners, speaking to them of the happy home of Heaven which awaits us all. One day at Sing Sing prison they visited a bitter young man who had been condemned to death. He declared that he was innocent and in his bitterness refused to listen to the sisters.

"We must do something to help him," the sisters decided. They appealed to the governor to delay the execution.

The young man was grateful for what they had done and listened as they told him about God's mercy. They visited him two days a week, praying with him and reading from spiritual books.

But no new evidence came forth to change his sentence, and the execution was rescheduled. The prisoner was plunged into despair. Praying harder than ever, the sisters begged for him the grace of resignation.

Two days before the execution, the prisoner became calm. "I forgive all," he said, "and though I am innocent, I accept my death as Jesus Christ accepted His." As he mounted the electric chair, he clutched a crucifix in his hands—the crucifix was later given to the sisters.

Another spectacular conversion took place in Nicaragua in 1893. A revolution had put in power an anti-religious government which ordered Mother Cabrini's sisters to leave the country at once. Carrying a few little bundles, the sisters filed out of the convent between a double line of soldiers, amid the sobs of their pupils. From all sides people flocked to say good-bye.

In the middle of the crowd was an anti-religious man, Don José Paos, who had come out of curiosity. As he stood there, a young pupil went up to one of the sisters and said, "How can you leave like this without even shedding a tear?"

"Why should we cry?" the sister replied. She lifted a crucifix she was carrying. "We had this with us when we came, and we have it with us now!"

Don José felt something stirring in the depths of his soul. He returned to his home, locked himself in his room, and refused to see anyone until the next morning. Then he went to the bishop and asked to be readmitted into the Church. Soon he was one of the most active defenders of the Faith. Years later he said, "A religion which inspires young sisters with such serenity, resignation and peace in times of hardship and strife must be the true religion."

When Pope Leo XIII celebrated his golden jubilee as a priest, Mother Cabrini paid him a visit to ask his blessing. "Let us work, let us work," the Holy Father urged her, "for after this there is a beautiful Paradise." The words struck home. No matter how much she had done there was still more to be accomplished. She must never stop; never rest; never say she had done enough.

On another occasion Pope Leo told her, "You know how much I am devoted to the Sacred Heart. I have consecrated the world to It, and you must help spread this devotion, since He has elected you for this purpose."

One of the new fields where the devotion—and even knowledge of religion—was sadly lacking was Denver, Colorado, in 1902. Many Italian immigrants had settled there as miners and factory workers but not enough Italian priests had followed them, nor were there parochial schools. Very few of the people went to Mass on Sundays; many children had not been baptized; some men and women thirty years old had not yet made their First Communion.

Mother Cabrini opened a school for the children, and also assigned two of her sisters to visit the homes, mines and factories with words of gentle encouragement. Soon many families had returned to Mass and the sacraments—so many that new churches were needed.

In New Orleans, many people were unkind to the sisters, but their opinion changed during the yellow fever epidemic of 1905. The sisters sent their orphans to a home outside the city and used the orphanage instead as a hospital for the sick women and children, whom they tended lovingly until the epidemic had passed. How grateful those people were!

That year marked the twenty-fifth anniversary of the Missionary Sisters of the Sacred Heart. They now numbered one thousand sisters in fifty houses on three different continents. Five thousand orphans were under their care, and they had tended over one hundred thousand sick.

Mother Cabrini died peacefully in one of her own hospitals in Chicago on December 22, 1917. It was fitting indeed that she should die in the land to which she had come out of obedience to the Holy Father and in which she had done such great good. She was the first American citizen to be canonized a saint.

Mother Cabrini felt that she could never do enough for God. One way that we, too, can be generous to God is by giving up some free time to do some chores around the house, even if we are not asked to do them.

Saint Therese

Patroness of the Missions

Saint Therese, born in Alencon, France, on January 2, 1873, was the youngest in a family of five girls. Zelie Martin, her mother, was a pious woman who died after a life of love and self-sacrifice when Therese was just four, so the child was raised by her elder sisters, Pauline and Marie.

When Therese and her sister Celine were still small, Marie made a wonderful suggestion to them. They could show their love for Jesus by making little sacrifices for Him—such as not saying sharp words or making complaints. They could keep track of these mortifications by using beads on a string. One hot day, Pauline asked Therese if she would make the sacrifice of not drinking, in order to save a poor sinner. "Yes," said Therese willingly. Already she wanted to save souls for Jesus. "From the time I was three," she once said, "I have never refused Jesus anything!"

Therese learned many things from Marie and Pauline. One day Pauline showed her how all the people in Heaven are completely happy even though some have more glory than others. This is how she did it: she took a cup and a thimble, and filled each with water. "Now," she asked, "which is the fullest?" Therese was puzzled, for neither of them could have held another drop. "That's how it will be in Heaven," Pauline said. "Every soul will be completely filled with happiness, but some will have more room for it, because they had a greater love of God while on earth." At once Therese decided to become a soul with great love of God.

Pauline taught her little sister all about the religious feasts. Therese's favorite was Corpus Christi, when the Blessed Sacrament was carried in procession and the children strewed flowers along the road in front of It. Therese thought that each flower was like a kiss to Jesus hidden in the Host.

School days gave Therese new chances to make sacrifices. She was a quiet girl, but her companions were rough and noisy. It was hard for her to hide her feelings and play with them, but she managed to do it.

Life also had its funny moments. Therese and her cousin, Marie Guerin, were walking down the street one day, playing "hermit." They pretended they were in the desert, and as they walked they took turns closing their eyes, as a mortification. But then, both closed their eyes at the same time, and walked straight into a stack of boxes piled in front of a grocery store. The desert forgotten, the "hermits" turned and fled.

On the beautiful day of her First Holy Communion, Therese told Jesus that she was entirely His. She was crying for sheer joy. Being united to the Model of all virtue, she listed her resolutions for progress: "I will never let myself become discouraged. I will say the Memorare daily. I will work to humiliate my pride."

When the Holy Spirit came to her in Confirmation, Therese felt another great joy, for she knew she had been given strength for the spiritual battles which would come in her life.

✿   ✿   ✿

Therese wanted to save sinners. She could not bear the thought of their going to hell, when Jesus wanted them to be happy with Him forever in Heaven. So she prayed often for their conversion.

Once, when Therese was fifteen, the newspapers were filled with reports about a murderer who was going to be executed but would not repent of his crime. This was her chance to pray for a *particular* sinner! "Dear God," she prayed, "send that poor sinner the grace of repentance, because of the merits of the Passion of Jesus!" She prayed long and earnestly for that poor man, and offered sacrifices for his conversion. At the same time she confided to Jesus: "He's my *first* sinner, so please give me a sign–any little sign."

Came the day of the execution. And what did the newspapers say about the criminal's death? Just before he died, the murderer asked for the chaplain whom he had ignored until then. The priest held a crucifix, and the poor man kissed it three times. He had repented! Therese had her sign, and knew that her "first sinner" had been converted.

Marie and Pauline had by this time entered the Carmelite Order. Now Therese, who wanted to draw closer and closer to Jesus, wanted to enter Carmel, too. She was not sure how she should tell her father, because he loved her in a special way and now that he was growing old he would feel all alone without her. But Jesus came first, so on a nice spring night when she and her father were walking together in the garden, Therese forced herself to speak.

At first her father didn't know what to say. This was a real blow to him, and he did not want to part from his dearest daughter. But after Therese had told him how much she really wished to go to Carmel, he agreed to let her go.

But that was just the first problem. Therese's legal guardian was her uncle, and he said that she was too young to enter such a strict order. Therese cried, but then she prayed and waited.

Three painful days passed. Then Therese's uncle changed his mind completely and consented. It was almost like a miracle!

Therese applied for admission to the convent. "You are too young," she was told. "We cannot admit a girl so young as you!" Not defeated, Therese appealed to the bishop, but he told her the same thing. What should she do now?

It was her father who suggested a pilgrimage to Rome in order to appeal to the Holy Father himself. That was a wonderful idea! Therese, her father, and her sister Celine set out for the Eternal City. On the way, they visited many beautiful and holy places, including the Holy House of Loreto where, according to pious legend, the Holy Family had lived, and which had been carried from Nazareth by the Angels hundreds of years before.

When the pilgrims went to see the Pope, a monsignor forbade Therese to speak to the Holy Father. But she had to! So when she went up to kiss his ring, she knelt there at his feet and begged the Holy Father to let her enter Carmel at fifteen. He replied firmly, "You will enter if it is God's will."

Poor Therese! It seemed that the journey had been in vain! She, Celine, and their father were greatly saddened, when they began their return to France. But Therese kept on praying.

There was a pleasant young man with the pilgrimage, and he paid a great deal of attention to Therese. She was cool toward him, but she told Celine privately she wished Jesus would soon take her out of the world, because her heart was weak and might begin to turn away from Him. She knew that when someone has a religious vocation, "trying life first" is a mistake—sometimes a fatal one!

About a month after she returned home, the bishop agreed to let her enter Carmel. How happy Therese was! She prepared herself well for the great day by making more mortifications and sacrifices than ever.

Of course, everyone cried when it was time for her to leave. Partings are always hard, especially in families where the members are very close to one another. But the children who become priests or sisters usually remain the closest to their parents and dear ones, because they are united to them by prayer.

Happily Therese began her religious life, offering her prayers, works and sacrifices for conversions in the missions. She had a strong desire to become a saint, but her poor health did not permit her to practice severe penances. She felt weak in many other ways, too. And yet she knew that Jesus would not have given her the *desire* to become a saint if she could not really become one. So she asked God's help and tried to do each duty in the best way possible only out of love for Him.

Her famous "little way" to sanctity consisted in prayer, humility and love. Once she wrote, "I prefer the monotony of obscure sacrifice to all ecstasies. To pick up a pin for love can convert a soul." She was faithful to each and every duty, eager to sacrifice herself, docile to all direction, and loved God so much that she was patient and kind with all for love of Him.

Therese always gave an extra bright smile to the sister who annoyed her the most. Or when someone didn't approve of her way of doing something, she would do it all over again as the other sister had suggested. She accepted everything that happened without complaining.

Her little cell was far from the others, and terribly cold in wintertime. She could hardly sleep at all, it was so cold. But she never let the others know about it, and even though she hadn't slept, she was as cheerful and full of energy in the daytime as she would have been after a full night of rest.

In chapel, Therese always sat next to a sister who kept jingling her rosary beads. This made it very hard for Therese to pray, but she never let anyone know about the trouble she had.

Her health became weaker and weaker, but she tried to hide the fact from everyone. Once when she felt very dizzy she was found cleaning high windows as if nothing were the matter at all!

Those small sacrifices were very important for Therese's progress in holiness. During her last illness she let the flies buzz around her and light on her face, without making a move to drive them away. She sweltered under a heavy blanket during the hot summer months without saying a word about it. She didn't complain about her hemorrhages and the painful sores which covered her body. She was smiling and pleasant till the very end.

The last night and day were filled with almost unbearable pain. Therese knew she was suffering not only for herself but to save many other souls. How much value that suffering had!

Then it was all over. Therese knew that she was dying. Happily she said her last words, "My God, I love You!"

*To St. Therese "little things" were what mat-
tered. Let us never be annoyed by the little
problems and sufferings but offer them to God as
acts of love.*

Saint Gemma

Example of Eucharistic Life

"But, Reverend Father," said the young mother, "I don't think we should call the child Gemma
as my brother-in-law wishes. I have never heard of
a saint in Heaven by that name—and I certainly
want my little one in Heaven one day!"

"Certainly ge٢s are to be found in Heaven,"
consoled the prie٢ 'Let's hope this child will be a
heavenly gem."

And so the day-old infant was baptized Gemma
Umberta Pia Galgani on the 13th of March, 1878.

Mrs. Galgani was a very good mother. She
went to Communion every day. When her children
were still small, she taught them the ugliness of sin
and the importance of pleasing God in every way.
Often she would show Gemma the crucifix and say,
"See, Gemma, this dear Jesus died on the cross for
us." Taking the child's hand she would place it on
the crown of thorns, the nails, the wound in the side.
Gemma would take the crucifix from her mother's
hands, clasp it to her, and kiss the wounds.

Every Saturday Mrs. Galgani would prepare Gemma's three older brothers for confession and she took them to church herself whenever she could. When Gemma turned seven and prepared for her first confession, her mother was very happy to see how serious the child was, how exact, and how sorrowful.

She said something that must have puzzled Gemma. "Oh, I wish I could take you with me! Would you come?"

"Where would we go?"

"To Paradise, where Jesus lives with His Angels."

"Yes! Yes!" exclaimed Gemma, her eyes shining at the thought.

"But never ask to die before the time God has planned for you."

❊   ❊   ❊

Young as she was, Gemma knew that her mother was very ill. Every day she became weaker and soon she could not leave her bed.

"This is highly contagious," the doctor declared. "The children must be sent away."

But Gemma cried and refused to go. "Who will encourage me to pray and to kiss Jesus on the cross?" After coaxing without result, her father sent the boys away and kept Gemma home.

She became her mother's little nurse and took care of her every need. When she was not busy about some task she would kneel beside her mother's pillow and together they would pray the rosary.

When Gemma received the Sacrament of Confirmation, her first thought after thanking God was to pray for her mother. It seemed to her she heard a voice asking, "Will you give Me your mother?"

"Yes," she answered silently, "but only if You will take me, too."

"No," was the reply. "You must stay with your father. I will take your mother to Heaven, but will you give her up willingly?" Gemma felt that she had to say "Yes."

When she reached home and saw her poor mother lying there suffering so patiently, Gemma began to cry but she did not say why.

Mrs. Galgani seemed to get better for a little while, then she began to be tormented by severe pains. Gemma knelt by her bed like a little statue. At last her father could not bear to see the little girl kneeling there so silently and he sent her away to stay with her aunt in another village.

Gemma felt as if the whole world had fallen to pieces. She wanted so much to stay with her mother, until her mother went to Paradise where she would have no more suffering and pain. But the little girl went off with her aunt without a complaint.

* * *

Months later Gemma came back to an empty house—even though it was full of children, and her father was there as always. Gemma hid her own sorrow and became the comfort of the whole family, for whenever she saw one of the boys crying over their mother, she would say, "Why are you crying? Mother is in Heaven. She is not suffering any longer—and she suffered so much!"

Every day the little girl trudged off to a school taught by the Sisters of St. Zita. She paid careful attention in class, and happily joined in the games during recess. The sisters liked her very much, because she always had a big smile for everyone.

First Communion day was one of the most wonderful days of Gemma's life. She prepared herself carefully, with sincere sorrow for all her sins, for she knew that soon Jesus Himself would be living eucharistically in her. Because of her good preparation and her deep longing for Communion, she felt Jesus' presence very strongly in her soul as soon as she had received the Sacred Host. Happy days followed, and for a time life was like Heaven on earth.

And then—suddenly—all joy was gone. Until now Gemma had felt a strong love of God, an attraction for prayer, a longing for Heaven. Now, she felt . . . nothing—nothing at all. Life seemed empty, aimless, without purpose or meaning.

She knew, with her mind, that God loved her, that Heaven awaited her, that prayer and duty and sacrifice were the means to Paradise—but she *felt* nothing. It became difficult to pray, difficult to work, to play, to laugh.

Something else tried to come in and fill the emptiness—the giddiness of the world. Suddenly Gemma was attracted by things and activities which had never interested her before. And yet she was determined not to give in to these new inclinations.

She kept herself at prayer even though a thousand distractions crept in. She smiled, although she felt only sadness inside. She pushed aside thoughts of going out with the other girls her age. She worked as energetically as ever, although she felt like doing nothing at all. She gave generously to the poor, as she had always done.

She was going through a period of spiritual dryness—something which many holy souls experience. It is a time when God seems many miles away although He is really very close. It is a time when a person can show a sincere love for God, because love of God consists in doing what He wishes of us whether or not we feel pleased by it.

In that time of darkness Gemma's faith and love grew strong, because she had to *force* herself to have faith; she had to *force* herself to love. When at last a feeling of happiness returned to her, she had become holier by far.

❋ ❋ ❋

Not long after the darkness lifted from Gemma's soul, another sorrow came into her life. Her brother Gino, who had entered the seminary, fell ill of a dangerous disease. He returned home and Gemma nursed him for many long, anxious months. Over and over the youth offered himself to God as a victim. Then he passed away.

Within three years, Gemma's father also passed away—and the children were left orphans and utterly poor.

Gemma was then nineteen. An aunt took her in and urged her to marry a nice young man, a doctor's son, who had fallen in love with the quiet, good-looking girl. He asked the aunt for her hand, and the aunt thought this was wonderful—but Gemma did not.

Perhaps Gemma did not wish to marry because her father had only recently died? No, there was another reason. Gemma wanted her heart to belong only to Jesus, and not to be divided with anyone else.

The young man persisted. So did the aunt.

"My Jesus," Gemma prayed, "deliver me from this distressing situation."

The deliverance was immediate and painful. Gemma developed a terrible pain in her spine, followed by deafness and almost complete paralysis. She suffered intensely, with the crucifix as her only consolation. Almost continuously she meditated on Jesus in His Passion, but even so, the devil began to prey upon her mind and imagination and she found herself fighting temptation. She prayed to St. Gabriel of Our Lady of Sorrows for help, and began reading a book on his life which some kind soul had lent to her. The temptations became less violent.

Gemma soon felt drawn to St. Gabriel, for she learned that he had had a great devotion to the Passion and to Our Lady, even as she had. One night that young saint appeared to her and told her she could make the vow of virginity. Overjoyed, Gemma made her vow the very next morning, after the priest had brought her Holy Communion.

She was growing weaker and weaker. The doctors could see no hope. Quite willing to die if it were God's will, Gemma waited patiently.

One night she heard a voice praying the Our Father. It paused in the middle, and Gemma tried to finish the prayer, although she was in such great pain she could hardly speak. Together she and her unknown guest said the Hail Mary and Glory Be— and repeated the prayers eight more times. It was a novena!

"Do you wish to be cured?" asked the unseen guest.

"It is all the same to me," replied the suffering girl. She only wanted to do God's will.

"Yes, you will be cured. At this hour every night I will come and we will pray together to the Sacred Heart of Jesus."

It was St. Gabriel.

Several nights passed in that way. The novena was almost over when the priest came to hear Gemma's confession and bring her First Friday Communion. After Communion Gemma could feel Jesus asking her, "Gemma, do you wish to be cured?"

Overwhelmed by His tenderness, the girl could not reply, but suddenly she knew that she had been cured.

"My daughter," said Jesus, "I give Myself all to you, and you must belong entirely to Me. I am your Father, and My Mother will be your mother.

My fatherly help can never fail those who abandon themselves in My hands. You will be all right even though I have taken away those who loved and helped you the most."

Gemma was cured! Everyone in the house cried for joy.

What a consolation it was to the orphan Gemma to have the Blessed Mother as her own mother! She had always loved Our Lady, but now she turned to her with all the trust of a small child. In every need she sought her Heavenly Mother's help. "Keep my heart with you in Heaven," she implored.

Often she would picture to herself that tender mother standing at the foot of the cross, suffering silently with her Son. Seeing those two most gentle Persons in such agony, she felt an intense desire to suffer with Them.

"How deeply I feel your sorrow, my Mother, seeing you at the foot of the cross, but do you know my greatest sorrow? It is that I cannot comfort you; on the contrary, I feel worse, because I myself have been a cause of so much of your suffering."

And so Gemma began asking Mary for the cross. Every day which passed without some suffering, she regarded as wasted.

"My Jesus," she prayed one day, after having been refused entrance to a convent because of her poor health, "I want to love You—oh, so much—but I do not know how."

"Do you wish to love Jesus now and forever?" a voice asked. "Then never cease suffering for Him. The cross is the throne of those who really love

Jesus; the cross is the heritage of the elect in this life."

Gemma found the cross in many ways. She found it when she went to live with a kind family, whose servants immediately became jealous of her. To one old servant who was especially mean, Gemma was very gentle. The woman had a horrible ulcer on her leg. Gemma would change the bandages for her, and would run all sorts of errands for her. Once she even leaned over and kissed the horrid wound.

She found the cross in the sufferings of Jesus' Passion, which He began to let her feel every Thursday night and Friday morning–in the hours when He Himself had suffered so terribly. During those hours, Gemma bore the stigmata–the gaping wounds in hands, feet and heart spurting blood. She felt the scourges tearing at the flesh of her back; she felt the thorns piercing her head. The pain was intense–and in addition to it she felt weighed down by the burden of the sins of mankind.

She sought the cross in her own penances, too, for often she beat herself without mercy for the forgiveness of sinners.

And yet Gemma feared pain! "I shrink every time I look at the cross," she wrote, "because I feel I could die thinking of the pain of it, yet in spite of this, my heart welcomes the sufferings. . . ." Why? Because Jesus had suffered, and Gemma loved Jesus very much.

After Communion one day, Jesus said to Gemma, "My daughter, I need strong, courageous souls who do not shrink from being victims of My Father's Divine Justice. . . . Oh, if I could only make you understand the anger of My Father with this world which has deliberately renounced Him. . . . He is preparing a severe punishment for the entire earth."

Gemma knew Jesus was asking her to suffer still more. "Of course I will sacrifice myself, dear Lord. There is no torment, however painful, that I would not endure for You; I would shed every drop of my blood to please Your Sacred Heart and to prevent sinners from offending You."

So Gemma suffered on, drawing strength and consolation from the Holy Eucharist. Her Communions were so fervent that she began to feel the joy of Heaven whenever she consumed the Sacred Host.

"Come, Jesus. Can there be any of Your creatures who do not love You? I feel You in my heart—what a mystery! I feel as if I am in Heaven. I forget all the troubles of the world, and taste and love only You."

Gemma's last months on earth were filled with the intense pains of a mysterious illness. The darkness of spirit she had felt years before returned to her. The devil tempted her. Life was empty of all joy.

Gemma turned to her Heavenly Mother, and asked her to intercede for her. She continued to talk to Jesus even though she could not feel His presence.

One day a nurse asked her, "What would you do if Our Lord let you choose between going to Heaven at once and staying on earth to suffer more and add to His glory?"

"It would be better to stay and suffer," Gemma replied. "Jesus' glory always comes first."

On Wednesday and again on Thursday of Holy Week, 1903, Gemma received Viaticum. Then on Good Friday, at about ten o'clock, she exclaimed, "I have to be crucified with Jesus."

Lying on her sickbed she extended her arms as if she were on the cross. She said nothing, and on her face was an expression of desolation and suffering, but also of love and calm. She remained that way three and a half hours. She continued to suffer the rest of that day and most of the next. Holy Saturday evening she received Extreme Unction and Viaticum. Then, bowing her head as Jesus had on the cross, Gemma Galgani commended her soul to God.

She was twenty-five years old.

＊ ＊ ＊

They buried her in the Passionist Convent of her city, Lucca, where she had longed to be during life. The inscription on her tomb ran thus:

"Gemma Galgani from Lucca, most pure virgin, being in her twenty-fifth year, died of tuberculosis but was more consumed by the fire of divine love than by her wasting disease. On the eleventh of

April, 1903, the vigil of Easter, her soul took its flight to the bosom of her celestial Spouse. Beautiful soul—in peace with the Angels."

In every sorrow, including her parents' death, St. Gemma turned for help to Jesus in the Eucharist and the Blessed Mother. We, too, will find sorrow easier to bear if we "talk it over" with Jesus and Mary.

Saint Mary Goretti

Martyr for Purity

St. Mary Goretti, the first 20th century martyr, is often called "The New Agnes"—for like that heroic young saint of the early Church, she gave up her life to preserve her purity unspotted for Jesus.

Mary was born in Italy, near the city of Corinaldo, on October 16, 1890, the oldest girl in a family of seven children. Her parents were pious, honest and hard-working, and Mary always imitated them and obeyed them cheerfully.

The little girl had a great devotion to the Sacred Heart of Jesus and to the Immaculate Virgin Mary. When her little hands were not helping with the housework, they were fingering the beads of her rosary, for Mary never passed up a chance to pray!

When she was ten, she lost her father, Louis Goretti, who had been taken ill with a fatal disease.

Mary missed him, for they had been very close, but she refused to become downhearted, for she recalled how fervently he had received the Last Sacraments, and how holily he had spent his whole life. Surely he was in Heaven, or at least in purgatory! So Mary showed her love, not with tears, but with prayers. Each time she passed the cemetery gate, she knelt and said a prayer for her father. Every day she said five mysteries of the rosary for the repose of his soul.

Now the Gorettis were poorer than ever before. Sometimes Mary's mother would become discouraged, as she wondered how they would manage to get enough food and clothing. At such times, the cheerful daughter would say: "Be brave, Mother. After all, we're growing up. Soon we'll be able to support the whole family—and until then, God will provide for us."

Generously, Mary would always do the most difficult and disagreeable parts of the housework, like scouring the pots and pans, scrubbing the floor, and, in fact, almost everything else, too. She was a second mother to her brothers and sisters, teaching them their prayers, looking after them, and urging them always to be obedient and modest.

In every little thing, Mary was helpful. For instance, whenever she and her mother had to cross a field, the girl would walk in front to scare away the snakes, because her mother was afraid of snakes.

Mary was humble, too. Whenever she was scolded, or whenever someone was a little tired and spoke sharply to her, Mary took it cheerfully, with no long faces!

What made Mary so good? Well, she wasn't really "born" that way. At times, it cost her a struggle to do the best thing. But she did it because she knew that God would be pleased. Her whole life was centered around God.

To go to Mass meant a two-hour walk, but that did not bother Mary. She was the first to enter the church and the last to leave, and she paid strict attention during the service. As often as she could, she went to confession, and she really tried hard to carry out the resolutions she made each time.

The virtue in which Mary especially shone was purity. She was very careful about the way she dressed, walked and spoke. She avoided any conversations which tended to be vulgar. Once, when she had met a girl at the village well who said indecent things, Mary told her mother, "I would rather die than talk as she does!" Mary knew that even the strongest soul will fall if it does not avoid the occasions of sin.

At that time, children received First Holy Communion at the age of ten, and we can imagine with what joy Mary received Jesus, after having waited for Him for so long! She had so much to tell Him! After Mass, the priest gave a special sermon for the young boys and girls who had made their First Communion. He urged them to preserve their purity always. And Mary's young heart renewed its determination to remain pure.

First Communion day

A great change came over Mary. After her First
Communion, she became much more devoted to
prayer and duty. Her conscience was more delicate.
Even her expression was more angelic. She received
Communion only four more times, but those five
Communions helped her to become very holy, be-
cause she was so wholehearted in corresponding
to God's grace.

The Gorettis lived with a family named Serenelli–a man named John and his son Alexander, who
was about twenty. Alexander was full of impure
thoughts and desires, mainly because he had read
the obscene magazines which his father had bought
and left around the house. Alexander had read
every filthy thing he could get his hands on,
and had gone around with companions as bad as
he, so it was no wonder that now he fixed his gaze
on the pure and innocent Mary!

Mary had to be home with the children during
the day, while her mother worked. One day, Alexander came up to her with a horrid, sinful demand.
Mary refused him and kept away from him. Ten
days later, the youth tried again, and the horrified
girl told him how detestable he was in the eyes of
God. He grabbed her–but she used all her strength,
broke away, and ran.

By now the girl was terrified. Should she tell
her mother? Oh, how she wanted to! But she didn't
dare. Already Alexander had told her he'd kill her
if she told her mother what he was up to. She didn't
dare tell. So she became silent and tearful, but she
never said what was bothering her.

"Mamma, don't go out to work! Please stay home!" There were tears in her eyes and tears in her voice, as Mary made the plea.

"But why, Marietta?" her mother asked in surprise.

"Don't go, Mamma," the girl begged again, but she wouldn't say why.

"She must be going through a stage," the mother thought. "Even good children have strange ideas sometimes, I guess." She put the notion out of her head and went to work.

Later in the same day Mary's mother scolded her daughter soundly for forgetting one of her duties. "I won't forget again, Mamma," the girl promised meekly.

The next day, the Gorettis and Serenellis were busy threshing beans. Under a blazing July sun, Alexander drove the oxen around and around the village threshing-floor, while Mary's young brothers and sisters rode in the wagon behind, and their mother did the winnowing. Around three o'clock, Alexander made an excuse to leave, and asked Mary's mother to take his place. He headed for the house.

John Serenelli was resting in the shade outside, for he had a fever. Mary was sitting on the outside stairway, in plain sight of the threshing floor— probably on purpose—busily sewing. She was mending Alexander's shirt, for her mother had asked her to do it.

Sullenly Alexander came up the steps. He passed Mary without a word and went into the house, where he went over to a box that held old pieces of iron and took out a piece that was about a foot long. One end had been sharpened to a point, like a dagger.

"Mary!" called Alexander. "Come here a minute!"

Probably Mary's heart froze within her. At any rate, she did not answer. She didn't even move.

Quick as lightning, the youth stepped out onto the landing and seized the girl. Mary struggled wildly as Alexander dragged her into the house and barred the door. She tried to scream; the boy stuffed a handkerchief into her mouth. Yet she managed to say, and to keep saying, "No, no, God doesn't want it; if you do it you'll commit a mortal sin; you'll go to hell!" She warded him off time and again. At last he seized the dagger.

She saw the choice, but for her there could be no choice. Mary braced herself to die.

Furiously, Alexander thrust the dagger into the girl time and time again. She crumpled to the floor unconscious.

"She's dead," Alexander thought. He turned away and went into his bedroom.

Slowly Mary came to. She was in an agony of pain. The door . . . she must reach the door . . . call someone. . . . Inch by inch, pain by pain, she dragged herself through the sticky, slippery blood to the door. She reached up and unbarred it. "John," she called, "Come! Alexander has killed me!"

But as soon as he heard her voice, Alexander rushed back into the room. He seized her by the throat and pierced her clear through with the dagger—six more times. "My God! My God!" cried the girl. "I'm dying! Mamma!"

Alexander ran back into his room and barred the door as his father came in with Mary's brother Mariano. When the little boy saw what had happened, he turned and ran in horror.

When Mary's mother and the neighbors reached the scene, the girl had been placed on a bed. She was still conscious, but her mother fainted from the shock. After she revived, she asked the pain-racked girl what had happened.

"Alexander did it."

"But why?"

"Because he wanted me to commit a horrible sin and I would not."

While the police came and took Alexander off to jail, friends tried to bandage the fourteen horrid wounds in Mary's body. They placed her in a Red Cross ambulance, and took her over rough roads—each jolt adding to the martyr's misery—to the clinic in a neighboring city. Mary tried not to show her mother how much she was suffering.

It was evening when they reached the clinic. A priest was called to hear Mary's confession, and as soon as he had finished, the doctors came in to stitch up her wounds. They knew that they couldn't save her, but it was all that they could do.

A picture of the Blessed Virgin greeted Mary from the wall of the little room into which she was taken. The girl looked at it lovingly. She prayed to it during those long, tortured hours when she was waiting to die. She prayed, too, to the Sacred Heart, and to St. Joseph, patron of the dying.

"Do you forgive your murderer?" she was asked.

"I do forgive him," she replied, "and I believe that God will forgive him too!"

Now a cruel thirst joined itself to the torment of Mary's wounds. But she was unable to take even a drop of water. "Think of Jesus on the cross," Mary told herself. "Think of Jesus, tormented in every member. Do it for Him."

Toward the end, they brought Jesus to her in Holy Communion. When she had received Him, her face glowed with a supernatural light. She kissed a picture of Him repeatedly, and another of His Mother. Then delirium came over her, and she no longer knew what she was doing.

In her last moments, the unconscious girl re-lived the nightmare of a few hours before. "What are you doing, Alexander?" she cried. "You'll go to hell!" She made a quick motion as if she were driving him back, then with a mighty effort she tried to leap from the bed. The strain was too great, and she fell back lifeless, while her pure and beautiful soul sped to Heaven.

The year was 1902, and the martyr was eleven and a half years old. But it was not the martyrdom which had made her a saint. It was her love of God and obedience to His laws. In her short life, her obedience, charity, humility, meekness, prudence and piety had been already heroic; her purity had been angelic. It was her daily practice of virtue in little ways which had obtained for her the grace to keep he   irity unspotted in the hour of greatest trial. ᴀ   rdom was the crown to an already holy life.

Mary hᴀ performed many miracles and obtained countless graces. One of them was the repentance of Alexander after Mary appeared to him while he was serving his long prison sentence.

Many sick persons also have been cured through her intercession. But she is most often invoked for the preservation of purity. She was canonized in 1950, in the presence of her mother and of Alexander himself.

The virtue of purity is safeguarded by the virtue of modesty. Modesty means dressing, walking, standing, and sitting with dignity, remembering that we are temples of the Holy Spirit. Modesty also means watching over our eyes and all our senses.

BIBLE STORIES

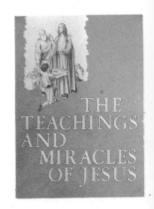

Bible
____for Children

God's message is one of saving love, and it unfolds admirably in the pages of this book. Covering both **Old and New Testaments** of the Bible, it majestically sets forth the more important happenings in the history of salvation. Their meaning is also explained in the light of recent biblical studies. Biblical maps are included; illustrations are in 2 and 4 colors. (Ages 8-12). 182 pages; cloth $5; paper $4.—CH0070

FOR THE
YOUNG

The Bible for
_____Young People

This dramatically illustrated **New Testament** in full color will make the discovery of the treasures of Sacred Scripture an enjoyable, unforgettable experience for young people (ages 9-13). 142 pages; cloth $5; paper $4.

—CH0080

The Teachings and
_____Miracles of Jesus

Daughters of St. Paul

Some of the best-known teachings and miracles of our Lord are retold in this volume for young people. Jesus has an answer to every question; He has words of everlasting life. His tender love for people and His divine power will strike unforgettable images on the minds and hearts of youth to aid them to work for His Kingdom. 136 pages; cloth $3.

—CH0690

Saints for Young People
for Every Day (2 volumes)

Daughters of St. Paul
365 sketches of saints from early Christianity down to our times. A beautiful treasury for 9- to 12-year-old boys and girls who will thrill to the challenge of imitating these holy men and women of God in simple, practical ways suggested. Each volume abundantly illustrated in two colors.

302 pages, Vol. I—CH0570; 338 pages, Vol. II —CH0580; cloth $5.00 per volume; paper $3.50 per volume.

DSP Encounter Books

A goldmine of enjoyable reading and wholesome inspiration, written in a smooth-flowing style for fourth to eighth graders (and their families). Great heroes and saints of God come alive with all the dynamism of their noble ideals. Each volume illustrated.

$2.25 cloth (unless otherwise noted); $1.25 paper (only starred titles are available in paper)

——**AFRICAN TRIUMPH***—Charles Lwanga, daring leader of the Uganda martyrs.
EN0010

——**AHEAD OF THE CROWD**—Dominic Savio, the teenager whose motto, "Death before sin," rocketed him to sanctity.
EN0020

——**BELLS OF CONQUEST***—Bernard of Clairvaux, conqueror of hearts and souls for Christ.
EN0030

——**BOY WITH A MISSION***—Francis Marto, the shepherd boy of Fatima who knew how to make a sacrifice with a smile.
EN0040

——**THE CHEERFUL WARRIOR**—Charles Garnier, who always had a cheerful smile in spite of the hardships and dangers of a missioner's life in the wilds of Canada.
EN0060

——**THE CONSCIENCE GAME***— Thomas More, who chose his God above his king.
EN0070

——**THE COUNTRY ROAD HOME**—John Vianney, the humble parish priest who brought thousands closer to God.
EN0080

——**THE FISHER PRINCE**—St. Peter, fisherman and apostle, the Rock of Christ's Church.
EN0090

____**MUSIC MASTER**—Herman Cohen, the talented musician who knew how to sacrifice all for the Lord he loved. EN0210

____**NOBLE LADY**—The gentle, valiant St. Helen who found the true cross. EN0230

____**NO PLACE FOR DEFEAT**—Pius V, the Pope who was a Dominican monk, renowned for his orthodoxy, his courage and mildness. EN0220

____**WIND AND SHADOWS***—Joan of Arc, the daring warrior-maid dedicated to her God and her nation. EN0250

____**CATHERINE OF SIENA**—The story of one of the greatest women in the history of the Catholic Church. EN0050

____**TRAILBLAZER FOR THE SACRED HEART**—The fascinating life of Father Mateo Crawley-Boevey, SS.CC., founder of the Enthronement of the Sacred Heart of Jesus in the home. His goal in life was: the whole world conquered for the Sacred Heart. $3.00 EN0245

____**GENTLE REVOLUTIONARY**—Saint Francis of Assisi, the man whose unbelievable witness of Christ-likeness rings in every page. EN0120

____**THE GREAT HERO**—St. Paul the Apostle—adventures of the greatest among the pioneers and saints. EN0150

____**NO GREATER LOVE***—Father Damien, the apostle to Molokai, who gave his life for his lepers. EN0219

____**PILLAR IN THE TWILIGHT***—Thomas Aquinas, the "Dumb Ox" who became a great teacher. EN0240

____**YES IS FOREVER***—Mother Thecla Merlo—the strong, faith-filled co-Foundress of the Daughters of St. Paul. EN0260

____**CAME THE DAWN***—Mary of Nazareth, the Mother of Jesus and ours, too. EN0045

Order from addresses on following page.

Please include 75¢ postage for each book and 15¢ for each additional book.

Daughters of St. Paul

IN MASSACHUSETTS
  50 St. Paul's Ave. Jamaica Plain, Boston, MA 02130;
    617-522-8911; 617-522-0875;
  172 Tremont Street, Boston, MA 02111; 617-426-5464;
    617-426-4230
IN NEW YORK
  78 Fort Place, Staten Island, NY 10301; 212-447-5071
  59 East 43rd Street, New York, NY 10017; 212-986-7580
  7 State Street, New York, NY 10004; 212-447-5071
  625 East 187th Street, Bronx, NY 10458; 212-584-0440
  525 Main Street, Buffalo, NY 14203; 716-847-6044
IN NEW JERSEY
  Hudson Mall — Route 440 and Communipaw Ave.,
    Jersey City, NJ 07304; 201-433-7740
IN CONNECTICUT
  202 Fairfield Ave., Bridgeport, CT 06604; 203-335-9913
IN OHIO
  2105 Ontario St. (at Prospect Ave.), Cleveland, OH 44115; 216-621-9427
  25 E. Eighth Street, Cincinnati, OH 45202; 513-721-4838
IN PENNSYLVANIA
  1719 Chestnut Street, Philadelphia, PA 19103; 215-568-2638
IN FLORIDA
  2700 Biscayne Blvd., Miami, FL 33137; 305-573-1618
IN LOUISIANA
  4403 Veterans Memorial Blvd., Metairie, LA 70002; 504-887-7631;
    504-887-0113
  1800 South Acadian Thruway, P.O. Box 2028, Baton Rouge, LA 70821
    504-343-4057; 504-343-3814
IN MISSOURI
  1001 Pine Street (at North 10th), St. Louis, MO 63101; 314-621-0346;
    314-231-5522
IN ILLINOIS
  172 North Michigan Ave., Chicago, IL 60601; 312-346-4228
IN TEXAS
  114 Main Plaza, San Antonio, TX 78205; 512-224-8101
IN CALIFORNIA
  1570 Fifth Avenue, San Diego, CA 92101; 714-232-1442
  46 Geary Street, San Francisco, CA 94108; 415-781-5180
IN HAWAII
  1143 Bishop Street, Honolulu, HI 96813; 808-521-2731
IN ALASKA
  750 West 5th Avenue, Anchorage AK 99501; 907-272-8183
IN CANADA
  3022 Dufferin Street, Toronto 395, Ontario, Canada
IN ENGLAND
  57, Kensington Church Street, London W. 8, England
IN AUSTRALIA
  58 Abbotsford Rd., Homebush, N.S.W., Sydney 2140, Australia